The Wealth of Coaching

A playbook for Coaching
in the Modern Workplace

ENDORSEMENTS

Susi Astengo's book *The Wealth of Coaching* is a compelling and timely contribution to the world of professional coaching. Drawing from a rich tapestry of personal experiences, experienced coaches, profound insights, and a deep understanding of human transformation, this book offers more than just a guide – it offers a mirror, a map, and a catalyst. Whether you're an aspiring coach, a seasoned practitioner, or an HR Leader, this book will challenge your thinking, awaken your purpose, and elevate your practice. Susi's voice is authentic, generous, and wise – an accurate guide in a world craving meaning and connection.

Ahmed Banderker, Director

Susi has worked with our company for several years and we have seen direct, measurable and impactful benefits from these engagements. Susi and her team combine deep insights, professionalism, enthusiasm, commercial nous, and a passion for excellence combined with a sense of fun that helps people develop the judgement, skills, and capabilities to be the best they can be. This book contains the insight and wisdom that we have benefited from, and distils a broad range of knowledge, data, wisdom, and humanity in helping people grow in the areas that really matter to build meaningful and lasting businesses, centered around healthy relationships. Given that successful teams result in high performance organisations, having the ability to build and maintain high-performing teams sits at the core of building lasting benefit.

Andrew Birrell - Chair, IDM group

A gem of a book for anyone interested in understanding the most effective way to implement coaching for both the individual and at scale. The insights are accessible, warm and astute. An easy read which belies the depth of thought, intellect, and experience which has shaped it. Susi Astengo brings her own blend of expertise and humanity to a topic which is increasing being seen as a foundational intervention within the learning and development arenas. Highly recommended for anyone interested in their own growth and development and for those of us who are already committed aficionados of the coaching genre.

Julia Dyssell, former CHRO, Sanlam

A complete and up to date practical reference on Coaching which takes into account a future journey, full of nuances.

Alessandro Pegoraro, EMCC Global Executive Board, Head of Development

The Wealth of Coaching is a wealth of information. It is a compelling and timely read for any leader, HR professional, or business strategist, considering the implementation of a tangible coaching strategy.

Susi Astengo not only brings together the wisdom and experience of a diverse range of seasoned coaches but also frames coaching as a powerful lever for cultural transformation and sustainable business performance.

The book offers clear insights into how coaching, when embedded strategically, becomes more than a development tool. It becomes a catalyst for engagement, accountability, and growth at every level of business.

Importantly, the book acknowledges the emerging role of AI in the coaching landscape by highlighting how technology can enhance access, consistency, and scalability without losing the human essence of coaching.

If you're serious about building a coaching culture that delivers real impact, this book provides both the inspiration and the practical roadmap to get started.

Craig McKensie, CEO, Four and One consulting

First published in 2025.

ISBN: 978-1-991272-39-3 (Printed)
eISBN: 978-1-991272-40-9 (PDF eBook)

Published by KR Publishing

Tel: (011) 706-6009
E-mail: orders@knowres.co.za
Website: www.kr.co.za

Typesetting, layout and design: Cia Joubert, cia@knowres.co.za
Cover design: Marlene De Lorme, marlene@knowres.co.za
Editing & proofreading: KR Publishing Team
Project management: Cia Joubert, cia@knowres.co.za

The Wealth of Coaching

A playbook for Coaching in the Modern Workplace

Edited by

Susi Astengo

kr
publishing

2025

ACKNOWLEDGEMENTS

We may not all have a book in us; however, it appears that we do all have a chapter. This book is dedicated to the team of coaches at Coachmatching, who, over the years, have been my friends, my mentors, my safe place, and my inspiration. You have made the past 17 years a joy, and it has been a privilege to walk this journey with you as both the industry and CoachMatching have matured.

This book would not have been possible without you.

To my son Gianluca, who has taught me how to be a better human being and whom I love with all my heart.

Picture a group of coaches gathered around a campfire. The flames flicker, casting shadows of the past while illuminating the road ahead. Each coach, from the seasoned veteran to the relative newcomer, shares stories of transformation, of obstacles overcome, and of breakthrough moments that changed everything. This book is our campfire moment, a place where we share what we have learned from the past and can see on the horizon for the future.

TABLE OF CONTENTS

FOREWORD

Compared to its big sister mentoring, coaching is still a young concept. Modern, non-directive, developmental coaching is even younger. It first appears in the work of Timothy Galwey in the 1970s, in the world of sport and only really gained traction in the world of employment and organisations in the 1990s. The origins of coaching lie in tutoring at university in England, as a directive form of learning.

Not surprisingly, the concept of coaching is still evolving. The rise of professional bodies focused attention on standards and competencies – on the doing of coaching rather than being a coach. The two main professional bodies, the ICF and the EMCC, took different paths. The ICF prioritised uniformity – which broadly meant adherence to approaches rooted in North American culture. The EMCC emphasised cultural diversity – which posed challenges in defining the core of what was and wasn't coaching. The ICF elected not to include mentoring or supervision; the EMCC saw these as complementary to coaching and to a considerable extent, overlapping. The increasing collaboration between these organisations, with many coaches being members of both, is an important part of the next stage in the development of the field.

I've been privileged to have played a role in these developments from the early 1980s, making me now arguably the only fully active survivor of the coaching pioneers. I am fortunate enough to have participated as a coach and mentor, a supervisor, a researcher and an educator in the field.

One of the big questions is whether coaching is a profession or a discipline. Being a profession requires high standards of regulation, based on agreed bodies of evidence-based knowledge and codes of practice. Currently, there is no global consensus on either of these, although the two international codes of practice (ethical codes) are quite similar in content. Moreover, the majority of coaching is done by line managers, who are typically unaccredited by a professional body. Mentoring tends to be seen as a vocation, being typically unpaid. I like the term "pro-vocation", which has multiple layers of meaning.

Another question relates to: what does a mature coach look like? The work of the Coach Maturity Research Group is unequivocal here. Its research, analysing the developmental journeys of mature coaches, shows that the more coaches "grow up", the less they focus on doing, and on helping clients achieve goals and find solutions. In contrast, the more they focus on being present and connected, and on using their wisdom to stimulate internal, reflective dialogue in the client. To a considerable extent, they merge coaching and mentoring.

A key feature of the coaching landscape is the context in which it operates. The business world is becoming more and more complex; the reactions of new generations to the world they have entered differ greatly from previous.

We now identify 10 levels of complexity in coaching, from basic 1-2-1 skills and performance coaching, through team coaching, to coaching the meta-system. To operate at higher levels of complexity – and hence add greater value to their clients and the world – coaches need high levels of system literacy. They also need to be at least as competent in thinking strategically as the clients who they serve. They also need to meet new generations where they are – and that means learning from them. Effective coaching is today increasingly a co-learning activity.

Having a sense of the history and future of coaching is, I believe, a valuable asset for leaders, HR professionals and coaches entering this world of informal development. It gives continuity and helps make sense of how and why we coach. We need to capture and value the experience of industry pioneers, such as Susi Astengo, who have seen it and done it for a long period, and who have dedicated themselves to raising standards for the benefit of coaches, clients and society. The lessons of history enable us to avoid the mistakes of the future.

Professor David Clutterbuck, *PhD (Hon), FRSA; Visiting Professor, Henley Business School; Practice Lead, Coaching and Mentoring International; Co-founder, EMCC Global*

ABOUT THE EDITOR

Susi Astengo

Susi has been the Managing Director of CoachMatching for the past 17 years, having established the business in 2008 after seven months of market research into the South African Coaching Industry. During her time as MD, she has received numerous awards, including Business Women of the Year, in the entrepreneurial category (2016) and an Africa Tech highly commended award for her contribution as a woman in technology (2024). She has built a team of 50 plus coaches locally and CoachMatching has an enviable long-standing and loyal client base. Commercially astute and technologically savvy, she has always focussed on delivering a blend of thought leadership, innovative products, and services that meet the current and future marketplace demands.

CoachMatching represents her personal values of Integrity and Partnership, and it is these two qualities that drive the organisational culture and create long standing relationships with her clients.

She spent a brief time with Deloitte when she arrived in South Africa in 2003 and prior to that she was an international management consultant based in London for over 10 years.

Susi is a single mother of a 20-year-old son, whom she raised whilst building the business and also a cancer survivor, having been diagnosed in 2020 in the midst of COVID.

Susi has published articles in The Business Day as a guest contributor, and has spoken at many conferences over the years.

Susi was educated in the UK and holds a Masters in Human Resource Management.

Susi can be contacted at: Susi@coachmatching.com

ABOUT THE CONTRIBUTORS

Lily Breuning-Ellis

Lily lives in Somerset West where she works as an executive and life coach as well as a grief and trauma facilitator in a lovely space called the Sanctuary of Light. In this safe space, her clients can explore both their own limitations and their potential. She has worked in the field of supportive intervention and life coaching for over 20 years and has a degree in psychology and diplomas in various related fields. She has recently done her certification in advanced breathwork – a powerful and growing field with some fascinating studies being done around breath, mental wellness, and long-term health and longevity.

Lily has a particular passion for supporting people living and working in high-stress contexts. She brings together cutting-edge information, heartfelt compassion, and deep listening as well as tools that are accessible to everyone and easy to incorporate into their daily routines. By also teaching the principles of healthy habit formation her clients can shift themselves towards greater resilience, efficient productivity, and vitalised wellness.

Lily lives in Somerset West with her husband and a menagerie of animals. She has three children whom she regards as her greatest achievements to date, loves time-out in nature, and swimming in cold sea water daily.

Lily can be contacted at: lily.coachmatching@gmail.com

Marcel Brunel

Marcel is a co-founding member of Dignity Inc., Marcel Brunel has dedicated the past fourteen years to working closely with various public and private organisations focused on developing emotional literacy and emotional regulation skills that change lives and organisational trajectories. Emotions enable deep healing work to occur within the self, the ego, and past trauma. He aims to shift our thinking to focus more on prevention than reaction." Marcel's approach to promoting emotional literacy and regulation provides focused insights beneficial to public and private professionals seeking to successfully navigate the evolutionary process of life, family, career, and retirement. As the co-author of Dignity in Policing: How Emotional Wellness Saves Lives, Families, and Careers, Marcel shares essential insights on enhancing performance through emotional regulation. Marcel gained these insights from working with close to 100 public safety agencies of varying sizes and observing the actions of more than 4,000 public safety officers.Marcel's background includes 4 years of service in the U.S. Army; he left service as a sergeant. He holds a bachelor's degree in psychology from Texas A&M and has served as an instructor with the FBI National Academy, the Caruth Police Institute (CPI), the Law Enforcement Management Institute of Texas Leadership Command College (LCC), Texas Constables Leadership College (TCLC), Dispatching with Dignity (DID), and the Fire Executive Management Training (FEMT).

Prof David Clutterbuck

David is one of the earliest pioneers of coaching and mentoring. Visiting Professor at Henley Business School, he is a distinguished research fellow at The Conference Board and Special Ambassador for the European Mentoring and Coaching Council. Author or co-author of some 80 books, he leads a global network of coach and mentor educators, Coaching and Mentoring International.

He can be reached on Linked In or by email david@clutterbuck-cmi.com

Vandena Daya

Vandena is a leadership and team coach with over 15 years of senior leadership experience in financial services. She holds a Bachelor's degree in Chemical Engineering and an MBA, and transitioned into coaching in 2021 to pursue her passion for helping individuals and teams flourish.

She now runs her own coaching practice, partnering with executives and senior leaders to deepen self-awareness, enhance emotional intelligence, and grow confidence and influence. She supports leaders in building mental fitness and resilience to lead effectively in today's complex and demanding environments. Vandena is a nurturer at heart – helping people and teams move beyond what limits them, surface the invisible, find their voice, and create what sets them free.

Her coaching draws on disciplines such as positive psychology, adult development theory, neuroscience, systems thinking, and mindfulness – guiding leaders to grow their inner capacity and shift how they relate to themselves and others.

Vandena contributes thought leadership through her newsletter and LinkedIn writings, where she explores topics such as mental fitness, the inner critic, the Thinking Environment, and the power of presence, gratitude, and sensory awareness. She also writes about working agreements as a powerful foundation for building collaborative, high-performing teams – emphasising that *how* teams work together is just as important as *what* they work on.

Vandena can be contacted at: vandena.coachmatching@gmail.com

Dr Neville Goldin

Neville is a consulting psychologist and executive coach in private practice. After a long corporate career in organisational and leadership development, he embarked on a second career, supporting leaders and leadership teams in their quest to become more authentic and effective in their leadership roles. He favours the systems psychodynamic approach to consulting and coaching, working holistically and systemically and often below the surface. Neville is also a coach supervisor, supporting other coaches in their work. In his previous professional publication, he co-authored an article entitled "Going full circle: Advancing coaching efficacy using 360° survey metrics – A case study", published in *The International Journal of Evidence Based Coaching and Mentoring* with Dr Hilton Rudnick.

Neville can be contacted at: Neville.Goldin@mweb.co.za

Savnola Goldridge

Savnola is a Neurodivergent Transformational, Executive, and Team Coach, Integrative Behavioural Strategist, and Master Credentialed Coach with over 30 years of experience in coaching, consulting, leadership, and entrepreneurship. Her career includes executive leadership roles in listed South African corporations and founding a successful consulting firm, which was later acquired, where she served as Executive Head of Professional Services. She now leads an international coaching consultancy that supports clients across the globe.

Savnola holds international Master Coach credentials and advanced certifications in the Enneagram, Systemic Coaching, Trauma, Bereavement, and Leadership Maturity. Her expertise is grounded in extensive training with world-renowned mentors in trauma-informed practices, personality systems, and adult development frameworks. She is known for applying a unique blend of behavioural science, developmental theory, and systems thinking to support transformation in individuals, teams, and organisations.

As a trusted advisor in high-stakes mediation, leadership development, and high-performance team coaching, Savnola has made a significant impact through her trauma-informed and Enneagram-based approaches. She regularly presents at international conferences, delivering masterclasses and workshops on topics including resilience, grief, trauma, and leadership maturity.

Savnola is the author of *The Memory Tree*, a children's book addressing grief and loss, and the creator of Enneagram typing cards – translated into multiple languages to promote accessibility across cultures. Her work is recognised for expanding the practical, inclusive application of the Enneagram as a transformational tool.

With a deep commitment to inclusive development and behavioural insight, Savnola continues to be a leading voice in personal and organisational transformation.

Savnola can be contacted at: savnola@savnolagoldridge.com

Karen Grant

Karen is a leadership and transition coaching specialist with a background in Business Economics. With over 15 years of experience as a global executive facilitator and Master Certified Coach (ICF), she helps professionals move through moments of change with clarity and courage – whether stepping into a new leadership role, preparing for tough conversations, or encountering critical transitions.

Karen's coaching is known for being deeply empathetic, blending strategic thinking with a human touch. Prior to embarking upon her independent career, Karen spent a decade as a key account manager and facilitator at Ernst & Young (EY) championing best practices in account management. Since 2008, she has partnered with leaders across sectors and geographies, playing a key role in shaping leadership development. Karen has been instrumental in the launch of Parental Transition Coaching to the South African marketplace.

She holds a Bachelor of Commerce Honours in Business Economics and is certified in multiple tools, including Clarity4D™, Neurozone Advanced Resilience Index™, the Enneagram and Persolog DISC. Karen serves as a coach trainer for the Thoughtsmiths Transforming Insights coach training and a mentor coach for SACAP (the SA College of Applied Psychology) She is a former ballroom dancer and ballet teacher, married to a film industry creative and mom to two grown sons.

Karen can be contacted at: karen@karengrant.co.za or www.linkedin.com/in/karengrantza/

Sam Isaacson

Sam is a coaching thought leader with rich experience gained from global professional services firms, leading the global consulting work for a pioneering unicorn coaching technology startup, and founding his own consultancy. His insights at the intersection of leadership, technology and coaching frequently appear in specialist and mainstream press and in a significant contribution to the coaching literature, including The Digital and AI Coaches' Handbook. He is a sought-after speaker at international coaching conferences and actively contributes to discussions on technology's impact on coaching.

Sam was Chair of the UK Government's Coaching Professional apprenticeship trailblazer group, which developed England's most popular accredited coach training programme, and he currently holds roles with AIcoach.chat, a non-directive AI coach platform, and as a Trustee with GivingTime, a charity providing pro bono coaching to school children.

Founder of the Coachtech Collective and lead trainer of the Coachtech Academy, Sam is dedicated to enhancing the impact of coaching and protecting the future of the profession through mature AI integration and coach skills development. He continues to explore the future of coaching in his LinkedIn newsletter, providing a lens on its evolution in harmony with emerging technologies, including blockchain, immersive technologies such as virtual reality, quantum computing and more.

Sam can be contacted at: sam@isaacson.uk

Shelley Lewin

Shelley is a leadership and relationship specialist with a background in applied psychology and over 6,500 hours of coaching experience as a practitioner, including deep work as a certified couple counsellor. Her practice spans global corporations, SMEs, and government sectors-coaching leaders from mid-level managers to senior executives. She is also the founder of *The Relationship Architect Coaching & Education* and author of *'Uncomplicated Love': A step-by-step guide for building a thriving relationship*. Shelley brings a rare blend of insight into both professional and personal dynamics, because thriving in one without the other rarely sustains.

Shelley has coached leaders from global corporations and government sectors-including professionals from Google, Disney, and the U.S. Space Force- through programs publicly acknowledged by BetterUp. Her work integrates systems thinking, attachment science, and her proprietary *Architecture of Relationship* framework, supporting clients to build connection-rich, high-trust environments. She is currently developing a suite of transformational 'blue ocean' retreat experiences designed for individuals and couples on Relationship Design and a Partnership Reboot, combining nature-based wisdom, the Enneagram, and relational mastery.

Shelley holds formal qualifications in counselling, along with certifications in coaching, and facilitation. She has contributed to multiple publications, panels, and interviews on leadership, modern relationships, and relational intelligence.

Shelley can be contacted at: shelley@tracoaching.com, URL: https://tracoaching.com/

Dan Newby

Dan is a long-time coach, coach trainer, author, and teacher. He is the author of six books on emotions, emotional literacy, and their role in life and work, including *The Unopened Gift, The Field Guide to Emotions, Dignity in Policing, and Dignity in Leadership*. He is accredited as a Professional Certified Coach with ICF, is the founder of the School of Emotions, and co-founder of Dignity Inc. He works with clients, individual and organisational, of all backgrounds from coaches and leaders to educators and health care professionals. Dan's passion is inspiring and enabling others to benefit from the often unrecognised value of their emotions.

Dan considers himself a practitioner and his approach to emotional learning is immersive and practice-based. His work explores the logic and relevance of emotions no matter what stage of life one is at or what work they are committed to. Emotions underlie every decision we make and are the basis of all our relationships. When we choose to ignore them, we lose one of our greatest human assets.

Dan has been fortunate to live in several countries, which has confirmed his understanding of emotions as an aspect of our humanity that unites us and can be the source of extraordinary collaboration. He lives in Spain with his wife and co-author Lucy.

Dan can be contacted at: dan@dignity-inc.com

Dr Ashika Pillay

Ashika is a medical doctor with over 25 years of experience across the medical and allied health fields, including a decade in senior roles within the pharmaceutical industry. Her background spans leadership, corporate communications, marketing, strategy, change management, and clinical research operations. She holds an MBA from the Gordon Institute of Business Science (GIBS) and is an internationally certified coach, mindfulness facilitator, and certified Chief Wellbeing Officer.

Ashika currently works as a leadership, wellbeing, and performance coach, and also facilitates wellbeing strategies and programmes for organisations. She is passionate about integrating the science of holistic wellbeing, preventative medicine, and longevity into her work with individuals and corporates, drawing on a multidisciplinary approach that blends medical insight with mindfulness and coaching.

Her corporate experience has given her deep insight, empathy, and understanding – not only of the challenges but also of the opportunities that exist to thrive as humans and as organisations. She believes that well-being is not just good for people; it's good for business. Her mission is to help people and organisations be at their best, so they can make a meaningful impact in the world.

She has appeared on various podcasts and television programmes and has spoken at local conferences on wellbeing and mental health. In, she contributed a chapter to the book Mental Health in the Workplace, and she continues to write regularly on LinkedIn and her personal blog.

Ashika can be contacted at: ashika@re-mind.co.za or visit www.re-mind.co.za for more information.

Brad Shorkend

Brad is a behavioural specialist and high performance coach obsessed with helping leaders, businesses, and everyone who wakes up in the morning to go to work to be better at the complicated job of being human.

Since 2005 he has worked with thousands of people around the world on how to 'better human' at work, and in turn how to build and lead organisations that are outstanding places for people to thrive at, and to deliver sustainable success in a world that has gone digital crazy.

He is a relentless entrepreneur, having founded and successfully (mostly) led over 20 businesses across numerous industry sectors.

Brad's professional career kicked off with him building his own architectural practice and specializing in architecture for business for over 15 years. It was during this time that he discovered his love for entrepreneurship, leadership, people development and the "thinking" space, and he is now a sparring partner for CEO's, MD's, Exco's, and leaders at all levels of organisation, high potential individuals, teams, and entrepreneurs.

Brad is also a TEDx speaker and a frequent contributor to many print and online publications and radio shows.

He co-authored *"We Are Still Human (and work shouldn't suck!)"* as his first published book and has contributed chapters to many others.

He is an adjunct faculty at GIBS and Duke CE business schools.

In-between all of this he finds time to escape to the mountains and has summited three of the seven summits, the tallest peaks in Africa, Australia, and Europe, and has expeditioned to Everest Base Camp.

Brad can be contacted at: brad@stillhuman.co.za

Liza Stead

Liza is the General Manager of a leading coaching consultancy, CoachMatching, joining in early 2023. Prior to this, she pioneered and led the Coaching, Mentoring and Mindfulness Centre within Rand Merchant Bank and the FirstRand Group, a global financial services firm. These 14 years are a career highlight where she was able to live her calling within an organisational context.

Liza has traversed three significant career re-directions during her professional life – 35 years in corporate - prior to taking early retirement to craft her career next. She was a working mother to two daughters in the earlier part of her career, and a life-long student. She completed a Project Management Professional (PMP) credential, MBA, and an array of coaching qualifications, culminating in being a credentialled Senior Coaching Practitioner and Coach Supervisor through the European Mentoring and Coaching Council (EMCC), and Coach Supervisor through the international Coaching Supervisor Academy (CSA).

Liza is a long-time leadership coach, transition coach, coach supervisor, mindfulness teacher and retreat facilitator. Her deep passion and commitment is to enrich and advance the coaching profession and to contribute to the maturity of professional coaches.

Liza can be contacted at: liza@coachmatching.com

Tessa Whyatt

Tessa started off her career as an Art Therapist nearly 20 years ago (MA Art Therapy, University of Hertfordshire 2006) and has worked extensively with individuals and groups, both in community and private practice. She currently lectures part-time on the Masters in Art Therapy at the University of Johannesburg (UJ). Tessa also holds the position of Art Therapy Co-ordinator for the South African National Arts Therapies Association (SANATA). She is registered with the Health Professions Counsil of South Africa (HPCSA). Tessa previously published a chapter based on her Art Therapy, Resilience, and Time To Think work combined in a program to help prevent school dropout in high schools [Time to Thrive: Youth Groups Combining Directive Arts Therapies and Coaching: International Advances in Art Therapy Research and Practice: Emerging Picture, Edited by Val Huet and Lynn Kapitan, Cambridge Scholars Publishing, 2020). She added training as a Grief Educator (2021). Much of her work is in the grief and loss space, paired with Resilience work to support and heal.

With an interest in Positive Psychology Tessa pursued further training as a coach, with an interest in strengthening client's self-leadership and EQ. Qualifications include Time To Think Coach (2012) and Time To Think Facilitator (2013), Management Coach (2019, University of Stellenbosch Business School), Resilience Coach (2020), Enneagram Coach (Aephoria, 2020), and Five Lens Certification (2021). The focus is on health and wellness from an integrative perspective, and Tessa is known as a Therapeutic Coach.

Contact information: tessawhyatt@gmail.com

CHAPTER AND FLOW OVERVIEW

A playbook for Coaching in the Modern Workplace

The book is a collaborative effort with a team of subject matter experts. The target audience and therefore intention is to provide for companies and individuals a practical understanding of the industry, hence the good, the bad and the ugly, as well as insights into the different types of coaching. Many of my team are already published in their own right, as stated below.

A user's guide to coaching

Chapter outline

1. **In case you missed it the first time by Susan Astengo & Prof David Clutterbuck –** Susi Astengo discusses how coaching has evolved. She explores the democratisation of coaching, different coaching models, and coach maturity.

2. **Coaching and therapy, the similarities, and differences –** Tessa Wyatt discusses coaching in detail to understand how it is different or similar to therapy.

3. **Coaching for better humaning –** Brad Shorkend. Takes us through the need for better humaning as we move from a knowledge economy to a relational economy and how and why that yields better results. Brad looks at the link between coaching and being better Humans, better businesses and a better world.

4. **From the bedroom to the boardroom –** Shelley Lewin "the relationship architect" shares that relationships are the cornerstone of all human connections, so it makes sense to examine them across all areas of one's life.

5. **From uncertainty to clarity –** Dr Neville Goldin/Liza Stead/Karen Grant focus on critical transitions throughout a person's employment. Through leadership transitions or retirement coaching and maternity coaching. As human beings, we are all exposed to key transitions, whether it be a simple promotion transitioning into a new role or a highly complex life transition, such as becoming a parent. Navigating these can be made easier with coaching.

6. **The role of Emotional Literacy in coaching –** Dan Newby states "most people are not taught about the full range of emotions to understand their purpose, why we have them, and what to do with them". Dan debunks many myths and helps us understand the crucial role emotional literacy plays in our lives and in coaching.

7. **The Mindful Professional: Integrating Neuroscience and Wellness Strategies** – Lily Breuning Ellis, Dr Ashika Pillay, and Vandana Daya. Well care is emerging as one of the most significant areas of concern for most organisations and individuals alike. The wellness industry has never been busier. From the worried well through to the burnt out individual, we all need to understand how the brain and body connection works and what we can do to help ourselves.

8. **AI and its role in coaching** – Susi with input from Sam Isaacson and Prof Nicky Terblanche examines how AI is disrupting the world of work, with the coaching industry being no exception. Coaches and organisations need to learn how to embrace technology to achieve optimal results.

9. **The role of assessments in coaching** – Sav Goldridge takes us through the role assessments play in coaching to create greater self-awareness as quickly as possible. This chapter will focus mostly on the Enneagram as our preferred tool.

10. **The Future of coaching** – Including the rise of the celebrity coach and coaching as entertainment– In this last chapter, Susi will guide the reader on the impact Social Media is having on coaching and the rise of an informal learning industry.

PART I

FOUNDATIONS AND FRAMEWORKS

Chapter 1

IN CASE YOU MISSED IT THE FIRST TIME

by Susan Astengo and Prof David Clutterbuck

After seven months of market research into the coaching industry in South Africa, I decided to start CoachMatching with a vision to "professionalise the coaching industry in South Africa". Little did I know that this was about to be one of the greatest adventures of my life and that my business CoachMatching was about to be birthed as my second child.

My research clarified that coaching is an industry and not a profession and, as such, there are few, if any, barriers to entry. They highlight that, currently, the coaching industry does not adequately meet several key criteria for professionalisation, including the enforcement of barriers to entry. This lack of standardised entry requirements allows individuals to practise coaching without consistent qualifications or oversight, raising concerns about the quality and credibility of services provided. I will discuss this more in Chapter 10, where we look at the impact of the rise of the celebrity coach and social media influencers.

Coaching is not a "new" thing and, in fact, coaching, as a concept and practice, has evolved significantly over the centuries. From its early roots in mentorship to its modern-day applications across various disciplines, such as sports, business, and personal development, coaching has continually adapted to meet the needs of individuals and organisations. This chapter provides a comprehensive overview of the history of coaching, tracing its development from ancient civilisations to its contemporary frameworks.

Early foundations of coaching

The origins of coaching can be traced as far back as to ancient societies where the transmission of knowledge and skills was primarily conducted through mentors and philosophers such as Socrates, Plato, and Aristotle, who employed a method of inquiry and dialogue that closely resembles modern coaching techniques. *The Socratic method,* characterised by asking questions to stimulate critical thinking and self-reflection, laid an intellectual foundation that continues to influence coaching practices today.[1]

Coaching in the 19th and 20th centuries

The term "coaching" itself originates from the 19th century, particularly in the context of sports. British educational institutions, such as Oxford and Cambridge, popularised coaching to improve athletic performance, focusing on the systematic development of physical skills and strategic thinking. By the late 19th century, coaching had expanded beyond sports to include academic tutoring and other performance-oriented fields.[2]

The 20th century witnessed a rapid expansion of coaching across various sectors, driven by industrialisation, organisational development, and psychological research. The rise of behavioural psychology, pioneered by figures such as B.F. Skinner and Carl Rogers, significantly influenced coaching methodologies. Rogers's **person-centred approach**, emphasising empathy, active listening, and non-directive guidance, became a cornerstone of coaching in therapeutic and organisational settings.[3]

Sir John Whitmore (Coaching for Performance,[4]) laid the foundations for performance-based coaching. By the 1990s, life coaching had expanded beyond the boardroom, driven by figures like Tony Robbins, whose motivational seminars and best-selling books introduced coaching principles to the masses.

Modern coaching and its professionalisation

Organisations such as the European Mentors and Coaches council (EMCC) started in 1991, the International Coach Federation (ICF), founded in 1995, established industry standards, ethical guidelines, and credentialing systems to ensure the credibility and effectiveness of coaching practices.[5]

Contemporary coaching draws upon various disciplines, including positive psychology, neuroscience, and systems theory, to offer a holistic approach to personal and professional development.

17 years ago, my role was as much about educating my clients regarding what coaching was and also could be and **should not be** used for. Back then, many of my clients wanted to use coaching as a remedial tool and they would often start with "one of our leaders/managers is not performing and their team is unhappy". To be fair, I still hear those words today but far less so. Coaching was seen as a silver bullet back

then and a way to solve performance related issues. There was also a phase when coaching was a badge of honour, with seemingly everyone wanting to be coached.

Things have settled down now and coaching has evolved significantly, with far more providers in the market. Not necessarily a good thing. Most requests we see now are for high potentials, talent management programmes and to support leadership development. Later in this chapter, I will share some approaches we have developed over the past two decades to "democratise" coaching.

This industry is grounded in the belief that, with the right guidance and support, people can unlock their potential, overcome obstacles, and foster growth. We will discuss this philosophy in more detail later, as over the past 17 years, my views on this have changed somewhat.

Creating a coaching culture and the democratisation of coaching

Democratising coaching is both a concept and the process: The concept of democratising coaching emerged around 2014 out of workshops Prof David Clutterbuck was conducting with coaches around the world. A recurrent theme from participants was resistance to the idea that there was one ideal way to coach. Different cultures have different approaches, derived from different traditions. The perceived repression of these approaches, in favour of a predominantly North American cultural perspective, as referred to as "cultural imperialism". The issue has been exacerbated by, for example, cultural insensitivity in competency frameworks and in the assessment of coach competence for accreditation.

Closely connected to the principles of democratising coaching is decolonising coaching. The dominant force globally in accrediting coaches is the International Coach Federation (ICF), which has formalised what it means to be a "competent" coach around a set of assumptions deeply rooted in North American culture. There is a growing movement in ICF to recognise that other cultures have very different perspectives on developmental relationships.

We have seen this at play with our international clients, where we try to support them either with local coaches or coaches who have the cultural sensitivity to navigate their nuances. There is a case for one size **does not** fit all and that the quality of the relationship between coach and coachee can be impacted either positively or negatively by the match. Equally, language plays a significant role as although English is recognised as the main global "business language" it is arrogant of the English-speaking world to think that being able to speak in their first language would not be a more effective option for the coachee.

In simpler terms, democratising coaching means enabling everyone in an organisation, big or small, to have access to some form of coaching or another. This is where external coaching intersects with internal coaching to help develop a coaching culture, and where we have had the most success in democratising coaching with our existing clients. This is also where Prof David Cutterbuck and I discovered our mutual passion to bring coaching to the masses.

Key aspects of democratising coaching include:

1. **Accessibility:** Ensuring coaching is available to people regardless of socioeconomic status, geography, or position in an organisation.

2. **Affordability:** Reducing the cost of coaching through scalable platforms, group coaching, or leveraging technology like AI-powered tools and online coaching platforms.

3. **Scalability:** Using digital tools and innovative models to expand coaching reach, such as apps, virtual coaching sessions, and automated resources.

4. **Equity:** Creating inclusive coaching opportunities that cater to diverse needs and underrepresented groups, addressing systemic inequalities in access.

5. **Empowerment:** Equipping individuals with tools, frameworks, and skills for self-guided growth and development, fostering a culture of continuous learning.

Our clients constantly face the challenge of managing shrinking development budgets and still meeting the demands to effectively develop and grow their people. Our approach is to offer a blend of coaching solutions and approaches to enable them to meet the fullest spectrum of coaching needs.

Coaching should not be a luxury reserved for the elite; it should be a fundamental right for anyone who seeks to grow, learn, and contribute meaningfully." – David Clutterbuck, Co-founder of the European Mentoring & Coaching Council

There are affordable solutions for all levels, and the trick is to understand how they can all work together. So, what to use, where and when and how to ensure that there is alignment, consistency and that the organisation's coaching strategy is addressing people's needs is key.

There is also a huge amount of information available on how leaders spend their day and this rarely varies between organisations and industries. Ironically, if you were to shadow a CEO and a junior leader for a week, you would probably observe them doing similar things:

- Chairing and attending meetings

- Setting goals, tracking, and managing performance

- Offering coaching and guidance on performance and career progression

- Making decisions and solving problems

- Leading teams and groups

- Gathering information and analysing data

- Communicating

What differentiates them is the degree of complexity, the levels of decision-making authority, the potential consequences of poor decision making, and the level of risk involved. Therefore, the coaching approach needs to reflect these factors.

The term democratising coaching has been co-opted by the IT industry to refer to the potential to reduce costs using Artificial Intelligence, while making it more readily available. The latter happens, at least in theory, because unlike a human coach, the AI coach is instantly available, day or night. AI is only a partial solution and we have successfully been developing coaching cultures by training leaders as coaches, creating an internal team of coaches, offering the Coach on Call, as well as implementing peer coaching and Coach Bots. We will discuss AI & Coach Bots in more detail in Chapter 8.

We developed a simple approach to examine the different options for different levels of leadership. The figure below shows the leadership focus areas and the possible coaching options that we consider to be effective:

HIGHER:
STAKES RISK
COMPLEXITY

One to one
coaching &
team coaching

HIGHER:
VOLUMES

Group coaching
Masterclasses
Leader as coach
programmes
Coach bots
Coach on Call

Vision and
strategy

Leading the
business

Leading leaders

Leadership development
and coaching individual
contributors and teams

Set goals, manage
performance and career

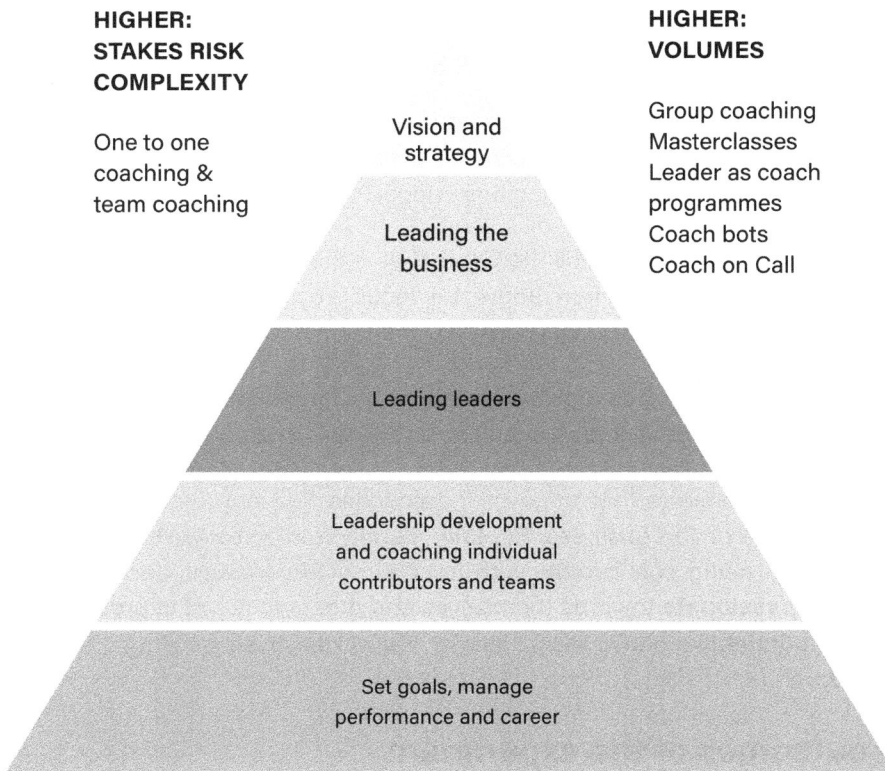

Figure 1: The leadership focus areas and the possible coaching options

Benefits of coaching

Clearly, I am a convert so, rather than me going on about the benefits of coaching I thought I would share a story as it articulates the benefits so clearly that you will be reaching for your strategy or coaching policy document to see where you can use coaching more effectively.

Time Etc replaced all of its managers with coaches. The notable experiment involving the replacement of managers with coaches was conducted by Time Etc, a virtual assistant platform. This innovative approach emerged as a response to declining employee engagement levels, which had reached a seven-year low in 2022, according to Gallup's annual survey. Only a third of workers reported feeling engaged at work, while almost a fifth (18%) described themselves as "actively disengaged."

"We started asking the people we were hiring what they needed from a manager. What stood out was how the list they gave us – goal-setting, feedback, personal, and professional development opportunities, autonomy – sounded much more like they needed a coach, rather than a manager," team at Time Etc. said.

The company decided to eliminate traditional management roles and instead employ coaches, adopting a ratio of one coach for every six employees.

The coaches' job was to help employees maximise productivity by offering close mentoring and feedback, encouraging them to identify how they work best, and making sure they are offered training and support to develop professionally

"Like managers, coaches are still there to act as a first port of call when challenges arise. But instead of directing from above, the focus is on empowering and supporting the employee to find their own way forward," the team added.

The company also organizes regular workshops, inviting external experts to conduct tailored classes on various topics, such as mindfulness and confidence building.

What is most notable is that none of the coaches had any technical experience of either the role or the business. So, they literally had to be **curious** all the time, **courageous** in being comfortable with not having the answers and trusting their people, **compassionate** towards themselves and others to assist in problem solving and able to **connect** with their teams quickly. We will discuss these four qualities later in the chapter.

Key outcomes of the experiment

increased Productivity: After implementing this coaching model, Time Etc reported a 20% improvement in employee productivity.

Enhanced Employee Engagement: The shift resulted in employees feeling significantly more engaged and happier at work. Time Etc consistently ranks in the top 1% of teams worldwide in terms of employee engagement, as measured by Gallup's Q12 Survey.

Reduced Turnover and Sick Days: The company experienced a decrease in employee turnover and sick days taken, which is noteworthy during the period marked by the "great resignation" when many employees were leaving their jobs

The experiment at Time Etc illustrates a significant shift in organisational management strategies, moving from traditional hierarchical structures to a more supportive coaching model.

Understanding coaching

To help understand how to get the best out of coaching at all levels, let's start with the basics. On a one-to-one basis, coaching is a dynamic and transformative process facilitates personal and professional growth. It involves a collaborative partnership between a coach and a client, where the coach employs various techniques and methodologies to guide the client in identifying goals, overcoming obstacles, and maximising potential. At its core, coaching is about fostering self-awareness, developing actionable strategies, and creating accountability. Coachees are encouraged to explore their thoughts and feelings, the context within which they operate, their unique skills and resources, which can lead to profound insights and breakthroughs. The coaching journey is not just about achieving specific outcomes but also about building a mindset and skills that empower individuals to navigate future challenges with.

I can share many stories of where this has been the case with textbook perfect results. A recent example that possibly you can relate to is of Jane, a senior leader in a financial services industry who is super successful, has been identified as high potential and who is struggling with a bit of Imposter Syndrome. We matched her (using our matching software) with a similarly successful female coach and within 1 day of receiving the request; she was up and running with her coach. Fast forward 6 months later and she has been promoted, is flourishing and all self-doubt and limiting beliefs set firmly behind her. "what did you do to her" asked her leader in a recent feedback session. I replied, "we got her the right coach". Our tag line has always been "the magic is in the match" and to this day, I still strongly believe that. This is just one person out of the thousands we have worked with over the years combining part science, part theory, and experience and a sprinkle or "magic" to enable individuals, teams, and organisations to access the highest calibre of coach to meet their needs.

However, coaching doesn't happen in a vacuum and so it is impossible to separate a coachee's experiences from their broader context, within which they experience them, whether that is at home or at work.

Mark Kahn, in his seminal work Coaching on the Axis,[6] introduced the notion of other critical stakeholders in this process; being the organisation and the line manager or HR. Over the years, I have experienced many Coaches, HR professionals, and Line Managers who struggle with this dynamic, some wanting to be involved in every aspect of the coaching whilst others erring towards abdication of all responsibility to the coach or coaching organisation. Navigating these respective views has presented many challenges and at times, I have needed to bite my tongue. Ultimately, I always return to meet the client where they are at – and that almost always resolves the challenge.

Not every organisation or individual within the organisation will have the same understanding of the relationships required for coaching to be a sustainable and successful development strategy. Also, why is coaching being seen as the go to developmental silver bullet by some and not others? Does coaching work? And if so, why is it so hard to get ROI data on coaching that convinces the powers and the decision makers to invest?

One time we had an HR lead in a large banking client who was a total control freak, had been in coaching herself and expected the coach to meet with her Line Manager every 2 months to update them on her progress. That was her reality, and as far as she was concerned, this was a perfectly acceptable and legitimate approach. It took some time and convincing to get to the point where she could understand why we weren't prepared to do the same but eventually the penny dropped and we could get back on track reporting to her on overall themes across the division and tying that feedback into other data and people analytics she had. By doing this, we could focus on the system whilst at the same time providing progress towards goal for the individual.

On another occasion, we worked with an organisation who gave us over R250,000 upfront to provide coaching to their executives and then for almost seven months never showed up for a single feedback and project supervision meeting.

As you navigate this guide, we will unpack the diverse coaching methodologies, tools, styles, types and best practices. Each chapter is dedicated to a specific aspect of coaching, be it relationship, leadership, or transition coaching, including stories, case studies, and hints and tips, that will enable you to make informed decisions either for yourself, your team members or for your organisation.

Coaching models and styles – What, why and how of coaching

The "WHAT" and "WHY" behind coachees' desires for coaching can be categorised as follows:

- **Performance Coaching:** Focused on enhancing an individual's skills and capabilities to achieve specific goals commonly used in sports and business settings.

- **Life Coaching:** A holistic approach that assists individuals in achieving personal growth and life balance across various aspects, including relationships, health, and career.

- **Executive or Leadership Coaching:** Aimed at developing leadership skills and strategic thinking within corporate environments.

- **Transition and Career Coaching:** Provides guidance to individuals navigating career transitions and professional development.

- **Transformational Coaching:** Focuses on deep personal change, addressing mindset, beliefs, and values to create sustainable growth.

- **Health and Wellness Coaching:** Supports individuals in making lifestyle changes to improve overall well-being and achieve health-related goals.

- **Sustainability coaching**: Focused on helping executives become better global citizens/ good ancestors, etc.

- **Coaching to manage Change:** Supports individuals, teams, and organisations in navigating transitions, overcoming resistance, and adapting effectively to new challenges.

- **Niche coaching.** This can include anything from bereavement and loss through how to parent and everything in between.

I know that there are many others, however, these are the ones we most frequently get requests to support. We break these down further into goal categories under the headings of leading self, leading others and leading the business.

Different coaching styles and their benefits (the how)

Different coaches employ a variety of styles, each suited to specific needs and goals. Understanding these styles can help in selecting the right coach and style for your unique situation.

1. **Directive Coaching:** This style involves a coach providing clear guidance, instructions, and structured action plans. It is most beneficial when clients require specific skills development, goal achievement, and performance enhancement, such as in corporate or sports settings. It is more aligned with mentoring.

2. **Non-Directive Coaching:** This approach focuses on active listening, asking powerful questions, and facilitating self-discovery. It is ideal for individuals seeking deeper self-awareness, long-term behavioural change, and personal development.

3. **Transformational Coaching:** A deeper style aimed at fostering profound change. This style helps clients shift their mindsets, overcome limiting beliefs, and achieve sustainable growth. It is most beneficial for individuals undergoing significant life transitions or seeking to align their values with their goals.

4. **Transactional Coaching:** Focused on achieving short-term goals and measurable outcomes, transactional coaching works well in corporate environments where performance and productivity improvements are the primary objectives.

5. **Holistic Coaching:** Incorporating elements from various disciplines, such as psychology, wellness, and leadership, holistic coaching takes a comprehensive approach to personal and professional development, making it ideal for clients seeking balance across multiple life domains.

6. **Solution-Focused Coaching:** This style emphasises identifying and leveraging strengths to overcome challenges and achieve goals quickly. It is useful in business and career coaching settings where results are a priority.

7. **Somatic Coaching:** This approach integrates body awareness and physical experiences into the coaching process, helping clients recognise the connection between their physical state and their thoughts, emotions, and behaviours. Somatic coaching is beneficial for individuals dealing with stress, trauma, or those seeking to improve their overall well-being and presence.

8. **Ontological Coaching:** Focused on the way individuals perceive and interpret their reality, ontological coaching explores language, emotions, and physical presence to create profound personal and professional transformations. This modality is beneficial for individuals seeking to enhance self-awareness, communication skills, and leadership capabilities.

9. **Internal vs. External Coaching:** Internal coaching involves coaches who are part of the organisation and have an understanding of its culture, goals, and challenges. It is useful for talent development, leadership growth, and aligning employees with organisational objectives. External coaching, on the other hand, brings an outsider's perspective, offering fresh insights, confidentiality, and unbiased guidance, making it suitable for executive coaching and complex personal growth journeys.

10. **Narrative Coaching:** This modality uses storytelling to help individuals reframe their experiences and reshape their personal and professional identities. Narrative coaching is beneficial for those dealing with change, transitions, or a desire to redefine their sense of purpose.

11. **Cognitive Behavioural Coaching (CBC):** Based on principles from cognitive-behavioural therapy (CBT), this coaching style helps individuals identify and change negative thought patterns and behaviours that hinder personal or professional success. It is especially effective in managing stress, overcoming limiting beliefs, and fostering resilience.

12. **Peer Coaching:** A collaborative approach where individuals coach each other based on shared experiences and mutual feedback. This is effective in organisational settings to build team cohesion and peer learning. While this approach fosters trust and mutual support, potential challenges include a lack of objectivity, as peers may struggle to provide unbiased feedback and often end up in them sharing advice. The absence of professional expertise can limit the depth

and effectiveness of the coaching process and, as such, Organisations should consider providing training or guidelines to ensure constructive outcomes.

13. **Systems psychodynamic coaching:** The primary task of systems psychodynamic leadership coaching is to provide developmentally and psycho-educationally focussed reflection and learning opportunities to the leader, to study, become aware of and gain insight into how task and organisational performance are influenced by both conscious and unconscious behaviour.

To increase the sustainability of behaviour changes and to protect the ROI of coaching, we have used peer coaching (we call them peer learning groups PLG) extensively to support individuals who have been through one-to-one coaching process. They are also often referred to as coaching circles.

We train them in the process and facilitate their initial PLG's to a point where they are confident in their ability to support their colleagues as part of developing a broader organisational coaching culture.

As you can see, there are many factors that impact on the selection of the best coaching style and model and depend on many factors, including those listed above. Layer on to that the personal preferences, as well as the areas to be developed and it is understandable why so many coachees I talked to during my initial research have had a less than life-changing experience.

Our deeper understanding of coaching over the past two decades establishes that the model a coach uses (the how) is less important than the quality of their relationship (the who). Many of our coaches are qualified in at least two different modalities and often more.

COACHING THE PATH THAT GENERATES LEARNING

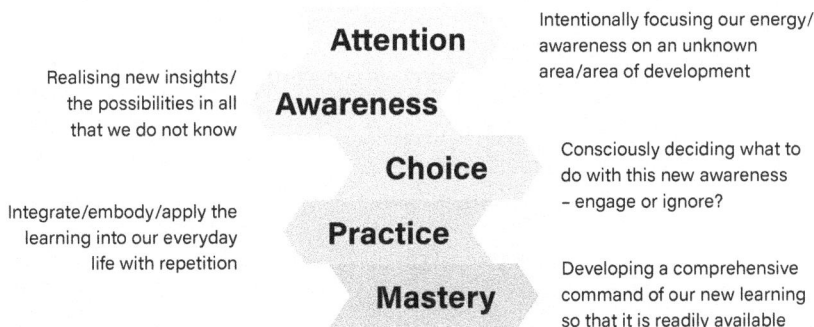

Attention — Intentionally focusing our energy/ awareness on an unknown area/area of development

Realising new insights/ the possibilities in all that we do not know — **Awareness**

Choice — Consciously deciding what to do with this new awareness – engage or ignore?

Integrate/embody/apply the learning into our everyday life with repetition — **Practice**

Mastery — Developing a comprehensive command of our new learning so that it is readily available

Figure 2: Coaching: The path that generates learning

As a basic principle, the above figure shows the path that coaching follows to achieve results. To round this section off, we also need to talk about the most common coaching models, as many of our clients might specify that they want "integral coaches only".

Popular coaching models include:

- **The GROW Model:** Developed by John Whitmore, it structures the coaching process into Goal, Reality, Options, and Will, offering a systematic framework for achieving objectives.

- **OSKAR Model:** Focused on Outcome, Scaling, Know-how, Affirmation, and Review, widely used in solution-focused coaching.

- **CLEAR Model:** Encompassing Contracting, Listening, Exploring, Action, and Review, used to create clarity and direction in coaching conversations.

- **Co-Active Coaching Model:** A relationship-based approach that integrates fulfilment, balance, and process to empower clients.

- **Integral Model.** Rooted in Ken Wilber's Integral Theory, it is a holistic, developmental approach that guides individuals through sustainable change by addressing multiple dimensions of their experience – cognitive, emotional, somatic, relational, and spiritual. It helps clients expand self-awareness, shift perspectives, and build long-term capacities for growth and transformation.

Not all coaches are created equal

Let me share a little more of my story. When I first started to explore coaching way back in 2007, it seemed that there were two main pain points to solve for and ironically, this hasn't changed much over the past decade. The first and most obvious was to understand what makes a great coach, is it credentialling, supervision, the model, or approach they use or experience and maturity, and the second was to understand how to get the right match.

So, what is it that makes the difference between an ok, a good and a great coach? In the absence of intimate knowledge of coaching understandably, most people rely on ICF/EMCC or COMENSA as the governing bodies to accredit coaches. The ICF/COMENSA and EMCC each have a clear set of competencies. However, just as passing a driving test ensures a basic standard is met, it does not guarantee an enjoyable journey, more just a safe one.

We all know that getting into a car with certain drivers is a more pleasurable experience than with others, even though both have passed their test! Coaching is very similar, not all coaches are created equal even if they have passed their test!. Their initial coaching qualification, in my view, is just the same as passing one's driving test. How the coach then applies and matures their skills is what makes for a great coach.

Based on many hours of research and meeting hundreds of coaches, I have a very clear view of what good looks like and reflected this in our rigorous coach assessment centre. Armed with a competency matrix and a ton of excitement, I approached the ICF to have my assessment centre accredited back in 2008, only to be told that it would not be possible as there wasn't an Internationally recognised standard for that. Thankfully, things have moved on since then and we now have CCMi endorsement for our coach selection process.

Over the years, I have met and assessed many "qualified coaches" and would say that standards vary enormously, so I have not been able to correlate accreditation with competence.

Back then, I started building a small team of exceptional coaches who were all qualified in one coaching model or another. However, their superpower was judgement. That elusive ability to instinctively feel or know when it was important to take the client's thinking to another level or in another direction. Their approach often led to the much lauded "Aha" moment. Judgement coupled with a genuine commitment to lifelong learning, I later discovered through my association with Professor David Clutterbuck, founding member of the EMCC, is the secret to success. He asserts that this reflected a level of coach maturity rather than a specific model, a process of philosophy.

Figure 3 below shows the various stages of coach maturity.

Different levels of coach maturity

Figure 3 below shows the various stages of coach maturity

1	**Models-based**	**Control**	How do I take them where I think they need to go? How do I adapt my technique or model to this circumstance?
2	**Process-based**	**Contain**	The present is difficult to describe, the future cannot be determined and decisions are risky.
3	**Philosophy-based**	**Facilitate**	How do I give enough control to the client and still retain a purposeful conversation? What's the best way to apply my process in this instance?
4	**Systemic eclectic**	**Enable**	Are we both relaxed enough to allow the issue and the solution to emerge in whatever way they will? Do I need to apply any techniques or processes at all? If I do, what does the client context tell me about how to select from the wide choice available to me?

Figure 3: Stages of coach maturity (Copyright David Clutterbuck, reproduced with permission of the author).[7]

In the absence of in-depth knowledge of the stages of maturity, many of my clients become attached to a particular coaching model as they believed that this would provide assurance of a consistent experience for the coachee and allow the organisation a means to monitor and measure the coaching. I have always believed that the model is less significant and what is important to the ROI, be that time or money, is ultimately the sustainability of the behavioural change achieved because of the coaching experience. Recent research by the Coach Maturity Research Group endorsed this perspective.

The shift in coaching is from doing to being

We were working with a major bank to support their High Potential Senior Leadership Programme and one of the delegates already had a coach. They asked would we be comfortable using that coach as part of the programme. I replied, "sure thing, as long as the coach goes through our assessment process". They did, and it was evident that they were operating at a very pedestrian level, using lots of encouragement and passive listening without much else. We declined them and stood our ground, suggesting that whilst the senior leader might be very attached to his coach, that perhaps he would be open to exploring our process, and if he still wanted the same person, then that was their decision.

I am delighted to report that they were open and were matched to their ideal coach and provided feedback to the organisation that the experience was "like night and day". Now, to be clear, I am not in the habit of taking business away from reputable coaches. I do, however, have a strong sense of integrity and ethics when it comes to ensuring that the coachee gets the best possible person to work with them.

Most great coaches become so after many hours of coaching and ongoing personal and professional development. Staying abreast of changes in the coaching industry and the business world is crucial to being able to understand a myriad of client's context. Whilst not impossible, its nonetheless improbable that a 25-year-old with limited work experience will be the most effective coach for a CEO, as they lack a frame of reference on which to draw, no matter how insightful their questions might be.

Over the past 17 years, we have held over 150 monthly coach development activities that have exposed our coaches to content as varied as wellness and wellbeing through to Artificial Intelligence and have developed specialists in the team who are also contributors to this book.

Accepting that effective coaching is a blend of the what, the who and the how I want to focus on two highly successful approaches.

The rise of the leader as a coach

Last year we collaborated with Prof Clutterbuck to support the development of both Leaders and Internal Coaches in a large public sector organisation, with over 10,000 employees. At that time, he introduced us, and then, to the 4 C's of coaching – Advocating that the behaviours that make for a great coach are also the behaviours that make for great leaders.

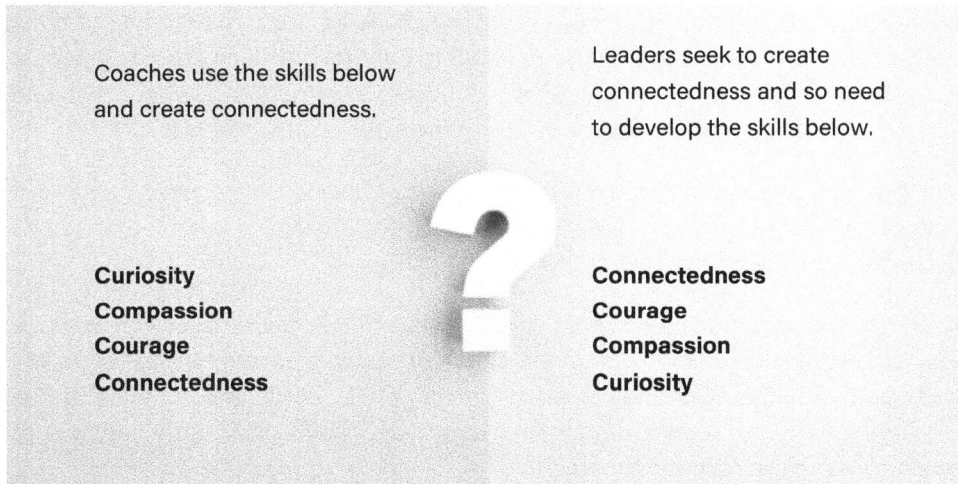

Coaches use the skills below and create connectedness.

Leaders seek to create connectedness and so need to develop the skills below.

Curiosity
Compassion
Courage
Connectedness

Connectedness
Courage
Compassion
Curiosity

Figure 4: The rise of the leader as a coach[8]

We developed three training tracks to enable leaders, with support from the organisation, to decide the level of coaching they wished to attain. Over the years, I have seen many coaches struggle to identify the transformational or overarching goals and objectives for the coaching, ending up with a series of transactional engagements with their coachee. It's a lose-lose situation. What happens as a result is that the coach ends up doing all the work, pushing for when the next session will take place and trying to maintain the momentum and cadence needed to be successful. In my experience this shows that the upfront contracting on the WHY of coaching between coach and Line Manager OR coachee in their Organisation, either has not happened as it should OR as is often the case the coaching has been offered to a diverse group of people not all of whom have bought into the opportunity.

Case study

i realised that there was an opportunity to address a need that the more traditional and transformational coaching approach didn't cater for. In 2020 we offered a large banking client "the Coach on Call", the principle being that many people within The Bank may not need or qualify for transformational coaching however, that pretty much everyone might have an opportunity or challenge that would benefit from a once of session with a coach. They decided to offer four sessions to ±300 people across one division as proof of concept. Suffice to say it was a huge success and three related employee engagement scores increased by four points.

What was fascinating to observe was that of the people who registered an interest in the coaching between 60- 80% took it up with the other 20% putting their hands up for fear of missing out (FOMO)!

Of those that used the service on average, 25% only needed one session, whilst a further 25% requested more. By managing the budget, we were able to be flexible and accommodate everyone's needs. The service is still on offer today and has followed a very consistent pattern that has aided us in understanding how to resource a project of that magnitude.

One of my team recently shared a situation that came up in a Coach on Call session, where a coachee came into the coaching having recently been diagnosed with cancer. Clearly, they were upset and wanted to talk to their coach, whom they have a great relationship with, and in a "safe" space, without having to worry about the coach would be feeling. While counselling them wasn't an option, the coach chose to listen to the coachee's fears and gently asked questions to help them identify resources that could support them in understanding the diagnosis, the treatment, and how to share the news with their loved ones. In subsequent sessions, the coachee expressed gratitude for that time and the coach's sensitivity and support, and they could focus on the original coaching goals.

Whilst this is the exception and quite an extreme situation, it indicates the special nature of the trusted relationship between coach and coachee, particularly when the match is right. The key focus of coaching includes enhanced self-awareness, improved goal-setting, and increased accountability.

Over several sessions, coaches help clients identify their strengths and areas for growth, resilience, and adaptability, equipping individuals with tools to navigate challenges effectively. As with the example shared above, also building personal resilience and a renewed view of resources

We are privileged to be working with a major player in the SA banking industry who recognise both the personal and professional importance of working with the "whole person", They recognise that what's good for the individual ultimately is also good for the organisation and have already seen multiple benefits.

In the next chapter, we will focus on the difference between coaching and therapy. We recognise that whilst people may think they need coaching, often it is a hybrid of coaching and mentoring or therapy. We are very clear regarding the boundaries. The Coach Maturity Research Group has also found that the most effective coaches merge these disciplines seamlessly into the service of evolving client needs. We operate on the 80/20 principle, in as much that all of our coaches need to be spending at least 80% of their time coaching, whilst the remaining 20% might be used to mentor of counsel.

Some questions to mull over?

- How is coaching being implemented in your organisation?

  _____

  _____

  _____

- What has shifted for you as a result of reading this chapter?

  _____

  _____

  _____

- How would you like to see coaching being implemented?

  _____

  _____

  _____

- What is one thing that you will do differently as a result?

  _____

  _____

  _____

Chapter 2

THE DIFFERENCES AND SIMILARITIES BETWEEN COACHING AND THERAPY

by Tessa Whyatt

What is Coaching? How is it different to therapy, counselling, psychology, and other helping/caring professions? And what are the similarities? These are important clarifying questions. And yet the more I have delved into these questions, the less distinct the answers have become! It is utterly grey in distinction and yet is also a wide rainbow spectrum.

In chapter 9, you will read more about our chosen assessment tool, the Enneagram. My personality type is leading from a main style Enneagram one. I like black and white answers, and for things to be clear. So I have been grappling with these kinds of questions all my life. In 2001, I wrote my Fine Arts Honours dissertation at UCT on the topic: The difference between Art and Craft. In 2013, I wrote my Time to Think Coaching assignment on the difference between Time to Think Coaching and Art Therapy. In this paper, I recognised so many synergies. These similarities included the deep listening, empathy, encouragement, noticing body language, and allowing for silence as a question. This was where I first started to blend coaching and my therapy work.

Now here we are twelve years later and I am once again investigating and delving into the murky grey waters of distinguishing between Therapy and Coaching, Coaching and Therapy! You may well ask: Why is this important? And why is it important to me? As a coach, therapist, supervisor, and lecturer, I navigate these spaces in my daily life. Sometimes it is okay to be more fluid and flexible, and other times requires more definition. So, we should probably start with some definitions, but already this is where it becomes tricky!

For the purposes of this book, it is important to clarify and define coaching, as well as to outline its specific benefits compared to other professions. These may be seen as similar professions with vague distinctions. Coaching is well established as a separate yet confusingly similar profession. I am attempting to make the distinction clearer. There are many interpretations, and my challenge is that it is not black and white. The best way to describe this would be as a spectrum. One of my coaching tools is to indicate an imaginary ruler or scale system, and to score yourself on that scale for various questions. This can be used for everything from emotions to stress levels to work-life balance. However, on this Therapy to Coaching to Therapy spectrum, it is difficult to define where something should be placed. For example, addictions counselling is clearly different to business coaching. However, wellness coaching may look quite similar to some forms of therapy.

A lot will obviously depend on the training, qualifications, personality, and way of being of the coach or therapist. How they define themselves and their niche becomes an important part of the distinctions.

For example, Trauma-Informed Coaching certainly leans towards the Therapy side of the spectrum. Wellness, life, and health coaching may be in the centre. Management, business, and career coaching would certainly be further away from the Therapy scale.

I refer here to the well-known and oft-quoted phrase, 'Beauty is in the eye of the beholder' (attributed to Plato). Similarly, I feel that Therapy versus Coaching is in the eye of (or in the mind of) the therapist and coach. I will refer to this later in the chapter as the Hat we are wearing. It is also based on the work we are contracted for, as this is critical to what is required of us by the client. Furthermore, it is based on our skillset, experience, and training as therapists and coaches. These are different professional areas that overlap in several ways.

What are we qualified for? A person who has experienced terrible grief will be able to hold space for and understand another person grieving with deep empathy. However, without the training, they are taking some risks to themselves and the other person. First, the person's story may be very upsetting and triggering to them, and risk re-traumatising them. Second, each individual's grief journey and situation is unique to them, and well-meaning advice can be harmful. Similarly, many people who have journeyed through addiction become specialist counsellors. This grief educator or addiction counsellor role looks similar to a mentorship role in leadership or entrepreneurship, for example. A mentor is someone who has relevant experiences that they can share with their mentee. They have 'been there, done that, and got the sticker' and this makes them an expert in their own life. Where this expertise may be valuable to another person, they are able to help support the person through their own experiences.

Sometimes mentoring can lean towards teaching. Teachers impart knowledge and concepts to aid the student's learning. But a good teacher, mentor, and leader will lean towards the coaching part of the spectrum. The leader-as-coach model has taken traction in many business spaces.

However, some teachers and therapists have a similar belief system, in that they are the expert and their role is to impart knowledge and guidance to another person. This creates a hierarchy. In this view, the client has agreed that there is something wrong that they need the therapist's help with. The therapist thus has consent in the contracting to use their expertise to promote healing and takes responsibility over the person's wellness. From a psycho-pathological perspective, the person arrives at the session with a problem or illness, and the therapist's job is to fix the problem and diagnose the illness. Here I think about a mechanic, plumber, or electrician. There is a problem that needs to be fixed and they have the skills and tools to be able to solve the problem. They have the hammer and know how to use it. To continue the metaphor, therapists and coaches have many tools, but we will usually avoid a direct hammer and nail approach. The closest to this direct approach would perhaps be business and management coaching, in particular where it leans towards mentoring.

A note on advice

Giving advice is something that many clients expect as part of a typical session. They arrive with a problem and want a solution. But this is actually something both therapists and coaches are cautious about. Good advice requires us to fully know and understand a particular situation, with all the history and nuances, all the multiple perspectives. This would allow the Therapist or Coach to set the person in a successful direction. However, it is best to err on the side of caution, with the understanding that we can ask questions and make suggestions, give ideas and guide rather than advice. In this way, we are handing responsibility back to the client, thus promoting equality between client and therapist to minimise the power dynamics and hierarchy inevitably present with an expert in the room. A client should be the expert in their own lives and, if absent, this self-belief needs to be nourished as part of sessions. The helpless feelings of not knowing what to do feed into the inequality and advice-seeking cycle.

My mother is a well-respected coach in the field. I remember phoning her once about a personal problem I was experiencing. After some long minutes I cried out: "What should I do? I just need you to tell me what to do! I don't need a coach right now. I need a mother and I need advice. Please help me!" I didn't want to work through my issues with a therapist or coach in that moment, to find my own voice and solution. I needed a mother's support and advice. This is important in the context of this chapter, because it speaks to agency, contracting, and clear communication about our needs and roles. My mother and I have had many other conversations where I have appreciated her enquiring mind and empathic listening skills, used to ignite my own thinking about my worries and problems.

Likewise, when we seek professional help, we also need to be clear about what we require. In that way, we are also wearing a 'hat' and can more easily find a suitable person to support us.

A teacher or leader using coaching principles does not qualify them to be called a coach. In the same way that a parent helping their child with homework does not make them a qualified teacher, an adult child nursing their elderly parent does not make them a nurse, and a good friend who is a great listener is not a qualified coach or therapist. It is important to make these distinctions, as qualification and training is one of the key ways that we *can* describe what we do and define between the different professions.

Another much-stated difference between Therapy and Coaching is in the professional registration. Therapists around the world are required by law to be registered with the necessary registration body to their profession. Here in South Africa, it is the Health Professions Council (HPCSA) responsible for the registration and compliance regarding continued professional development (CPD). The HPCSA registers a wide variety of professions, including doctors, psychiatrists, psychologists, therapists (including Arts Therapists, Occupational Therapists, Physiotherapists) etc. These titles are protected in that unqualified, unregistered people may not use the name. Most therapists have a Master's degree, equivalent or higher qualification.

The Allied-Health professionals are registered with a different body, but for most it is not a mandatory registration. In a similar way, coaches are encouraged to be members of their professional body and to register, but they do not have to join. Locally, we have the self-regulatory body called Coaches and Mentors of South Africa (COMENSA) and worldwide, there is the International Coaching Federation (ICF). There are many highly qualified and experienced coaches. However, the name 'Coach' is not a protected title, and many people call themselves this without significant training, qualification or registration. This is something to be wary of when seeking support.

Is there a spectrum?

I was wondering if there was a way of creating a spectrum from Therapy to Coaching but soon realised that the similarities are probably too strong. There is no huge chasm between two polar opposites. To create a full picture of the differences, we need to acknowledge the similarities, the colours, and gradients, as well as the multitude of in-between, and not just black and white.

Image 1 attempts to map the spectrum, the distinctions present from my research, according to experts in the field. There are many myths/misconstructions that are (un) helpful distinctions. Many of these profess to clearly define the difference between the Coaching and Therapy professions. There is also a narrative or hierarchy around Therapy. However, this does not fully explain all the overlap, the blurred boundaries, or the similarities. Like a rainbow in the sky, the colours are sometimes difficult to distinguish as separate and the edges are blurry.

Psychoanalysis, Clinical Psychology, Trauma Counselling	Health and Wellness, Life Transitions, Career Counselling, focus	Business, Executive, Management, Leadership, Mentoring work, focus on goals
Focus is on the Past		Future focus
Unconscious		Conscious
Diagnosis, Fixing	Helping, Support	Learning
Problem focused		Solution focused
Identifying weaknesses		Identifying strengths
Pathology, illness		Goal orientated
Dysfunctional clients	Salutogenic approach	Functional clients
Unhealthy clients		Healthy clients
Abnormal emotions		Normal emotions
Healing focus	Wellness, Health focus	Performance focus
Help people get better		Help people think for themselves
Slow progress		Fast progress
Long term?		Short term?

Figure 5: Is there a spectrum? Some generalised ideas about the difference between coaching and therapy

[Salutogenesis is a term coined by Aaron Antonovsky, a medical sociologist. It is a theory that focuses on promoting health and well-being, rather than those factors that cause disease. A salutogenic approach moves from sickness to wellness, Disease (Dis-Ease) to Ease.]

Table 1: Similarities and differences

	Coaching	Therapy
Client population	Mostly Adults, some Adolescents	Children, Adolescents, Adults
Individual versus group	One-to-one as well as Team Coaching	One-to-one as well as Group Therapy
Lifestyle, Work-life balance, Wellness	Yes	Yes
Careers	Yes	Yes
Business, Executive, Management	Yes	Sometimes
Grief counselling	Sometimes	Yes
Trauma work	Sometimes, specialist Coaches	Yes
Childhood memories	Sometimes	Yes
Long term vs Time Limited	Sometimes	Sometimes

Coaching emerged in part from the field of Positive Psychology, which focuses on enhancing a person's strengths, well-being, and personal growth to help them achieve their goals. It is a move in psychology, from helping people cope with trauma and loss, to helping people thrive in life. From victims to survivors, from surviving to thriving. This is a Salutogenic versus Pathological approach. Coaching leverages the principles of Positive Psychology with an emphasis on identifying and utilising an individual's strengths towards achieving their goals.

Coaching is based on the premise that human beings are inherently learners. We start learning about the world from the day we are born. As learning beings, we seek information to help us navigate the world. Coaching provides a context in which the person can learn about themselves. A good coach will encourage and enable their clients to learn *for* themselves and come up with their own solutions. There is a belief that people are the expert in their own lives. To help people to come up with their own ideas, we must first listen. This way, we acknowledge the client's power and autonomy to make their own decisions.

Some of the key forerunners of Coaching as we know it today were sports coaches dedicated to the simple goal of improving the game of their players. The field of coaching emerged with a focus on enhancing the client's overall well-being and life satisfaction, not just performance in a specific area.

A most notable example from sports coaching would be the tennis teacher stating the player should "Watch the ball" versus the tennis coach asking the player to count the ball's rotations. The latter is asked as a question.

Questioning

Both therapists and coaches use a combination of deep listening and skilled questioning with their clients. Questions are used to help and guide. They are one of the tools that can offer a way out of cyclical thinking and stuck-ness. By asking a well-chosen question at the right time, a client's thinking can be reignited. Nancy Kline's *Time To Think Coaching* model is based on listening with palpable attention, but there are specific questions used to ignite the mind. She also uses silence as a question and speaks to *waves and pauses* in the Thinker's thinking. In Kline's work, "The person who holds the problem also holds the solution"[9] and our job as coaches is to help the coachee/ thinker to get there, using the Ten Components of a Thinking Environment™.

There are many types of questions that are used in coaching – mostly open questions that encourage clients to think for themselves. One generalisation is that therapists may be perceived to be more empathetic listeners attuned to emotions. Although there are forms of clinical psychology that practice with minimal questioning, most therapists use questions. Similarly, a generalisation about coaching is that it uses more direct questioning. However, as with most of this chapter, it is not so clear-cut. It requires flexibility based on *what the client is bringing* to the session, and at that moment in time. Thus, there are often nuances in how much questioning is utilised in one particular coaching session versus another, as indeed in therapy.

One question I often ask my clients, both in Therapy and Coaching, is: What have you tried before? What has worked for you in the past? In this way, the client can identify positive moments in their lives when things were not as bad as the current situation. And we can help them learn from their past mistakes and successes. In this way, we start with a learning, growth mindset. I sometimes jokingly refer to myself as an investigative detective versus a therapist or coach. I enjoy the process of peeling layers and figuring things out. This positive enquiry also leads towards a solution-focused approach, i.e. if we can figure out what is not working, then we can see what options are available to us and work towards a future goal.

The distinction assessed

The professional world is often competitive, and this world cares about these distinctions and worries about them on a regular basis. Some professed differences may seem arbitrary and focused on labelling. Others are misconstrued and based on untrue assumptions about the 'other' profession.

In her first *'Fine Points'* blog of the year (13th January 2025) Nancy Kline writes about "Therapy". Having already had this chapter approved, I read her notes most avidly. She speaks about the "impossibility of compartmentalisation":

> "The fact is that the human mind flowers in the presence of presence" and "The compartments also obfuscate the fact that what matters is what *happens for* people in the session, not whether or what it is labelled. Yes, we need expertise. But what we call it does *not* matter".[10; 11]

The interesting thing is that I both agree and disagree with this statement, however, to end this chapter with such an answer would do a disservice to my fellow contributors to this book. And so I plough on, eager to come up with some distinction, some way of explaining my thoughts and coming up with a comfortable answer that makes sense to me.

I thought I might delve into some 'light' reading to help tune my initial blurry thoughts. I looked first to my office shelves, heavily laden with both psychology and coaching books. There was no light reading or clear answer to be found in all these important texts. Each author shares a deep belief in their own model and expertise. Several books have chapters on different types of therapy or coaching models. However, I couldn't find what I was looking for. Thus, it was that I sat back at my desk to type my enquiry into the search engine. Artificial Intelligence (AI) gave some summarised guidance. There were hundreds of articles and blogs. Some professed to have the answers – stating the main differences, where others posed their titles as a question: Is there a difference?

To me, there is a deep difference. And that is based on the requirements of the client, the clear contracting of what their needs are, and the "hat" the professional is wearing in the sessions. As a person who is qualified to wear both hats, I have to be particularly careful as to be clear which hat I am wearing at each moment. If a client comes to me for coaching, then I must put on my Coaching Hat. In this way, whatever content comes from the client is viewed by me through this coaching lens and not a therapy lens. The case example below will illustrate this point.

It is interesting to note that as a Therapist I will sometimes offer my 'Coaching Hat' to my clients in order to share tools. But I never offer a 'Therapy Hat' to clients who come to me for coaching. Some of my research for this chapter speaks to the idea of more therapists leaning towards a coaching style in their work. Coaching has been so successful: proven to work and to help people faster. Cognitive-Behaviour Therapy is goal-orientated similarly to coaching.

People coming to therapy are often there to find a solution. Their goal may be to get 'better' and my role is to help them define this goal: What does "better" look like to them? And how can I help support them towards getting there? In this way, the therapy is both goal-oriented *and* future-focused. These are some of the main differences that emerged from my reading. One of the well-publicised so-called differences is that Coaching is about goals and learning and a focus on the future, whereas Therapy focuses on the past. Such distinctions are, to me, unhelpful as they profess that there *is* a clear distinction. Not that I want to confuse the matter, but to me, this is an easy, simplified answer that is simply untrue.

When coaches should refer clients to therapy

Coaches work with a variety of clients. Some clients are there for straightforward executive, business, management or career coaching. They bring clear work problems to the sessions and stick to work content. Many are successful, high-functioning individuals. Some of the work is focused on 'preventative' medicine: wellness and resilience-in-advance (coined by Linda Hoopes as Prosilience). Sometimes we refer to these clients as 'The Worried Well.' However, there are also clients in crisis, with stress, burnout, anxiety, depression, grief and loss. Coaches can also work with clients who are at the end of their tether and are in desperate need of support. These are sometimes specialised wellness or life transition coaches, with the wisdom to support particular clients. For example, trauma-informed coaches work with trauma from a clear coaching perspective, with a focus on resourcing the client. These coaches work in the present with clients, through validation of what has happened to them, un-shaming, and resourcing towards the future. The dangers of this work are for people working with trauma who are not trained to do so and can risk re-traumatising the individual, but also risk traumatising themselves from what they are hearing when they are not qualified to safely hold this information.

At times, a coach will come across a client that they don't feel qualified to work with. Or whom they feel would benefit more from a therapist than a coach at that particular moment in their life. No matter how qualified a coach is, and how clearly they contract with a client, life 'stuff' inevitably creeps into coaching sessions. Life is not so clearly delineated into personal life and work life. We cannot separate our past from our present either. For example, one's hellish boss at work might be triggering because of the relationship one had with their own father. Or a person's grief at the loss of a loved one may impact on their concentration at work and performance in the workplace. Many things impact on our work life, because we cannot separate problem areas such as low self-esteem, or issues around family history, culture, sexual preference, physical health.

A good coach will notice and address these issues where relevant to the sessions, and be able to provide insight, suggestions, and support when these issues may be part of a problem. One of the suggestions may be for the person to seek a different kind of support. We may refer a client to a psychiatrist for potential medication or a diagnosis, for example, for chronic anxiety. Or we may refer to a specialist therapist with grief or trauma counselling experience if it is required, and the coach does not have the necessary experience or training to deal with this from a coaching perspective. Specific reasons that I, as a coach and therapist, would refer to a specialist would be for anything that would benefit from a diagnosis such as psychosis, depression, chronic insomnia, anxiety disorder etc. as well as some things such as an adult diagnosis of Attention Deficit Hyperactivity Disorder (ADHD) or Autism Spectrum Disorder (ASD) as this kind of diagnosis can often help people to feel more in control of their life as it can help them understand themselves better. I would also refer to issues of active addiction where the problem is getting out of control and affecting both work and family life. In addition, I am likely to refer, even sometimes temporarily, to a specialist in body/ somatic work, in particular for clients with severe trauma and Post Traumatic Stress Disorder (PTSD). Specialisms such as for Eye-Movement Desensitisation and Reprocessing (EMDR) or Trauma Release Exercises (TRE) have been proven through strong research to be effective tools in trauma work. Referring to parallel practice does not mean that the coaching or therapy cannot continue, but sometimes necessitates a pause.

On a personal note

Through my Health Professions Council of South Africa (HPCSA) registration, there are very clear guidelines around these hats. I may have dual registration but may not work with the same individual in this dual capacity. I must ensure to avoid conflicts of interest when providing services. And I have to inform the client of my profession at the start of the working relationship, with clear informed consent.

However, there are times when I have had to restate this within the sessions.

In some of my more personal coaching sessions, I have noticed that we are moving towards the therapy side of the continuum. In these cases, I may refer to my therapy qualification and mention to the client that the work we are getting into might be better placed within a therapy session. This would not be with me. Even though I am a therapist, I could not easily refer the client to myself! If I believe that I cannot support the client within my training and experience, then I would refer out.

In my therapy sessions, I will sometimes find it appropriate to mention my coaching hat and offer some appropriate tools to support their health and wellbeing. However, this would be in a therapeutic relationship and *always* with permission. To an outsider, this part of the session may *look* like a wellness coaching session.

It is clearly part of my contracting and informed consent intake that clients know that I am an Art Therapist by training and a coach. They are signing up for therapy and that is the professional capacity within which I will work with them. I am registered and trained as an Art Therapist. However, I do have many clients who choose not to do art in the sessions. They know that is my training and have signed an informed consent form to agree to therapy sessions.

One insight I have found useful to my work is that when I am sitting with a client, I am there with my history and training as an Art Therapist. That means it is the hat and lens I am most often wearing. I thus often use imagery, metaphor, and visualisation, even with my clients who prefer to lean towards talk therapy and in many of my coaching sessions. For example, I had a client who told me they felt like they were in a race and couldn't stop. This was causing a lot of stress and the coaching was to assist her anxiety. I asked her to explain what kind of race she was in, in order to get a better understanding of her situation. I was expecting something about road running as I knew this person took exercise seriously for her wellbeing and try to manage the stress. But she proceeded to describe a horse race in quite some detail. The feeling of running in circles, the sense of other horses nearby pushing her into the railing and breathing down her neck, the sense of wearing blinkers. All this visualisation enabled me to understand her current circumstances more clearly. We continued to use this metaphor on her coaching journey. With another client, they described driving on a large roundabout and being unsure which exit to take. They wanted direction but were feeling stuck despite still driving around in circles. This cyclical thinking is a common reason that people seek help from coaches. I asked them to describe the type of vehicle they were driving versus one they would prefer to be in. I asked them to think about finding a way to stop the vehicle, perhaps get out and stand in the middle of the traffic island and take some time to pause and assess the options available. We spoke about gratitude for having options and choice.

A note on confidentiality

Both Therapists and Coaches are bound by important ethical and moral codes. This is part of our training, our way of being, and our registration with regulatory bodies. Similar to the Hippocratic Oath, we believe in not doing harm.

Therapists are under strict confidentiality restrictions, whereby it is only under certain conditions that confidentiality can be breached, such as harm to self of another person, or where instructed by the court. Clients can feel safe building trusting relationships with their therapists and sharing difficult thoughts and feelings within this container.

Coaches are also bound by confidentiality, unless it is explicit in the contracting. This is one of the main differences, particularly in management or business coaching, and where the company is paying for the coaching service. Often, as with Coach Matching, the company is referred to as the client, and the individual person coming to coaching is referred to as our coachee. Under these circumstances, the coachee agrees to certain information being shared about the sessions, and three-way meetings with their line manager are common practice to improve the coaching experience. However, the Coach will probably keep personal and detailed information confidential in order to maintain an important trust relationship with the coachee. Most coaches will give a generalised summary of the main points of the coaching sessions without going into details, such that much of the personal content of sessions can preserve coachee confidentiality. Therapists may also need to practise this kind of summarised depersonalised information at times, for example, with children's parents or teachers who require some sort of feedback about how the sessions are progressing. The Therapist would still need to maintain strict confidentiality.

Case study example

*Name has been changed to protect confidentiality.

Samantha* is a woman in her 40s who lost her husband to Covid. She was referred through her manager for coaching. Sometimes this is described as 'Corporate Therapy' as it is well-known that therapy has a stigma surrounding it for some cultures and generations. As a coach, therapist, and grief educator, I was well-placed for the 'match'. Samantha was granted four coaching sessions, which occurred online over the course of two months. When I first saw her, she was in the deep grief of the first month. I was contracted to work with her as a coach, but my hat was firmly present as a care/therapeutic coach with strong grief counselling experience. Also, my training, and for most coaches, is to let the client lead the content of the session. So, in that first session, Samantha shared her narrative, and I listened with empathy and compassion. Any outsider looking into our session would not have been able to distinguish if this was coaching or therapy. The important thing was for her to have the chance to tell her story, without interruption or fear of judgement, nor well-meaning but unhelpful placatory remarks. Samantha expressed her sadness as well as her anger. At that stage, Samantha was in shock, and the trauma surrounding her husband's death was very prevalent. She felt heard.

The second session was much the same but occurred after the first month anniversary of her husband's passing. I shared information about the stages of grief (Elizabeth Kubler-Ross)[12] as well as resource material that I thought might be helpful. She was still definitely not in a place to take in lots of new information, so the resources were an image and a three-minute video. In session three, Samantha shared that she was struggling with sleep and sometimes could feel her husband's presence. The grief paired with her lack of sleep was impacting her work, particularly her focus. Prior to this, everyone at work had been very kind and patient. But now she felt that everyone had forgotten her loss. Life carried on for everyone else and she was angry about that, too. Some psycho-education came into this session regarding her anger and neuroscience, as well as her sleep problems related to lack of concentration at work. When we are in trauma, our brain function is affected. Trauma-informed coaching focuses on validation and resourcing of our clients. In session four, some of the focus was on sleep science to help improve her health and well-being. As this was our last contracted session, I was also aware of giving Samantha some tools for continued self-coaching. She was in a high managerial position at work and needed to return to full functioning. We talked about compartmentalisation, about when and with whom she could continue to safely share her thoughts and feelings. Towards the end of the coaching journey, I believe that an outsider may have been able to distinguish this as coaching. It was partly more directive and informative, sharing resources and helping Samantha to understand her grief. But this was also because it was contracted as a short-term intervention. If Samantha had come for therapy instead of coaching, I imagine it would have been a longer period of support and building the therapeutic relationship. The first year after a loss is the hardest, with all the firsts without the loved one's being particularly difficult, including the first anniversary of their death. Grief has no timeline though and thus, given the circumstances, I felt that I was able to provide good-enough support for Samantha. I did also refer to future therapy needs as a recommendation for coping with the loss and her further healing.

The importance of supervision

One other thing to note is the role of Supervision. In Coaching and Therapy, this is an important space to discuss our clients, to work through any concerns about them, to think of new ways of working with them and resolve any ethical issues. It is also where we grapple with our own emotions and triggers that may come up as countertransference (our often-unconscious reactions towards our clients). Supervision is a critical learning space, to engage in reflective practice, to discover more about ourselves as practitioners. Through doing regular supervision, we help our clients, but it also helps to prevent carer fatigue and burnout.

Supervision is a large part of any therapy and psychology course, particularly at the Masters level, where students are working with clients for the first time as part of their clinical practice modules. Students engage in both individual and group supervision spaces to help them learn about themselves as future therapists and to think through problem areas with their clients. For therapists, supervision is not mandatory after qualifying, however, it is strongly recommended as a crucial part of sound, ethical clinical work. Many places of work offer supervision as part of the job. Usually, a supervisor is present in both individual or group supervision. However, sometimes people engage in peer supervision to support one another as professionals.

In coach training, supervision plays a less central role, and although it is recommended for coaches to engage in supervision, there is less emphasis on the importance of it. However, at Coach Matching, we engage in several supervision spaces. Coaches have small group supervision on a quarterly basis. And bi-monthly coaching circles in small pods where we engage in peer learning spaces that include an element of peer supervision. We also have qualified supervisors as part of our coaching team if we need to reach out for additional individual supervision. This recognition of the importance of supervision is admirable.

In my own practice, I engage in the Coach Matching offerings, as well as individual supervision of my therapy work, a monthly peer supervision space, and a weekly Thinking Session with a colleague. All of this helps me to reflect on my practice and become more skilled and attuned. It helps to grow my own emotional intelligence with a growth mindset, so that I can nourish this in others.

Conclusion

This chapter explores the distinctions and overlaps between coaching and therapy, emphasising the complexities of defining them separately. I have reflected on my personal experiences and professional journey, examining coaching and therapy through various lenses, including training, qualifications, and practical applications. The chapter outlined a spectrum where coaching and therapy co-exist rather than being entirely separate disciplines. Ultimately, I have suggested that rather than rigidly defining coaching and therapy, professionals should acknowledge the vast spectrum and focus on the needs of the client while maintaining clarity in their own role.

Perhaps I should have retitled this chapter to the similarities between Coaching and Therapy! The similarities are numerous. There is so much synergy. Both are part of the caring professions. Both coaching and therapy focus on enhancing wellness and self-awareness, on personal growth and development. That is the premise to both.

We can research: What is Therapy? And What is Coaching? because it is true that we can define types of therapy and particular tools and techniques, and types of coaching models. But to distinguish them as different from each other? There are many interpretations. Although many other people will try to give you answers, that challenge is not one that I profess to have succeeded at. But I hope in this chapter that I have provided food for thought if not clear, definitions.

In attempting to define Coaching and find clear distinctions between Coaching and Therapy, I have gifted myself some clarity. Seven is my favourite number. Here are the main points I am taking away from my journey in grappling with the greys to find the rainbow:

1. Red: **Coaching and Therapy Exist on a Spectrum** – There is no absolute boundary; different coaching styles may resemble therapy, while some therapy models take a coaching-like approach.

2. Orange: **The 'Hat' We Wear Defines Our Role** – The clarity of role (coach vs. therapist) is crucial, and professionals must be explicit about which perspective they are working from.

3. Yellow: **Training and Qualifications Matter** – While both fields use similar techniques, professional qualifications, and regulatory bodies define their scope and ethical boundaries.

4. Green: **Coaching is More Goal-Oriented, Therapy Addresses Deeper Issues** – Coaching generally focuses on future goals, performance, and solutions, whereas therapy may explore past traumas, unconscious patterns, and emotional healing.

5. Blue: **Supervision is Essential for Both Professions** – Reflective practice through supervision helps maintain ethical standards and safety for the client, as well as the coach's or therapist's emotional well-being and professional growth.

6. Indigo: **Questioning and Listening Are Shared Tools** – Both coaches and therapists rely on deep listening, questioning, and creating a space for client transformation, but the intent and depth of exploration may differ.

7. Violet: **Referrals Are a Professional Responsibility** – Coaches must recognise when a client's needs go beyond coaching and require therapeutic intervention, ensuring ethical practice.

In conclusion, and just to begin the confusion anew and perhaps a fresh investigation, in my paintings, collages, mosaics of rainbows, I always include pink as the eighth colour. This way it blends beautifully with the purple and red to complete a rainbow circle (see colour wheel).

Questions for consideration

- What do you need help and support for in your life right now? Consider your needs and requirements to determine the best fit for you. Ensure good contracting to understand the service you will be receiving.

  _____

  _____

  _____

- Are you looking for a long-term solution or a quick fix? Are you looking at long-term or short-term goals? Take note of the goal-focused approach in coaching versus the more diagnostic and healing-centred approach in therapy.

  _____

  _____

  _____

- Do you have a problem that needs a thinking partner to help you come up with your own solution, or is your 'problem' of a more serious nature requiring professional support and a possible diagnosis and medication?

  _____

  _____

  _____

- Is the coach or therapist suitably qualified to meet your needs? Check the qualifications and registrations of professionals to ensure you are getting quality care. Professional identity is important – – therapists and coaches must be clear on their role based on training and client needs.

  _____

  _____

  _____

PART II

COACHING IN ACTION

Chapter 3

BETTER HUMANING. BETTER BUSINESS. BETTER WORLD

by Brad Shorkend

"The real danger is not that computers will begin to think like men, but that men will begin to think like computers." – Sydney J. Harris[13]

If Harris was looking at us as a society right now, what might he be saying?

Undoubtedly, one of the prevailing mindsets of today's workplace economy is that humans are expendable, that their labour – and possibly their thinking – should be reduced or even eliminated as a cost wherever possible.

This mindset doesn't work!

The rules of humanity

Many organisations tend to forget about people being people... still desiring, creating, and responding to human experiences. Even in this heavily digitised age, humans are at the heart of business.

Simon Sinek says that: "100% of employees are people. 100% of customers are people. 100% of investors are people. If you don't understand people, you don't understand business."[14]

Reading his words inspired me to build on them and share that:

"If you don't care about people, you don't care about business."

We need to reconsider the way we think about this fast emerging 'next world of work.'

For any organisation to maintain its humanity and its human relevance, they need to be deeply embracing the diverse intellectual capabilities and the people-based behaviours that live in the human capital fabric of our daily work environments.

The companies and leaders who get this right are flourishing and will continue to achieve amazing results both at a transactional and at a culture level. They understand that digital isn't something that you do, it's something that you become while still making people matter.

They embrace the human factor and they are relentless and obsessive about humaning better! In fact, even better than better... they make *humaning* a non-negotiable!

Organisations who have made the shift to the "relational economy" reap the benefits. Let's look at the statistics:

- **21%** increase in productivity – *Gallup*[15]
- **23%** achieve above average profitability – *McKinsey*[16]
- **5%** increase in customer retention equates to 25-95% increase in productivity – *Bain*[17]

Teams with deeply Human Managers experience:

- **34%** increased performance
- **15%** increased productivity
- **21%** increase in innovation

The lingering complexity of recent years has been **how to** more meaningfully connect with our people and access their next levels of ability in this digital new normal.

Regardless of technology or the speed of innovation, people are still people and the rules of humanity still apply!

What does this mean for us humans who have the privilege of earning our living as empathetic thought provokers and delivering our methods and impact to other human beings in the various coaching formats that we do?

As coaching professionals, it is easy to fall into a thinking lane of "I do my *peopling* as the informed and qualified guide on the side", and while this is true, it is only part of the truth.

Yes, each of us has those mindsets (preferred), methods (tools, systems, and processes) and muscles (skill sets) that are productised and packaged as the services that we offer – and powerfully deliver to our coachees, whether individual or group.

This is the obvious area of engagement where we are directly in the spotlight and our humaning (coaching skill in our case) is most being put to the test. It's easy to fall into the trap of thinking that this is what clients are watching, assessing, and ultimately scoring when they are giving feedback on our services and the quality of the experience that they had with us.

And also what they are contemplating when they are considering inviting us back for more, or thinking about referring to us.

And we're not entirely incorrect, and then also completely wrong.

There is the entire additional aspect of how we show up and the experience that we create in every single other moment of engagement besides our in-session activity; the critical human experience touchpoints of business, whether as a professional coach or any other business pursuit.

And this applies whether we are a business comprising 1, 10, 100, 1 000 or 10 000+ people.

That connection needs to extend way beyond just the clocked hour. Every touchpoint of the relationship with our clients, their organisations, the purchasers, and decision makers needs to elevate to a humanness that they don't want to lose, choose not to quit on, and keep coming back for more... these are opportunities to WOW people, in all the best ways possible.

These WOW moments become their narrative that they share with others, and in turn they want to experience again and again.

This is well demonstrated at an organisational level as well.

Technology giant Microsoft has over the past few years undergone a ground-breaking transformation. The organisation's commitment to fostering diversity, equity, and inclusion (DEI) within the organisation has been emphasised by their CEO, Satya Nadella as he has deeply embedded the importance of building a culture where every employee feels valued and empowered to contribute their unique perspectives.

Nadella once remarked, "*Diverse teams outperform homogeneous teams, and diverse companies outperform homogeneous companies.*"

Microsoft's initiatives include unconscious bias training, flexible work arrangements, and investment in programs aimed at attracting and retaining diverse talent. Through their incorruptible focus on creating an inclusive workplace where employees from diverse backgrounds can thrive, Microsoft has not only enhanced innovation and overall organisational effectiveness but also strengthened its reputation as a socially responsible corporation.

There is significantly improved workplace harmony, much reduced employee attrition, and this has been achieved because of 'better humaning.'

If we bring it back to the coach/coachee interplay, our entire approach to the end-to-end journey that we coaches create for our clients is going to need to evolve to an even higher level of better humaning, humaning awesomely – and in order to do this we need to have a significantly better understanding of the current state of humanity.

It's all a bit of a mess!

Relational risk realities

Why do I say that it's all a bit of a mess? Or actually a lot of a mess...

The lighting fast advancement of digital technology has gifted us with many obvious benefits, such as increased access to information and multiple improved and convenient communication channels.

That's fantastic, and necessary.

However, it has also led to a decline in face-to-face interactions and a hugely increased sense of disconnection from other people, other humans.

This disconnection (whether sensory or actual) is proving to have severe consequences on many people's mental and emotional well-being. Their human beingness is being stretched in unhealthy directions.

In many cases, this disconnection is leading to increased loneliness.

A recent study by the American Psychological Association found that 47% of Americans reported sometimes or always feeling alone, which can lead to depression, anxiety, and other mental health issues.[18]

Research by the University of California, Los Angeles, found that people who spend more time on social media than in active engagement with others are more likely to experience decreased empathy and increased narcissism.[19]

The *mess* intensifies even more than digital communication frequently leads to misunderstandings, misinterpretations, and a clear lack of emotional intelligence, which can hinder effective communication and significantly damage relationships.

So, in a world where technology is increasingly dominant and even misinterpreted for its true value, it is becoming even more crucial that we enthusiastically prioritise better humaning.

We need to be cultivating emotional intelligence, empathy, and compassion in our daily interactions, we need to be intentional about building stronger and more meaningful relationships and amplifying the level of care that we demonstrate as we enhance the way we human with each other – and how we make each other feel.

This is the heart of the issue...

How we make other people feel is a skill!

And it is a skill that does not necessarily come naturally to many people, or in many cases is taken for granted and assumed that we are doing it well.

> What if we are NOT, and if we lose that distinct humanness and the ability to human well, then how different are we from machines when it comes to the experiences that we create?

Human vs machine and where humans win!

The most distinct difference between humans and machines lies in their capacity for perception, empathy, and emotional understanding.

Machines don't feel!

And they don't care or need to care about the quality of the experience that they create for another being, whether human or machine. Yes, I just referred to machines as beings... it can get very confusing at times.

While machines can process vast amounts of data and perform tasks with incredible efficiency, they lack the ability to perceive and understand the world (and people) in the same way that humans do.

We cannot escape the fact that even in a digital world, human beings are critical to shaping the future of business.

Sure, machines deliver, but humans over-deliver.

Machines automate, but humans innovate.

Machines apply reason, while humans apply reason and emotion.

It is these subtle nuances that can make the world of difference to the degree of relevance which consumers assign to a brand and brand experience.

There are certain human skills and behaviours that cannot (yet) be duplicated by machines. Curiosity, imagination, and creativity are still very human attributes.

And so is care, critically so.

> Machines cannot 'people' better than people (will they ever?), and people cannot 'machine' better than machines.

Humans are still winning in these areas of activity, but just doing is no longer good enough... we need to be continuously improving, and fast. This is a critical message and should be in front of mind for everybody.

> Machines can gather and analyse data, but they do not possess the same level of perception as humans, and they do not have intuition or gut feel.

As coaching professionals, we need to be leaning in hard to developing an even greater connection to our own instincts and intuition and bring that 'feeling' even more strongly into our coaching environments. Susi spoke in Chapter 1 about the need for coaches to mature from doing to being and coaches at that level will be the ones who significantly outperform other man/woman or machine.

This will probably be a significant experiential differentiator from the programmed and mechanical machine-based coaching and may just be a decision tipping point for many purchasers of coaching services – for those who are still hanging onto their story, "I want a human being with feelings".

> Humans can perceive and understand complex situations, including social and emotional cues which are essential for human interaction.

Humans have the capacity to empathise with others, which involves understanding and sharing the emotional state of another person.

And the nuances of where that person may be at.

This is a fundamental aspect of human social intelligence and is difficult (dare I say impossible, for now) to replicate in machines.

As coaches, our ability to connect the dots, to sense the layers of deep emotion, to be there with another human in the moment, and to hold that space with an authentic heart still remains one of our unique human advantages.

It is non-transactional, unprogrammed, and purely a way of being.

Machines lack the ability to understand and respond to human emotions in the same way that humans do. They are programmed to recognise certain cues but cannot truly comprehend the depth and complexity of human emotions.

These differences highlight the unique aspects of human intelligence and the limitations of machine intelligence.

Up till now...

And then this happened...

GenAI (Generative AI) arrived in our reality, delivering two outputs that change the game.

Firstly, GenAI is able to engage in analytical and logical thinking (the human left-brain stuff) and secondly it can also at the same time create almost anything that you ask it to across all platforms (multimodal) which is likened to the human right brain stuff.

When these two are overlapped, integrated, combined, connected, or however you might see them becoming mutual with each other the AI can now start to interact with us humans with an elevated type of intelligence that can only be measured and viewed as even beyond human genius and in many ways even feeling like human interaction.

Even more significant is that AI's intelligence is doubling every five to six months now, and that will get even faster.

And even more 'human' in the way it will engage.

Thinking human – being human – being relevant

The rapid advancement that I have described here is going to force us to have to find an even better level of humaning. Even beyond the *awesome* that I casually mentioned earlier.

As coaches what is going to be relevant to our coachees, what we share with them in session will be one thing, but the way we understand their worlds and create a complete experience for them from start to finish is where the rubber is really going to hit the road. We're going to have to human at a level that we may not have even imagined previously. It's going to be where our relevance and our future success is going to be created.

And this is going to look different for all of us. We are each going to have to find our own human magic and our own ways of elevating the human experience that we create in line with what I have described.

> We're not going to have the luxury of choice. Awesomeness is going to be essential.

> We're going to have to be even better, even more impressive, even more positively impactful.

In order to remain relevant, businesses have to be very aware of, and very adaptable to, what is going on in the broader environment – again, awake, mindful and switched on. Being switched on, tuned in, and adjusting to suit.

This is where people come in, because people – not machines – have been and can (maybe?) remain the visionaries and the disruptors.

People notice, people intuit, people respond, people innovate.

What?... No, how!

The 'what' is changing so fast these days that if we obsess about what, then we will almost always be in the wrong place. We need to improve significantly our 'how', the way we react, and the relevance of our responses to the present.

Again, better humaning.

For as long as we have been thinking about existence on this planet, caveman times, it's been about survival of the fittest. Darwinism. Long term efficiencies. This is no longer true... it is now about the survival of the fastest. A significant mindset shift, massive method adjustment, and a whole new set of muscles are needed to move from the fittest to the fastest.

This will also evolve the way that we show up in terms of how we do what we do, not only how we think.

Clear states that:

> *"We don't rise to the level of our goals, we fall to the level of our systems."* [20]

I very much agree with this, but only if we apply a modern lens.

In the past, excellence equalled accurate repetition and duplication in pursuit of an objective. But this is like quicksand if we are repeating and duplicating systems that no longer meaningfully respond to the current state of humanity, business, technology, etc.

It is not only a technological transformation, it's a consciousness transformation – for those who get it... we are having to evolve significantly as human beings in terms of our own state of awareness, and our own operating systems.

Without awareness, awesomeness is going to be a tough ask!

A gentle caution

While Generative AI offers us unprecedented advantages in crafting coaching tools and methods, when not 'humanly filtered', it also poses ethical considerations and challenges that demand careful and conscious navigation. (see chapter 8)

Striking a balance between technological efficiency and ethical use is essential for responsible deployment and emphasises the need for a dynamic interplay between AI and human skills.

As GenAI continues to shape the future of professional coaching, deeper human intentionality will be instrumental in harnessing its potential while ensuring a harmonious integration with the human experience.

Transformation also comes loaded up with an emotional obstacle course for people on the journey.

There will be the anxiety of loss, and often times sadness of having to let go of what we have been so familiar and comfortable with for so long.

Deeply engrained in our personal identities.

There will be the awkwardness of the unknown 'middle', the daunting space that we may find ourselves hovering in as we venture beyond our safe comfort zones, on route to a new space of comfort.

We might (probably) have limited mindset, method, or muscle to be highly functioning in this space as we find our feet there, but once we find our flow and become enthused by the possibilities ahead, we will emerge into a space of renewed excitement and meet the obstacles with openness and expansion.

We will be tested to the core of our being and what we believe matters to us most, and what we may define consciously or unconsciously as our values.

Our authenticity will be tested as it is so humanly easy to default back to what use to make us comfortable...

> And we must not! We need to dig deep, awesomely deep!

The values lie

in the day-to-day operating of my workplace advisory business, I have the privilege of perspective and access, and I obtain a very meaningful understanding of what makes my clients tick.

Their businesses, their people, and their systems and processes.

I spend a lot of time debating, challenging, designing, trash-canning, and re-crafting the values of many of the organisations that I work with, and I'm always intrigued by the initial default to the generic values being the 'must haves' that so many organisations feel compelled to display in their corporate reception areas and websites:

- Integrity (the all-time champion!)
- Customer centricity
- Innovation
- Communication
- Respect
- Collaboration
- Trust
- Passion
- Quality
- Teamwork
- Responsibility
- Loyalty

- Reliability
- Excellence
- Courage
- Service

... to list a few.

Significant investment is provided by organisations for the crafting of these values. Expensive agencies are contracted to come up with them, and they are enthusiastically signed off because that 'box is ticked'.

They are then displayed on wall posters, reception area signage, on the company website, and even on corporate clothing and stationery.

However, when I ask the executives in these organisations what these values look like when genuinely demonstrated in daily practice, I'm often met with blank stares. When I ask how these values impact organisational strategy, more blank stares and sometimes attempts at saving face.

And when I ask what happens when employees, including leaders, behave in ways contradictory to the articulated values – there is silence.

And then most often a response of "nothing".

This is what I call the values lie.

Of course there are some people who have good awareness, understanding, and application of their respective organisational values, but from what I've experienced in the many organisations that I've worked with around the world, this figure is scarily minuscule compared to what it could be.

As a coach or a thought leader, are you being authentic to what you share with the world?

How is this contributing to the human awesomeness that you stand for, hopefully?

And by 'awesomeness', in this context, it means is the quality of having extremely high behavioural standards for yourself, and being extremely effective in your ways of engaging, showing up in all your interactions with others evident?

Perhaps this would be easier and more accessible if I simplify the whole conversation. Yes, you may keep all the other values stuff that you want to add in because it feels like it needs to be there, but single out one even bigger overarching value... awesome humaning!

When employees are not having a great experience, they check out. They either check out physically and leave the organisation, or they check out psychologically, but they stay in the business. The latter is arguably the more destructive of the two.

Often referred to as **"quiet quitting."**

This phrase gained popularity in recent years to describe employees who do the minimum required of their role without going above and beyond, often because of burnout, disengagement, or dissatisfaction with the organisation or leadership. They're still on the payroll, but their emotional and cognitive investment in their work has significantly diminished.

The same then applies to partners, colleagues, associates, and anyone within your network, even if you don't have employees.

These people continue to show up every day but leave their innate brilliance at home, hence only grudgingly bringing the bare minimum that they need to get things done – drip-feed contribution, base level survival stuff.

This results in them dispassionately doing just what they need to and nothing more to retain their jobs/contracts. It's a game of playing safe, keeping head above water, doing the bare minimum and literally slowly but surely 'infecting' the business, team, and clients with their negativity.

Don't take my word for it. What's the impact of not HUMANING Better?

Gallup[21]

- Only **32%** of U.S. employees were actively engaged at work.
- Nearly **18%** were actively disengaged (i.e., quiet quitters).
- The majority – **50%** – were "not engaged," suggesting a potential for quiet quitting.

Cost to Businesses

- Gallup estimates **disengaged employees** cost the U.S. economy **$483 billion to $605 billion** annually in lost productivity.

Productivity Decline

- Research by McKinsey [22] found that disengaged employees are **20-25% less productive**, even when present.

- Turnover & Culture

- Organisations with high rates of disengagement experience **59% more turnover** and report greater difficulty maintaining a healthy workplace culture.[23]

Wellbeing Impact

- Quiet quitters often report **lower job satisfaction**, increased **burnout**, and **poor psychological safety**, further perpetuating disengagement.[24]

QUIET QUITTING
THE HIDDEN COST TO ORGANISATIONS

Definition

Employees who mentally disengage from their wok while remaining physically present – doing the bare minimum without going above or beyond

Key Statistics

18% of global employees are actively disengaged (Gallup, 2022)

32% Only 32% employees are engaged at work

$8.8 trillion Disengaged employees cost the global economy over $8.8 trillion annually in producity

Quiet quitting contributes to higher absenteeism, lower morale, and increased

✓ Foster psychological safety (Amy Edmondson)
✓ Encourage open dialogue
✓ Promote growth and development

ORGANISATIONAL IMPACT

Decreased productivitiy

Higher staff turnover

Longer project timelines

Increased recruitment and onboarding costs

Poor customer service and biand representation

Team morale suffers

What Can Leaders Do?

✓ Encourage open open dialogue
✓ Pronogise and reward effort
✓ Ensure clarity in roles and expectations

Figure 6: Quiet Quitting: The hidden costs to organisations

Think about the last time a receptionist gave you a warm welcome, or a colleague lit up when you asked them how their weekend was; how did it make you feel? Human beings are hard wired to want to connect with other humans. If ever there was a reason to do what feels good anyway, this has to be it.

Amy Edmondson, the Novartis Professor of Leadership and Management at Harvard Business School, is widely recognised for her pioneering work on psychological safety in the workplace. It is a concept that describes an environment where individuals feel safe to take risks, voice their opinions, and make mistakes without fear of punishment or humiliation. Translated as being treated as a Human.

Her influential book "*The Fearless Organisation*",[25] underscores the critical role of psychological safety in fostering innovation, team learning, and engagement. Edmondson's research has helped to shape modern leadership practices and has been adopted globally across industries seeking to build more inclusive, high-performing teams.

In consideration of this, the primary intention of a leader should be the highly complex and often mislabelled 'soft' (it's not soft, it's mission critical!) people related behaviour that sits alongside the long list of 'hard' transactional activities.

There should be zero tolerance for breaking of the value of people and counterculture behaviours.

Zero!

As coaches, we need to hold up the mirror for the people that we coach, and also for those that we ourselves work alongside in our own businesses.

And we need to look in that same mirror ourselves.

With this in mind and through active participation in many culture and employee experience projects with my clients, I have crafted a set of principles for even better humaning.

They are 10 principles that guide the human behaviours that I believe go a very long way to creating the conditions for success for businesses and the people inside those businesses (and their clients, etc)

The still human principles of awesome humaning (and high performance)

- *Seek and create clarity* (obsessively and relentlessly);

- *Be accountable!* (be willing and obligated to accept responsibility and to account for one's decisions and actions);

- *Do what i say i will do, when i say i will do it* (incorruptibly);

- *Have the backs of my team, and strive to do so for those even beyond my team* (generosity and abundance);

- *Look for the win-win* (fairness across the board);

- *Deliver excellence only* (anything less is inexcusable, find a way);

- *Be intentional in everything* (do the right things, the right way);

- *Be curious* (maintain a relentlessly wondering mind about yourself and others);

- *Anticipate* (be awake and aware, conscious of "what if");

- *Be human, a kind human* (not soft, kind! No assholes).

I started to incorporate these principles into my work sessions with other clients to test them and see how they live alongside the Still Human "Method for Organisational Culture – Build Your Story, Lead Your Story, Live Your Story, Own Your story" – and I found that they superbly complemented the Method with the added benefit of now giving people a set of guiding principles to set intention around while crafting their own business culture frameworks.

During one session with a corporate CEO, the client paused and pondered for a moment after reading them and he said to me; "Brad, if we as humans do these 10 things consistently and CREATE LESS HARD MOMENTS, it will massively amplify and protect what we stand for and the culture we are building."

And that was exactly the point. Mission accomplished.

Mindset, method and muscle

What I have been describing here boils down to these three aspects: Mindset, Method, and Muscle.

We can't run or hide away from the technological advances taking place in the world, but we can evolve our thinking and mental frameworks around them. Without a Mindset reset or refresh, we are prone to wheel spinning in the same quicksand that we have been stuck in for years or even decades.

And if we don't get the base mindset right, then the behaviour that follows is, well, lesser quality humaning.

For too long, we have made decisions from a mindset of protection, not expansion. When we start to think through a lens of 'thrive' instead of a lens of 'survive', awesome becomes possible.

The possibility of evolving massively as humans with and alongside technology.

The Method component would then be the systems and processes that give us the rigour and shared language to build consistency in application of the Mindset that we are implementing.

And the Muscle then refers to the skills and capability set required to actually do the work that is required, and this is often the overlooked aspect. We all need to be in constant growth, our personal skills development project should be a constant – and relevant.

So now what?

I have been sharing here how I believe we can amplify our human awesomeness and, in doing so, how we can build incredible human powered businesses in an increasingly digital world.

We don't know what's coming next. How can we?

What we do know for sure, however, is that if we don't apply ourselves meaningfully to a higher level of humaning we are going to be left behind.

And in the words of another client of mine in a recent session, 'It's not complicated, it's just hard.'

> But we need to choose our hard.

I personally prefer the 'hard' of getting out of my comfort zone in the interest of progress and awesome humaning – on mostly my own terms.

This feels way better to me than the 'hard' of being stuck in my comfort zone while the world goes flying by – none of it on my terms at all.

I wish for you the courage of optimism, enthusiasm, and awesome humaning as you add your own magic to making the world an even better place.

Take care of yourself.

Take care of each other.

HUMAN AWESOMELY!

What are your rules of humanity going to be? What are you making matter most?

Questions for consideration

- Has this caused you to stop and pause to reflect on your own values articulation, and how you are living them meaningfully in your own business?

  _____

  _____

  _____

- Do you have a carefully articulated values construct? Do you hold yourself to them?

  _____

  _____

  _____

- How do you, with integrity, challenge the human being opposite you in a session with regards to their own delivery on their values?

  _____

  _____

  _____

Chapter 4

A SURPRISING REVELATION: FROM THE BEDROOM TO THE BOARDROOM

by Shelley Lewin

When I first began my formal training in applied psychology, my focus was clear – I wanted to support couples to improve the health and quality of their intimate relationships. I believed (and still do) that intimate relationships and partnerships are the cornerstone of personal fulfilment. What I hadn't anticipated was that everything I was learning for success in the bedroom -or home front- had profound relevance and validity in the boardroom.

For over two decades, I have worked closely with couples as 'The Relationship Architect' in unravelling their conflicts, fostering deeper connections, and helping them shift from dysfunctional patterns to healthier dynamics. Constructive communication, trust-building, and power dynamics are at the heart of my work. As my career evolved, something unexpected happened. When I began coaching executives, I quickly realised that the same principles that helped couples build thriving relationships were just as applicable – if not more crucial – for leaders in the corporate world.

Leaders, like partners in a marriage, need to build trust, navigate conflict, and create environments where people feel seen, heard, and valued. Without relational intelligence, both romantic and professional relationships crumble under misalignment, miscommunication, neglect, and power struggles. This realisation led me to refine and adapt my approach, transitioning from counselling intimate relationships to **coaching professional relationships** in a way that empowers leaders to build thriving, human-centric workplaces.

Introduction: The leadership shift toward relationships

Leadership is evolving. In an era where traditional industrial-era leadership focused on efficiency, productivity, and hierarchical control, modern leadership is experiencing a fundamental shift – one that places relationships at the core of success. We are now firmly in the **relationship economy**, discussed in the previous chapter, where trust, collaboration, psychological safety and emotional intelligence have become the new currency of influence.

More succinctly, we are moving from command-and-control to coaching and co-creation environments.

HR professionals and leadership coaches are at the forefront of this transformation. Leaders are no longer solely measured by how well they execute tasks but by their ability to motivate, guide, inspire, connect, and create inclusive environments where their people can become high performers.

Leaders setting their teams up for success sounds a lot like parenting, don't you think?

The skill of relationship building is no longer a 'soft skill' – it is a strategic advantage, helping leaders develop meaningful connections that drive engagement, retention, and performance. The need for this shift is driven by several factors:

1. **Technological Advancements**: the rise of remote work and digital communication tools has changed how teams interact, making relational skills more critical than ever. Years after the pandemic, a significant portion of the workforce continues to work remotely, underscoring the need for leaders to foster connection in virtual environments.

2. **Generational Changes**: Millennials and Gen Z now comprise a significant portion of the workforce, and they prioritise work-life balance, flexibility, and meaningful connections. Companies that adapt to these preferences by fostering strong leadership and innovative, people-first policies are seeing higher employee engagement and satisfaction.

3. **Emphasis on Mental Health**: Investors and organisations are increasingly recognising that poor mental health practices contribute to increased absenteeism, high turnover, and difficulty in attracting top talent. Investing in workplace mental health initiatives has proven financial benefits, with studies showing a significant return on investment.[26]

A leadership story: From a results bias to people-centricity

Consider the story of a seasoned manager who excelled in task execution but struggled with high team turnover. Initially, she approached leadership with a command-and-control mindset, focusing on productivity metrics above all else. However, as disengagement grew, she realised something needed to change. Through our coaching and the 'people centred or relationship lenses', she learned how to build trust, foster open communication, and prioritise the human aspects of leadership. The transformation was remarkable – her team became more engaged, retention improved, and overall performance increased.

This story illustrates the profound impact of relationship economy. Leaders who invest in relational intelligence not only enhance their own effectiveness but create workplaces where people **want** to stay, contribute, and grow. Over the last two decades, my observations have reinforced a simple truth: People don't leave companies; they leave people.

In contrast to that, we know 'why people follow'. Based on the Gallup Polls of more than 10 000 people that asked followers to describe what leaders contribute to their lives, four themes or basic needs emerged. Those were **trust** (also described as honesty, integrity, respect), **compassion** (also described as caring, friendship, happiness, and love), **stability** (described as security, support, strength, and peace) and **hope** (other words cited by followers included: direction, faith, and guidance).[27]

In the following sections, we will explore practical frameworks, strategies, and case studies to help leaders navigate this shift effectively. The future of leadership is relational, and relationship coaching is the key to unlocking its full potential.

The architecture of relationship: A framework for leaders

In the space between any two people lies a **third entity** – the relationship itself. This concept is beautifully captured by the **Vesica Piscis**, a sacred geometric symbol representing the space where two individuals overlap. **This space is the relationship**, and it has its own dynamic, separate from the two people involved. The strength and health of this third entity determine the levels of cooperation and willingness of each individual to collaborate. When the connection is strong, it is like an invisible thread thickening over time, forming a deep bond. And when there is a bond, we are inspired to want to go the extra mile, to show up as a team player, to be considerate and to 'follow you wherever you go' (personally or professionally speaking).

When we, or the 'U.S', is healthy and harmonious, it creates an environment where the individuals living within it can thrive. When its discordant or chaotic, it can diminish, toxify and erode at the wellbeing of the individuals. Each person – 'ME' and 'YOU' – is either nourishing or neglecting, helping or harming, contributing or contaminating the 'U.S.' space.

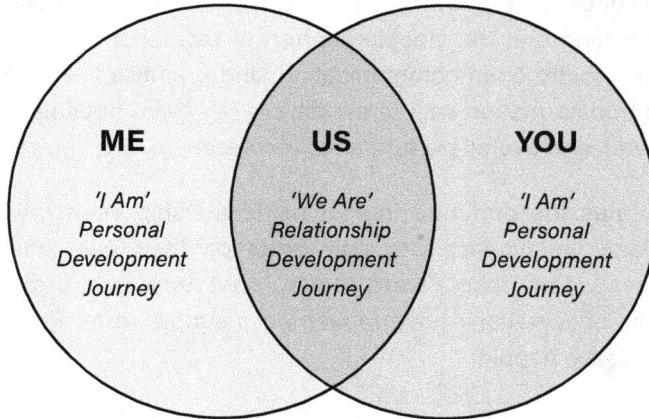

Figure 7: The Architecture of Relationship: When 1 + 1 = 3

Understanding the third entity

Rather than viewing relationships as a static connection between two individuals, the Architecture of Relationship emphasises that relationships are **co-created and dynamic**. They require intentional **maintenance, balance, and alignment** to function effectively.

A thriving relationship is characterised by:

- **Clarity of Shared Purpose:** What are we trying to create together?

- **Mutual Respect and Boundaries:** How do we maintain autonomy while nurturing our mutually beneficial relationship?

- **Commitment to Growth:** How do we evolve together rather than apart?

It has been my experience that when leaders understand that **1 + 1 = 3;** they recognise that the quality of their leadership is not just about obtaining obedience and compliance from their subordinates, instead it is about generating an environment where they foster collaboration, elicit buy-in and inspire collaboration.

The two essential lenses: Connection and power dynamics

So far, I have highlighted that we are moving out of the traditional industrial economy into a relationship economy, the reasons for that and the importance of evolving our leaders into relationship builders. I have also provided a framework to illustrate the relationship as a third entity. Now I would like to move on to how leaders can actively shape this **shared space** by focusing on two essential guiding lenses; the components that shape the quality of relationships.

Connection and Power. Each contributes to the dynamics within any relationship in distinct ways.

1. **Connection** is about trust and rapport, making it easier to influence and collaborate with others. It's about harmonious resonance which encourages open communication, safety, and a sense of belonging.

2. **Power** is about authority, rank, and credibility, people are more likely to follow and be influenced by those they perceive as knowledgeable and competent. Power, though, when used forcefully, can be a blocker to connection so let's begin with connection.

Connection: The glue that holds relationships together

At their core, relationships are defined by the resonance they create. When any two things are combined, the alchemy of their connection will result in one of two outcomes: either a harmonious reaction, producing beautiful cohesion, or a dissonance of chaos, leading to a disruptive impact. Therefore, the glue that holds relationships together will either be complementary or corrosive.

> *"People will forget what you said, they will forget what you did, but will always remember how you made them feel."* – Maya Angelou

This quote serves as a powerful lens for assessing the health and quality of your connections. How we make people feel is where we exert the greatest influence – and where we can have the most lasting impact. Or not.

A harmonious connection allows individuals to become better versions of themselves, or at the very least, creates a space for each individual to be their authentic selves. This is the foundation of a healthy relationship, encompassing trust, emotional intelligence, psychological safety, and effective communication for ongoing feedback and growth.

Without a healthy bond or harmonious connection, individuals in a relationship have little incentive to work toward shared goals – unless fear is their driving force (for example, fear of losing their job). In the absence of fear, indifference often takes its place, leading to apathy toward the job and its outcomes. Neither fear nor indifference are compelling reasons for anyone to show up and perform beyond expectations.

In my experience working with thousands of executives, even when a client was high-performing and engaged, if their motivation stemmed from fear or apathy, their commitment eventually deteriorated. Over time, their engagement withered, often leading to burnout. The corrosive nature of their connection with their leader gradually eroded their self-worth, confidence, and mental well-being. This, in turn, significantly diminished their loyalty to their leader, the organisation, and belief in its mission.

Mini case study

A department head began noticing increasing disengagement among her employees. After engaging in relationship coaching, she realised that her leadership style lacked warmth and emotional availability. By incorporating regular check-ins, active listening, more frequent recognition, and personal acknowledgment, she witnessed a transformation in morale, engagement, and overall productivity.

Power: Understanding the Three Power Differentials

Power in relationships is not a fixed state – it is dynamic and shifts depending on context and hierarchy. Every relationship involves **power differentials**, and in leadership, these dynamics can either create alignment or tension. Relationship coaching helps leaders navigate three different power differentials. Each power dynamic influences the strategies required to **build trust, foster connection, and create alignment** within the relationship space.

An awareness of these **three power differentials** allows leaders to **adapt their leadership style** to different contexts, ensuring that they foster connection while maintaining authority in a way that uplifts rather than diminishes relationships.

Every professional relationship exists within one of three power differentials:

Horizontal power (equal partnership)

in this type of relationship, both parties have equal power, rank, and authority. Decision-making is shared, and responsibility is distributed evenly. Examples include life partners, peers, team members, and siblings.

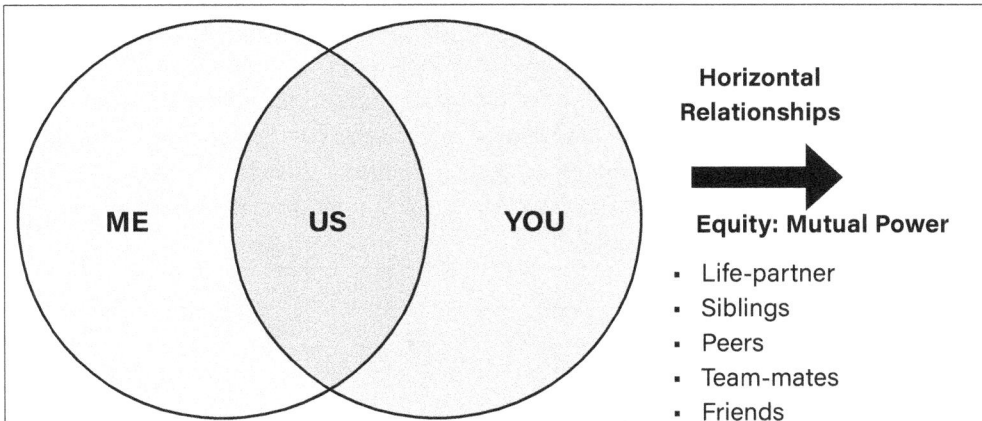

Figure 8: Horizontal Power: equity and mutual power

Navigating horizontal relationships (partnering peers and equals)

- Foster collaboration rather than competition.
- Lean-in to mutual respect and clear communication to maintain alignment.
- Encourage shared decision-making and joint accountability.

We are equals in this union. To create connection, I need to FOSTER COLLABORATION.

In a horizontal relationship, fostering collaboration is essential because you are a teammate. For a team to succeed, each member must trust that others have the team's best interests at heart. Mutual respect and trust ensure that individuals work together rather than against one another. Each party must value the other's input and expertise, creating an environment where everyone feels heard and aligned toward a unified goal. Without a unifying goal, a team can easily become a group of individuals pulling in different directions.

To foster collaboration, there must be a clear, shared agenda that is mutually beneficial to all parties involved. Clearly defined roles and objectives help prevent confusion and ensure that expectations are aligned. Partnerships and teammates share power and decision-making responsibilities, reinforcing their collective ownership of outcomes.

Opposition may arise because of differing perspectives or approaches. Healthy dynamic tension between individuals with opposing opinions is both normal and beneficial. The key is to navigate disagreements constructively rather than destructively. The ability to problem-solve and engage in fair conflict resolution is crucial for maintaining connection. Active listening is a fundamental skill in psychologically safe problem-solving, as it allows individuals to fully explore challenges without fear of judgment.

Mini case study

A people's leader was receiving feedback from colleagues that, although she was excellent at getting things done efficiently, her bias for action often led her to reactively enter 'fix-it mode' without fully exploring the root cause of the issue. As a result, problems would resurface, creating frustration among her peers. When the issue was raised, she initially became defensive, offering quick solutions instead of engaging in deeper dialogue. Her peers expressed frustration over her inability to truly listen to their perspectives before taking action.

Through coaching, she devised a plan to shift into a 'curious detective' mindset instead of a 'fix-it' mindset. She intentionally practiced active listening and asked multiple clarifying questions to ensure that each teammate had fully elaborated on their perspective.

As a result, she quickly transformed into a true collaborator. Her peers noticed the shift and praised her for becoming more cooperative, leading to stronger relationships and more effective teamwork.

This case study illustrates how a leader can **foster collaboration** by shifting from reactive problem-solving to a curiosity-driven approach, using active listening and team alignment to create stronger partnerships.

Vertical Power Above (Authority Over You):

This occurs when someone else has greater authority or rank, making decisions that impact you. Examples include parents, senior leaders, line managers, and customers.

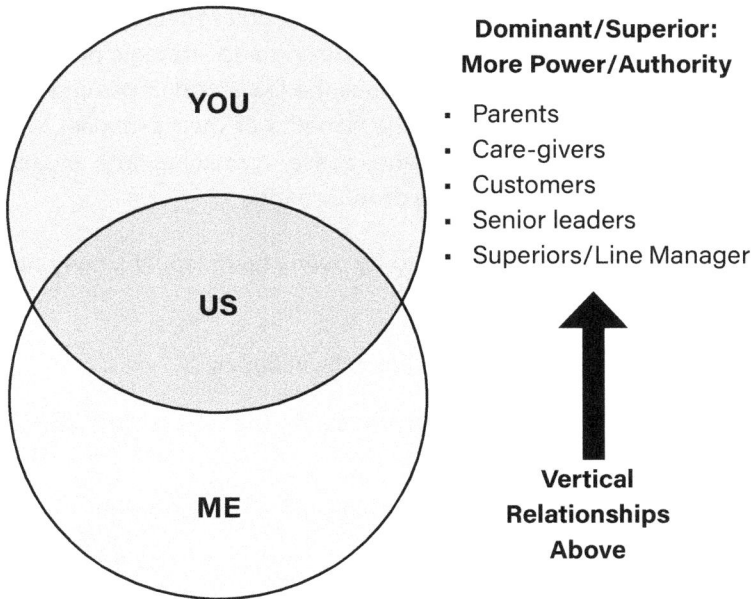

Dominant/Superior:
More Power/Authority

- Parents
- Care-givers
- Customers
- Senior leaders
- Superiors/Line Manager

Vertical
Relationships
Above

Figure 9: Vertical Power Above: you are the subordinate one with less authority

Navigating power above (influencing upward):

- Build credibility by understanding and aligning with superior priorities.
- Leverage storytelling and data-driven insights to gain buy-in.
- Recognise power imbalances and adapt communication accordingly.

We are not equals in this union. To generate connection when you have less power, you must ELICIT-BUY IN from your superiors.

When a coachee or client wants buy-in from their customer, line manager, or senior leadership, the first step is to demonstrate understanding, commitment, and a willingness to align their efforts with their superior's strategy. Once it is clear that they have their superior's best interests at heart, it creates space to position their own agenda while highlighting what's in it for the person with authority. This approach builds credibility and trust, demonstrating that they understand their superior's priorities and opening the door for negotiation – instead of facing a hard "no."

Eliciting buy-in involves presenting ideas in a way that resonates with their superior's priorities and values, using persuasive storytelling and strategic positioning. They can influence decision-making and increase the likelihood of gaining approval for their initiatives by clearly presenting the benefits of their proposal. An effective way to elicit buy-in is by building a business case – providing data and evidence to support the feasibility and impact of a proposed idea.

A strong business case doesn't need to be overly technical; it simply needs to be structured, relevant, and compelling.

A clear and persuasive business case typically includes:

1. The Problem or Opportunity – Clearly define the issue or the opportunity for improvement.

2. The Proposed Solution – Explain your idea and why it's the best course of action.

3. The Expected Benefits – Use data, case studies, or real-world examples to highlight the advantages of implementing your solution.

By structuring their pitch around these three elements, individuals can effectively present their case, demonstrating alignment with leadership priorities while showing the value of their proposal.

As a parent, my husband and I encourage our son to pitch to us and persuade us why he thinks something is a reasonable idea – especially when we disagree with him. His task is to change our minds with a compelling argument. *(Side note: I fully support youngsters joining a debate club at school, as it teaches an excellent transferable skill for life.)*

Mini case study

My client was the General Manager of a large hotel group. In coaching, he shared his challenge – he felt intimidated by his skip-level boss, the Global MD of the group. In the presence of this senior executive, he often felt fearful and fell silent, which was problematic for building visibility and credibility in senior leadership meetings. This was particularly concerning because he wanted to implement changes at his hotel and needed buy-in from the regional and global team. To explore this, I asked him about his comfort level when dealing with hotel customers. He immediately reassured me that he was at his most confident when engaging with guests. His twenty years in the hospitality industry had prepared him to handle even the most difficult customers with ease.

I then posed a question: "Let's suppose your skip-level boss was an 'intimidating' guest at the hotel. How would you relate to him, then?"

His response immediately revealed multiple solutions for handling this type of personality. I pointed out that the power differential was exactly the same – he already had the skills, charisma, and competence to engage powerfully with the senior leadership team, just as he did with difficult guests.

He was astounded by this realisation. With renewed confidence, he implemented this perspective immediately.

When he returned for a coaching session, he was delighted to report back that, after a recent senior leadership meeting, his line manager approached him with surprising feedback:

"I couldn't believe what I was seeing from you today with my boss. Whatever you did or ate for breakfast – please keep it up! You were a completely different person in there today."

This shift transformed his leadership presence and empowered him to engage with senior leaders as a hotel guests, rather than as an intimidated subordinate.

This case study highlights how reframing a power dynamic and leveraging existing interpersonal skills can help a leader shift from Self-doubt into confidence, strengthening their ability to **influence upward**.

Vertical Power Below (Authority Over Others):

Here, you hold authority, rank, and decision-making power over another person. Examples include any children, dependents, and direct reports.

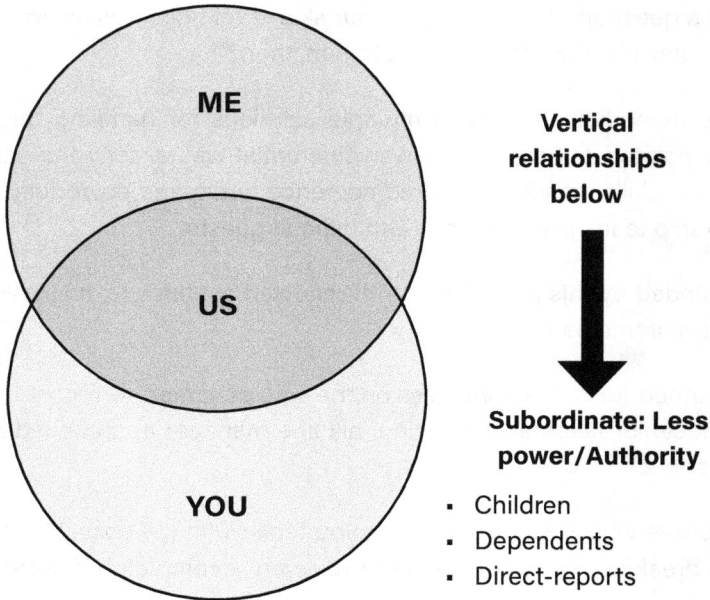

Vertical relationships below

Subordinate: Less power/Authority

- Children
- Dependents
- Direct-reports

Figure 10: Vertical Power Below: you are the dominant one with authority

Navigating power below (leading direct reports)

- Establish psychological safety through active listening and inclusion.

- Set clear expectations while encouraging autonomy and ownership.

- Recognise the responsibility of decision-making while ensuring fairness and opportunities for growth.

> We are not equals in this union either. To generate connection when you have more power and authority, you must INSPIRE CO-OPERATION from your subordinates (instead of insisting on obedience and compliance).

There is an outdated approach to parenting and leadership that follows the principle: *"Do as I say, not as I do."* While this tone may have worked historically, it is no longer effective in contemporary homes and organisations. Whether leading children or adults, the directive *"Do it because I said so!"* is becoming increasingly redundant. If you want cooperation from those you lead, there must first be a strong connection, paving the way for meaningful engagement and cooperation.

As a parent, I have observed that insistence often leads to resistance. At home and in the workplace, obtaining cooperation requires patience and genuine curiosity. Building connection with direct reports or children takes time and requires attentiveness to what matters to them. Every leader should know who and what is important in the lives of those they lead. Curiosity and care cannot be faked. Actively listening and demonstrating a sincere interest in the people you lead fosters trust and psychological safety, encouraging them to share their challenges openly.

To create a psychologically safe environment, leaders must engage in active listening, regular one-on-one meetings, and open, transparent communication. When subordinates and children do not fear making mistakes, they feel safer and more empowered. Instead of worrying about being scolded or fired, they are encouraged to learn from failures, seeing them as opportunities for growth rather than threats.

Encouraging autonomy is empowering. Focusing on progress rather than perfection, acknowledging contributions, and providing positive reinforcement is motivating for people of all ages. This approach is precisely what modern organisations expect from people leaders. We are in the relationship economy era, not a hierarchical command-and-control era.

Referencing the four pillars of "why people follow" from Gallup's research – trust, compassion, stability, and hope (with additional words cited by followers, including direction, faith, and guidance) – highlights a crucial point:

When people choose to follow, they are willing to be led. That is the ultimate definition of cooperation.

Mini case study

My client held a senior director position overseeing EMEA and APAC. In our coaching sessions, she expressed frustration with one of her direct reports, whom she perceived as regularly condescending and lacking professionalism at the leadership level. She frequently found herself thinking and saying, *"I can't stand how she talks to me,"* or *"She is so rude to me."*

Through coaching, she agreed to experiment with shifting her approach – setting aside her frustration and defensiveness to explore the root cause of her direct report's negative tone. The goal was to lean into curiosity and care, identifying whether there was an underlying issue contributing to her behaviour.

In parallel, she also needed to set clear boundaries around what she was willing and unwilling to accept in their interactions. Instead of defaulting to a reactive stance of *"You can't"* statements, she reframed it as **"I don't"** statements, reinforcing her own standards for engagement.

For example, she practiced responses like:

- *"I don't accept you raising your voice with me, and I won't respond to that volume."*

- *"I don't like the direction this conversation is going, and it doesn't work for me to have an unproductive dialogue."*

During her one-on-one meetings, she discovered that her direct report was experiencing burnout symptoms and felt unsupported – which was the root cause of her resentment. By demonstrating empathy and offering support in prioritisation, they identified tasks that could be delegated or removed from her workload.

As a result, the quality of their conversations shifted dramatically. Through building a better connection, my client not only taught her direct report how she expected to be treated but also modelled the respect she wanted in return.

This case study illustrates how a leader can **inspire cooperation** by shifting from frustration to connection – building psychological safety, practicing active listening, setting clear boundaries, and demonstrating empathy.

Typical challenges in navigating power dynamics

Many senior leaders resist vulnerability, equating it with weakness rather than recognising it as a leadership strength. This resistance can prevent them from building trust and authentic connections, ultimately limiting their ability to inspire cooperation.

Teams often remain stuck in old paradigms, struggling to transition from hierarchical control to relationship-driven leadership, which requires mindset shifts at every level. Navigating conflict and difficult conversations is another common challenge – without the right tools and skills, disagreements can escalate into destructive conflicts rather than opportunities for constructive growth and problem-solving. *(I regularly reframe conflict with my clients as "negotiation with teeth.")*

Relationship coaching equips leaders with the ability to manage these conflicts effectively, fostering collaboration rather than discord. Below are some of the typical challenges within each of the three power differentials, which can be overcome through relationship coaching:

1. Horizontal Relationships (Partnering Peers & Equals):

   • **Power Struggles:** Competing for influence can create friction rather than collaboration.

   • **Lack of Clear Roles:** Without defined responsibilities, confusion can hinder progress.

   • **Unresolved Conflict:** Differing opinions can escalate if there isn't a structured way to address them.

2. Navigating Power Above (Influencing Upward):

   • **Fear of Speaking Up:** Employees may hesitate to voice concerns or propose ideas.

   • **Misalignment of Priorities:** Leaders may struggle to make their case when their goals don't directly align with senior leadership.

   • **Limited Influence:** Without strategic persuasion techniques, gaining buy-in can be challenging.

3. Navigating Power Below (Leading Direct Reports):

   • **Over-Reliance on Authority:** Leaders may default to commanding rather than coaching.

   • **Low Engagement:** Employees who feel micromanaged or undervalued tend to disengage.

   • **Resistance to Change:** Without psychological safety and trust in their leader's vision, subordinates may resist innovation, fearing uncertainty or unintended consequences.

Key takeaways for leaders

1. The relationship economy demands leaders who build trust and foster collaboration across teams, rather than simply executing tasks.

2. Leadership success is increasingly measured by emotional intelligence, relational agility, and emotional literacy (*see the chapter by Dan Newby*), rather than technical expertise alone.

3. Understanding the Architecture of Relationships helps leaders prioritise the third entity – the relationship itself – rather than focusing solely on individuals.

4. Power must be balanced with connection. Leaders who rely solely on authority risk eroding trust, disengaging teams, and weakening collaboration.

5. Effective leadership is context-dependent. Recognising whether you're operating in a horizontal, upward, or downward power dynamic ensures you apply the right leadership approach in every situation.

6. Collaboration fosters success. Whether partnering with peers, influencing upward, or leading others, creating a culture of respect, shared purpose, and psychological safety drives stronger outcomes and higher performance.

Why relationship coaching matters in leadership?

Traditional coaching often focuses on performance metrics and goal achievement, but relationship coaching shifts the focus to how leaders interact, communicate, and build trust within their teams. Unlike competency-based coaching, which enhances what leaders do, relationship coaching enhances how leaders engage – strengthening their influence, collaboration, and ability to inspire cooperation.

Leaders who develop relational intelligence unlock:

- Higher Employee Engagement – Employees thrive in environments where they feel valued, heard, and connected, leading to greater motivation and commitment.

- Stronger Collaboration – High-trust teams work together more effectively, breaking down silos and fostering innovation.

- Long-Term Success – Organisations with strong people and relationship cultures consistently outperform competitors in retention, morale, and business outcomes.

Hints and tips for HR professionals and coaches

- Encourage leaders to prioritise connection over correction – trust must be built before effective feedback can be given.

- Use coaching questions that help leaders reflect on their relational impact and influence, not just performance outcomes.

- Implement peer coaching and mentorship programmes to reinforce relationship-based leadership at all levels.

- Facilitate training on psychological safety, active listening, and conflict resolution to strengthen relational intelligence.

- Guide leaders in shifting from command-and-control to coaching and co-creation, fostering a culture of engagement and empowerment.

Final thought: The future of leadership is relational

HR professionals, leadership coaches, and organisational developers have the power to redefine leadership. By embracing relationship coaching, we don't just help leaders manage teams – we help them architect thriving, connected workplaces.

If the future of leadership is human, then relationship coaching is the bridge that ensures AI's role in shaping the future of work serves people- not replaces them.

Chapter 5

THE POWER OF EMOTIONS IN COACHING

by Dan Newby and Marcel Brunel

"There is an ironclad connection between your emotions and the way you show up for yourself and others". – Marcel Brunel and Dan Newby

I recall a coachee telling me recently that she was an "impatient person" and that it was the one thing she most wished she could change about herself.

As a coach, there are several ways we could understand her statement. We could hear that she is indeed impatient and begin inquiring what she might do to be more patient or less impatient. We might question what provokes her impatience or where she believes it comes from.

However, If we look at her statement through the lens of emotions, we might ask how she knows that the emotion she is experiencing is impatience. Pursuing that line of questioning, my coachee attributed her behaviour to impatience, a conclusion she had accepted uncritically from her parents. But, her description of those moments – being full of energy and having the desire to get things moving – her emotion sounded more like enthusiasm, excitement, or exuberance to me.

When I invited her to consider what emotion she might be experiencing if it wasn't impatience, those were some of the ones she mentioned. After discussing what we believed each meant and why they might be closer to her experience, she came to the conclusion that the emotion she was experiencing often was exuberance rather than impatience.

The change in her self-regard was immediate and notable. She said she no longer felt ashamed of her energy but saw it as natural for her. She also reflected on it, making sense for her parents to label her emotion as impatience because that is what it probably looked like to them. She was the oldest of four siblings, outgoing, full of energy, curious, and a bit restless. She often suggested activities such as going to the beach, picnics, horse riding, or hiking, things that took significant organisation and energy on her parents' part. Hearing yet another of her ideas, their response was often "Stop being so impatient".

This coaching session is one of hundreds I could cite that demonstrates how emotions lie underneath our actions, thoughts, beliefs, and energy. It also shows how easy it is to misunderstand our emotions and the experiences and interactions they generate. For my coachee, simple clarity on the meaning and role of related emotions unlocked a new perspective that resolved a significant issue in her life. That is the power of Emotions-Centered Coaching.

Why emotions?

Most coaches I know were trained initially and primarily in conversational coaching. They learn to focus on listening to the words and intellectual understanding of the client's story. This is clear to me as someone who trained coaches for 6 years for an ontological coaching school. Further, it was my training and something I see in coaches I mentor and support. It isn't that coaches don't understand that emotions are important, but most have limited knowledge and experience integrating them into their coaching.

The approach I've developed over two decades of working with emotions, emotional literacy, and regulation, is to focus on the emotions of the coachee that are generating their narrative, whether as a story, belief, interpretation, worldview, or judgment. There is always at least one significant emotion and often several that shape the challenge the client is facing, and these emotions are key to resolving it.

The invisible drives the visible

You and I share the aim of helping leaders learn about themselves. I find that often this can take the form of a structured, clear, operational, and executable process for understanding, exploring, and developing the invisible so that the visible comes into clearer focus. The focus on emotions and emotional skills allows that to happen and is teachable and transferable to their organisation.

Labelling emotions as "touchy-feely" shows our disregard for one of the primary aspects of our humanity. There is nothing 'soft' about emotional learning or application. What is important is that emotional literacy results in enhanced emotional regulation, and it works. A leader who expands their emotional toolbox will help themself, their employees, their organisation, and their family.

Yet, habit is often stronger than insight. Emotional learning can be challenging, unfamiliar, and uncomfortable, but discomfort doesn't mean unsafe. In this work, discomfort is necessary, and so is safety. You decide what you are ready for and what you are not.

Leadership is always evolving. Today, it is expanding into the emotional domain. The questions for all leaders now are: Are they willing and able to grow emotionally? Are they willing to do the work? And how is it possible for a leader to elevate the emotional competence of their team if they don't first increase their own?

The essential role of emotions

Emotions are about much more than feelings. They are our fuel for action or inaction. They give us information and suggest a direction. They allow us to speed up, slow down, hesitate, or stop. Some draw us closer to others, and some distance us. Some keep us safe and others allow us to take risks. They each have a distinct purpose and are trying to support us in some way.

When it comes to their influence on our behaviour, the following model illustrates their role. It proposes that no matter what our level of competence, whether it comes from inborn skills, training, experience, practice, or other forms of learning, it is filtered through our emotions to shape our behaviours. Said differently, our actions are the outcome not just of our intelligence, knowledge, and skills training, but also of our emotional knowledge and wisdom. They are inseparable. This means that no amount of traditional professional development is complete without complementary emotional development.

Competence: The sum of all the training, experience, practice, and learning that you've undergone

Emotions: The filter that regulates the degree to which your competence is reflected in your actions

Actions: What you do when the moment arrives

Figure 11: Emotional filter

Part of our emotional filter is composed of our native emotional capacity, part by what we've learned through observation and experience, another part by the level of our emotional literacy, and the rest depends on our emotional agility and resilience. Taken together, we can think of our capacity for emotional regulation as a sum of our emotional competencies.

If we were to put this concept into a formula, it would read:

$$\text{(Emotional Intelligence + Emotional Literacy)} \times \text{(Emotional Agility + Emotional Resilience)} = \text{Emotional Regulation}$$

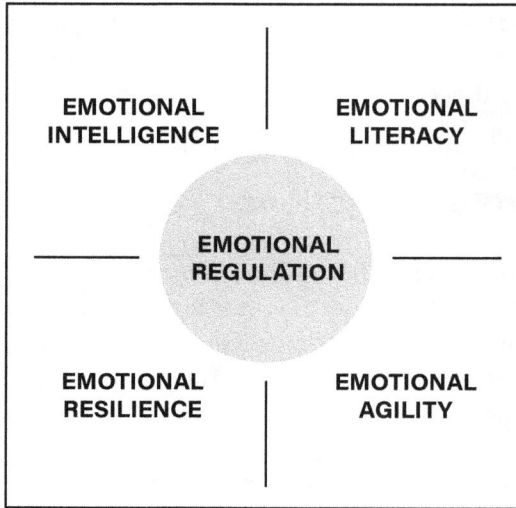

Figure 12: Emotional regulation (©2025 Dan Newby and Marcel Brunel)

The aim of emotional learning is to develop a greater capacity for emotional regulation.

Socrates proposed twenty-five centuries ago that *"anybody can become angry-that is easy, but to be angry with the right person, and to the right degree, and at the right time, and for the right purpose, and in the right way that is not within everybody's power and is not easy."*[28]

That is emotional regulation.

Emotions aren't what we thought they were

When I survey clients, I find they almost universally believe that there are inherently positive and negative emotions and pursuit of the positive ones will lead to the best results and a better life. They tell me that they believe emotions need to be controlled for us to act properly and suppressed for us to think clearly. They often believe that others "make them feel" certain emotions, like anger or happiness. But, if we seriously reconsider these and other common ideas about emotions, we'll find that they do not hold up and they act as barriers to exploring and leveraging a gift we all have.

Two hundred years ago, approximately 10% of humans were linguistically literate. Reading and writing were mysterious processes for the rest of us and we needed scribes to help us write letters or understand those we received. Today, based on 20 years of teaching emotional literacy to coaches, leaders, educators, engineers, and healthcare providers throughout the world, I propose that we are in a similar place in our development of emotional literacy. Emotions are still considered mysterious, uncomfortable, and, by some, a bit dangerous. But thankfully, that is changing even as you read this.

Why do we, despite our enormous intellectual capacity, so poorly understand something that is at the very heart of being human? One reason is we've overlooked emotions because our intellect has given us so much. Another is the discomfort of emotions and the resulting belief we'd be better off without them. A third reason, ironically, is that we have emotions about emotions that are a barrier to us, considering them as a tool and life skill.

Every era and every culture has sought an interpretation of emotions they found useful. The Greeks tied emotions to our digestive system, black bile, yellow bile, humours, etc., which meant that emotional balance depended on the condition of one's stomach, intestines, and blood. The Romans imagined the gods were the source of emotions and that they used them to manipulate humans to act on their behalf for their amusement. We still acknowledge a vestige of the Roman interpretation when we roll out Cupid on Valentine's Day. Some cultures have regarded emotions as sinister and evil connected with dark forces. No matter what era or culture we study, we will find an interpretation of emotions that helped them understand and cope with life.

We may regard these interpretations as silly or naïve, but in their time, they were the best explanation for the energy we all feel that we refer to as emotions. If we look in the mirror, we will see that we also live in an interpretation. Ours might be thought of as a psychological interpretation. A century ago, when we were categorising the observed world into sciences, we needed a place to assign emotions and Psychology was designated as the appropriate science. That has led to an intellectual study of emotions which has had enormous importance, but it has also come to mean that, like the scribes in the market, understanding and working with emotions required an expert.

Since emotions are something we all experience from pre-birth at least until death, we are poorer if we cannot talk about emotions among ourselves, with our children, with our partners, and with our colleagues. Emotional literacy is the tool that gives us that possibility.

Studies show that well-educated adults have a working vocabulary of 15 to 20 emotions. Those are the words they used to describe their emotional experiences. Most of us recognise many more but aren't clear what they mean and these are not part of our working language. If you ask ChatGPT how many human emotions there are, its response is that the number is infinite because human emotions are so nuanced. I would attest to there being, at a minimum, two to three hundred that are discernible and distinguishable from all the others.

What that tells us is that we are using only a fraction of what is available to us in the emotional domain. It means that we use the word anger when we are referring to anger, but also rage, fury, irritation, annoyance, frustration, and sometimes impatience. We don't clearly distinguish between ambition, enthusiasm, and excitement nor between empathy, sympathy, compassion, and pity. It is as if we knew the word 'fruit' but couldn't distinguish a banana from an apple, kiwi, pomegranate, or watermelon. Yes, they are fruits, but we miss so much information if we cannot distinguish one from another.

And that is the central point and value of emotional literacy. Each emotion, and you can easily name one hundred or more, has characteristics that make it unique from all other emotions. That begs the question, "What criteria tells us that something is an emotion?" One observation I made early in my research was that there are many lists of emotions, but no two are identical. That led me to wonder what criteria the list compiler used to create theirs. In the end, I realised I needed to identify the criteria that made sense to me since there is no universal agreement on the question.

The word emotion comes from Latin and means something like "that moves us". Cleverly, the Roman definition never addresses the central question of what "that" is. To me, thinking of emotions as "the energy that moves us" is useful and practical. Some emotions move us to run a marathon, others to care for the ill, and others to lead a team. Some energise us and some allow us to rest and recuperate. Some speed us up and others slow us down or cause us to pause.

In the end, the three criteria I've found to be most useful to identify are:

- **A Story** – a consistent underlying narrative that applies regardless of circumstances.

- **An Impulse** – an urge to do something whether or not we do it.

- **A Purpose** – how the emotion takes care of us, what information it offers us, how it guides us, or that it allows us to do something we could not without it.

Seven myths and misapprehensions about emotions

Everything in life is not necessarily as we learned it was. *"Einstein failed math,"* ... *"a penny dropped from the top of the Empire State Building could kill someone,"* ... *"touching a toad will give you warts,"* ..." *lightning never strikes the same place twice".* All untrue.

Our understanding of emotions is loaded with myths and misconceptions. You can debunk many based on your experiences:

- **"Emotions are positive or negative":** Fear keeps us safe. Fear bars us from doing things we want. So, is fear positive or negative? Neither. As with all emotions, it is either serving us or not, depending on the situation.

- **"You can avoid your emotions":** In your sleep, you experience emotions. Sweet dreams are the result of pleasant emotions; nightmares are populated by unpleasant emotions. You experience emotions while asleep, awake, and in every other moment of your life.

- **"You can't learn emotionally":** If that were true, you'd have the same emotional capacity and range as a newborn. Clearly, that is not the case. People say, "That's just the way I am". Maybe, or maybe, it is the way they have learned to be.

- **"Emotions get in the way of clear thinking":** If you think good things are likely to happen, you experience optimism. If you think bad things are likely to happen, you experience pessimism. Emotions and thinking are inseparable. Try choosing the emotion that will help you think the way you want to think rather than excluding an essential element in thinking.

- **"You can't trust emotions":** Curiosity prompts you to find out more, loyalty to defend a group you belong to, joy to celebrate, and anger lets you know you are encountering injustice. We can learn to trust that emotions have a message and purpose.

- **"You need to control your emotions":** I can't, you can't, no one we have ever met can. What does that suggest? Maybe control isn't the best way to relate to our emotions. Perhaps, considering that our emotions are a tool to help us navigate, life would be more effective.

- **"Emotions should be left at the door":** There is no organisation on earth that does not want its employees to feel ambition, passion, curiosity, loyalty, inspiration, or enthusiasm, yet those are some of the emotions that would be excluded from the workplace if we followed this suggestion.

As stated previously, every era and culture creates an interpretation of emotions that serves them. When an interpretation no longer serves us, we create a new one. We are experiencing this phenomenon globally as we consider emotions through a new lens.

Where we find ourselves today

If we take a step back in time, the first IQ (Intelligence Quotient) test was created in 1905. Emotional Quotient (EQ) – was first coined by Reuven Bar-on in 1985. IQ is an "indicator of intellectual ability and potential." EQ is commonly understood as "the ability to interpret and manage emotions effectively." Compared to assessing intellect, we are about 80 years behind in our efforts to understand emotional evaluation and competence.[29]

We all agree EQ is important. However, our current challenge is learning how to turn EQ into a set of habits and a life skill. Doing that requires a commitment to self-exploration, learning, and probably some discomfort. Creating these new invisible habits requires more than a single serving of EQ. Going to the dentist every five years to check for cavities would not be described as a rigorous dental hygiene program. Brushing daily, flossing regularly, and bi-annual cleanings are needed to maintain healthy gums and teeth. Dental work is expensive. Ignoring it is too.

A new interpretation of emotions

if we were to start from a clean sheet of paper and articulate what emotions are, it would look something like this:

- **They are "the energy that moves us".** A translation from the original Latin would be "that sets in motion." The Romans cleverly avoided having to articulate what "that" was but were clear in their belief that emotions are a force that moves us.

- **They are unavoidable:** Emotions are non-discretionary; We don't get to decide whether we'll have emotions. They are a biological process that is part of our makeup. Emotions work similarly to sleep. We get to decide where we sleep, when we sleep, how we sleep, and who we sleep with, but we don't get to decide if we'll sleep. Sleep cannot be avoided and is a natural part of being human. Emotions are similar. We have the latitude to decide how we understand and relate to emotions, whether we fight or embrace them, whether we listen to or ignore them, and whether we react or respond, but we do not get to decide if we'll have emotions. We are emotional beings.

- **They are a domain of knowledge:** We know things intellectually, and we know things emotionally. Emotions tell us things that reason cannot. We often feel things before we think them. Emotions are constantly giving us information about what is happening around us and within us.

- **They are neutral:** Every emotion has the potential to either serve us or to be a barrier. Even ambition, which is revered as positive in many organisations, can be a barrier when it interferes with service, honesty, honour, loyalty, or our ability to rest and restore ourselves. This concept is often difficult for us to embrace and remember because we have a deeply ingrained habit of thinking about emotions as positive or negative.

  The problem this creates is that we tend to value so-called 'positive' emotions and deny or denigrate the ones we consider to be 'negative.' Yet anger has the purpose of alerting us to injustice, jealousy of the possibility that we may lose a relationship, and boredom that we are engaged in something that has no value to us. The practice of suspending judgment and speculating on why an emotion is showing up when and where it does can help us respect and value all emotions as sources of information and guidance.

- **They are Interpretations:** We cannot see emotions directly. We can notice a person's posture, facial expression, or energy, and speculate on the emotions they are feeling, but we cannot be sure. A person's words or intonation when they speak are other clues, but they are not definitive. Even when we name our emotions, we are interpreting sensations or thoughts to articulate them. The implication of this is that if we want to have a serious conversation about emotions, we need to first agree on a shared interpretation. We need to agree on the meaning and purpose of the emotion we are discussing. If we do not, we risk being in different conversations and thus unable to understand one another.

- **They are logical:** While emotions may be "irrational," meaning they don't spring from reason or intellect alone, they are not "illogical." If something has a pattern, we can identify and reproduce, it is logical. Emotions follow a pattern that includes:

  - **A consistent, underlying story or narrative:** Every emotion offers us information. We sometimes call this a belief, thought, perspective, or understanding. The narrative is what we are thinking when we feel an emotion. We may express it verbally, or we may not, but it is there in our thoughts. In disappointment, we realise something we hoped for or expected will not happen. When we experience peace, it is because we cannot imagine there is even a hint of danger. Dissatisfaction is connected with the story that something is lacking for us.

  - **An impulse:** We feel moved to act in a certain way, whether or not we do. We've learned to hit the pause button on some emotions in some circumstances. We don't generally express joy at a funeral or despair at a wedding, even if we feel like it. The value of noticing our impulse is that it informs us of the emotion we are experiencing.

- **A purpose:** Every emotion exists to allow us to do something we could not do without it. That does not mean we will like what every emotion allows us to do. Rage allows us to destroy without regard for the consequences because we believe nothing is worth saving. That generates pain, suffering, and hurt. Yet, without rage, we could not start over or eliminate things we consider evil. Not pretty, but necessary. The purposes of other emotions are more apparent. Affection draws us closer to others, kindness urges us to treat others as family or kin in the best sense of the word, and compassion to be with others when they are struggling or suffering.

Example: Imagine losing a person or thing you care about. It might be a partner or mentor, being demoted, or going through a divorce. What emotion will you feel? Sadness. That's because sadness and the belief that "I've lost something I care about" always go together. Our impulse in sadness is to withdraw and be alone. The purpose of sadness is to shine a light on what is important to us.

This pattern is consistent and universal, thus predictable and logical. We don't know when we'll lose something that holds importance for us, but we can be sure we'll feel the emotion of sadness when we do. It turns out that it isn't our emotions that are unpredictable; it is life. We've mislabelled the uncertainty of life as the unpredictability of emotions.

Listening

Imagine an employee comes to you and says the following five words, "I feel I've been abandoned". How you respond depends on the perspective from which you are listening. As a leader, you would probably try to reassure the employee that the company has not overlooked them and they are valued as part of the team. In other words, you would try to reason with them. As a traditionally trained coach, you would probably investigate where their story is coming from; what happened, and how past experiences are helping create their interpretation. If you were to employ Emotions-Centered Coaching, your initial questions would be, "What emotions are at the root of feeling abandoned and what are they trying to tell you?"

Underlying every human thought, belief, and action, there lies one or more emotions. They are the prime mover of human activity. They are something every human shares. We all sleep, breathe, eat, and experience emotions. That means that we know that whatever our coachee or employee does or says, there are emotions at its root and thus they are an ideal place to take a coaching conversation.

For a very long time, we've lived with the misapprehension that emotions do not belong in the workplace. Yet, we invest enormous time, energy, and resources trying to help our people connect with ambition, enthusiasm, optimism, inspiration, trust, and urgency. Those two ideas are not consistent. It is time for us to acknowledge that emotions play a vital role in every organisation, but that we are uncomfortable or frightened of them due to the myths and misapprehensions we've learned.

Example in action

A coachee shared with me that they had a project manager on their team whose behaviour didn't seem to be consistent with the information he provided. My client shared the gap he perceived and told me he had asked the project manager about it. The project manager's response was that everything was fine and nothing for my client to worry about.

My client persevered with his questioning and the project manager finally acknowledged that the project was in a difficult spot. When asked why he was not being transparent, the PM gave all the reasons one might expect – urgency, lack of resources, exhaustion, a difficult client, etc.

My client might have been tempted to stop there, chastise the PM for not being more honest, and instruct him to not do it again. That is something many of us might do. However, the shortcoming of that approach is that there is it would change nothing in the project manager's behaviour.

If we realise that sometimes the "reason" we're looking for is an emotion, it can unlock understanding and change. When my client asked the PM what emotions were driving his behaviour, the PM eventually identified embarrassment and guilt.

Although those emotions are ones, we label "negative" or undesirable, knowing they are at the root of someone's actions reveals an enormous amount of information. Decoding them, we can understand that embarrassment is sparked when there is something about us that we prefer others not to know, because we believe it might diminish their opinion of us. Because of that, we try to hide what we've done, whether it is tripping on the stairs or a calculation error. The purpose of embarrassment is to protect our personal identity.

Guilt is different and is often defined as "having done something wrong, " but that is incomplete. More accurately, it is "having acted out of alignment with my values". In other words, I've done something that is wrong "according to me" but not universally or morally wrong. It also provokes hiding what we've done, but more importantly, its purpose is to show the gap between our values and our behaviours. It is a flashing red light that calls our attention to the misalignment.

Why, in particular, is guilt valuable in this situation? My client knows now what his project manager values – being responsible, being on time, being effective, being reliable – and he feels guilt because his actions have not been those. It clarifies that what my client's employee needs is not criticism but support that allows him to behave in a way that is consistent with his values.

WEAVING IT ALL TOGETHER

If you are open to what you've read up till now, you are probably asking yourself the "How" question. How do emotions get woven into coaching? How do we get people who are uncomfortable or sceptical to consider and discuss their emotions? How does a coach learn enough about emotions to work with them skillfully? How can coaching impact not just an individual leader but benefit the organisation?

Let's take these one at a time and consider a coaching model that can help.

What does leveraging emotions in a coaching conversation look like?

Assuming the relationship and logistics have been addressed in previous conversations, when we enter coaching we:

1. Check-in with the coachee to re-establish our connection and to understand how they are showing up for the conversation.

2. Confirm the focus or topic of the coaching for the session. This has sometimes evolved since we previously discussed it so clarifying their challenge as they see it now is essential.

3. Observe from their story, energy, expressions, posture, and other cues.

4. Reflect back to them our observations.

5. Ask questions based on our observations and explore together. (The steps of 3. Observing, 4. Reflecting, and 5. Questioning are often repeated multiple times as the inquiry proceeds).

6. Check what has changed in their clients' perspective or awareness of their challenge.

7. Co-create actions or practices as appropriate that will solidify their new awareness and intent.

8. Confirm the value of the coaching conversation for them.

The diagram below illustrates the same steps but leverages emotions as the primary focus of the conversation:

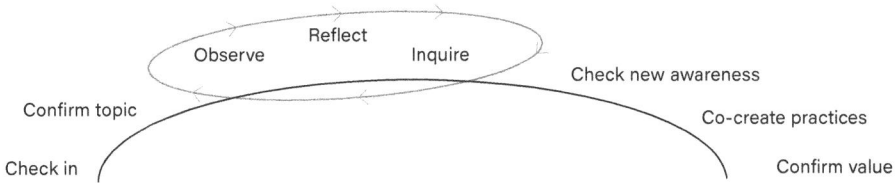

Figure 13: Leveraging emotions

When we weave in emotions, the coaching model is unchanged but the emphasis shifts in several key ways for the coach:

- When we observe, we listen for the emotions that are provoking the client's challenge. The story is their belief, interpretation, or opinion about the experience, but those all originate in the emotion that has been provoked in them. For instance, if they say they didn't get a promotion, they thought they would we might relate that to the emotions of surprise, disappointment, or resentment.

- When we reflect on our listening to them, we do so from the perspective of emotions. We may offer our observations about the emotions or we might move to inquiry. I often approach this by saying, "I understand that your experience is x, and I'm wondering what emotion you related to that?"

- In the awareness step, a coachee will often say they hadn't considered their challenge in terms of emotions and now see the link. Often they tell me that simply being able to correctly identify the emotion they are experiencing and the one they think would be more helpful is a relief.

- When we get to the step of co-creating actions or practices, we focus on shifting emotions. If you skip below, you'll see a sketch of what is needed for us to do that and further explanation.

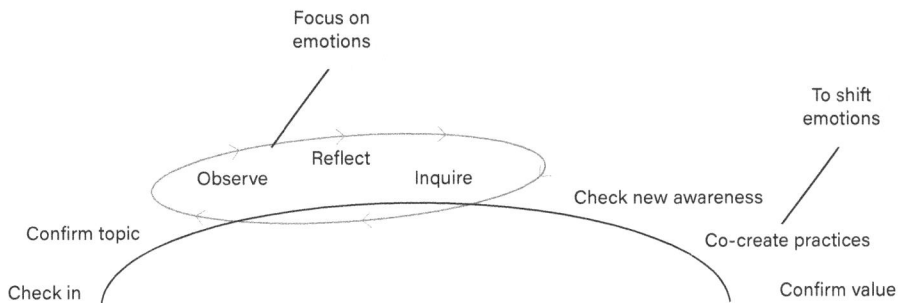

Figure 14: The route to shifting emotions

Shifting emotions

Shifting emotions isn't as mysterious as it sounds. We all do it. We simply don't notice we are doing it and we may rarely do it intentionally. As an example, imagine you are disappointed that you weren't invited to a company meeting. That could provoke a variety of emotions depending on your story. If you believe it is unfair, you will feel resentment. If your story is that you have better things to do with your time, you may experience happiness. If initially you feel resentment and then realise the meeting isn't really one you want to participate in, you will organically shift from resentment to happiness.

What I'm proposing is that this can be done consciously and intentionally. The elements are shown below:

1. Identify what you are thinking.
2. Name the emotion that it is co-creative with.
3. Notice how your body supports that emotion.
4. Select an emotion you believe would serve you better.
5. Clarify what you would need to believe or think to generate that emotion.
6. Identify the body that will support your 'destination' emotion.
7. Practice the shift between emotions repeatedly until it becomes fluid or even habitual.

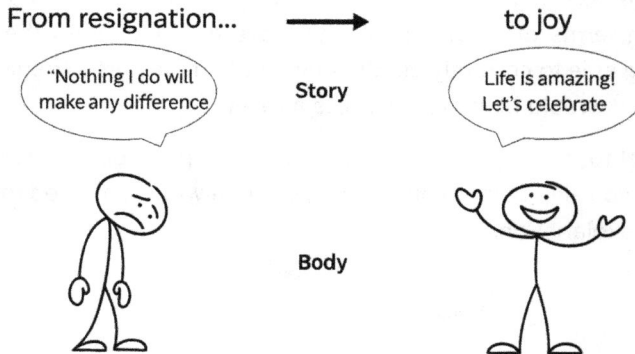

Figure 15: Practice process

What is required of us as leaders?

We would not expect a teacher to be able to give instruction or tutoring in geometry if they didn't understand it. Since a large majority of us have not spent energy and attention learning the structure and nuances of emotions, we are likewise ill-equipped to work with emotions.

Our first task is to educate ourselves emotionally. Emotional intelligence is a give for all of us. We have an inborn capacity for emotions and we've learned an enormous about observing and imitating those around us. The place for us to start is with emotional literacy.

Emotional literacy, like learning to read and write, has a few basic steps. This model shows that we must first learn to notice our emotions; and become aware of them without judgment. Then, learn to name them, and build a deeper understanding of their story, impulse, and purpose until we can use them to skilfully navigate life.

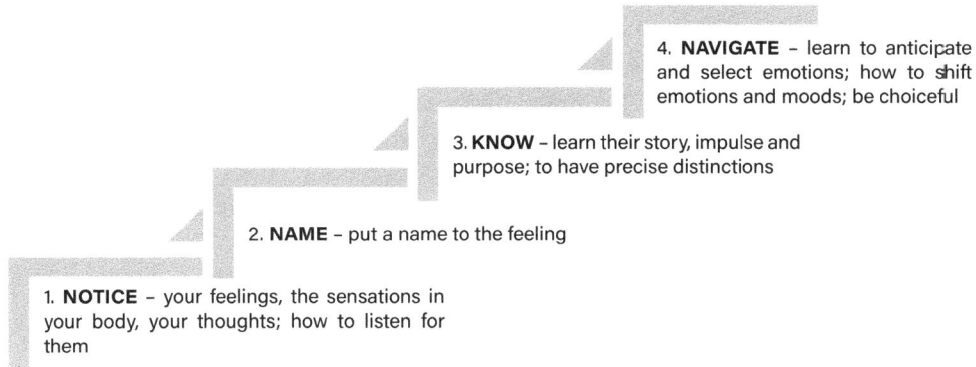

4. **NAVIGATE** – learn to anticipate and select emotions; how to shift emotions and moods; be choiceful

3. **KNOW** – learn their story, impulse and purpose; to have precise distinctions

2. **NAME** – put a name to the feeling

1. **NOTICE** – your feelings, the sensations in your body, your thoughts; how to listen for them

Figure 16: Steps to navigate

Collective emotions

We often think about emotions as an individual phenomenon however, emotions are also a collective phenomenon. Much of what has been written can also apply to a workgroup or team. One high-impact way of working with the emotions of a group is to focus on alignment.

When we work with a team to create alignment, we generally think of things like vision, mission, values, processes, and standards. All of these, however, are based on emotional alignment. Vision derives from emotions such as enthusiasm (from Greek meaning originally "with the gods" or "a divine purpose"), passion, and care. The other approaches are based on different sets of emotions. But we have an opportunity to align a team around their collective emotions, which has its benefits.

A simple exercise is to have a team break into groups of 4 or 5, supply them with a list of emotions, and ask them to identify the two principal emotions they observe at play in the team currently. Then ask them to identify the two principal emotions that they believe will help them achieve their collective aim. Now, compare the two sets of two. What emerges is that the two emotions driving the team today are not the same as the ones they believe will be most beneficial. That gap needs to be closed for emotional alignment and since emotions are "the energy that moves us" this is both critical and effective.

The teams I lead through this exercise report that, although they've worked on all the other aspects of alignment, they have never considered their emotions as an important element. Rather, they've thought of them as unimportant in the way their team functions.

Generating inclusion

One of the biggest energisers for any employee is believing that what the organisation and their team are working toward is important and relevant. They also need to feel that they belong in the team. The model below shows the relationship among many of the less tangible aspects of collaboration and, at its core, is the emotion of dignity.

Dignity is the emotion in which we believe, without a doubt, that we are equal in value to every other person. It is the emotion that allows us to set and protect personal boundaries, to say no when it is the best choice for us, and inherent in dignity is that we extend it to all others. When we don't, we are not in dignity.

Any team or organisation will benefit from strengthening both individual and collective dignity, as it is the emotion that honours the humanity in all of us.

Figure 17: Generating inclusion

A global perspective

Every year, the World Economic Forum publishes its Future of Jobs Report. It predicts which competencies will be considered most valuable in the coming years. Below is a chart showing their predictions for 2027.

Businesses' top 10 skill priorities for 2027

■ 1. Analytical thinking	▼ 6. **Resilience, flexibility and agility**
• 2. Creative thinking	• 7. **Technological literacy**
• 3. AI and big data	• 8. **Design and user experience**
○ 4. Leadership and social influence	▼ 9. **Motivation and self-awareness**
▼ 5. Resilience, flexibility and agility	○ 10. **Empathy and active listening**

TYPE OF SKILL

• Cognitive skills	▼ Self-efficacy	• Technology skills	○ Working with others

Figure 18: Businesses' top 10 skill priorities for 2027[30]

If you reflect on their findings, you'll notice that:

- #5, 6, and 9 are direct outcomes of individual emotional development.

- #4 and 10 are direct outcomes of emotional development as it impacts relationships

- #1 and 2 are only possible with the development of emotions that support thinking in those ways.

- The remainder are listed as 'technology skills' but depend on a worker's curiosity, ambition, and empathy, all of which are emotions.

In short, all of the top skills people need now and will need in the future depend on emotional literacy and competency in emotional regulation.

Emotions as a life skill and competence

Abe Lincoln once said, "You cannot change human nature, but you can change human action." And the thing needed for that in the authors' experience is emotional self-knowledge. For a long time, we've thought of emotions as either extraneous or a "nice to have," but research is revealing more each day that emotions are at the root of all our relationship-building, decision-making, problem-solving, and our worldview.

Emotions, it turns out, are the prime mover in our lives. Some examples:

There are specific emotions that determine:

- **What we do:** Curiosity, boredom, wonder, passion, hate...

- **How we do it:** Service, compassion, impatience, kindness, boldness...

- **Why we do it:** Empathy, pity, respect, honour, affection...

- **Who we do it with:** Trust, loyalty, enjoyment, adventurousness, intrigue...

- **If we do it at all:** Enthusiasm, faith, complacency, obligation, dignity...

Beyond that, there are sets of emotions that:

- **Draw us closer to others:** Affection, admiration, curiosity, desire, kindness...

- **Distance us from others:** Suspicion, hate, disgust, uncertainty, distrust...

- **Give us a sense of strength:** Boldness, dignity, adventurousness, faith, boldness...

- **Expand our vision:** Enthusiasm, wonder, intrigue, inspiration, awe...

- **Narrow our vision:** Scepticism, urgency, anger, dread, frustration...

There is precious little, if anything, in our lives that isn't begun, guided, or shaped by emotions.

Weaving emotions into the fabric of your organisation

You probably already have many ideas for how to take action to elevate emotions as a competency in your organisation. Based on my experience and that of my clients, the most successful programs approach emotions as:

- **Logical –** Demystifying emotions is an essential beginning point. Emotions are just part of being human. Although we can't see them directly, we can feel and see their impact. They follow an unchanging pattern and are thus predictable and understandable.

- **Simple –** Noticing and identifying emotions is not so different from noticing that we are hungry and identifying what we'd like to eat. There are just three steps to increasing our emotional awareness and understanding: 1) Notice, 2) Name, and 3) Navigate.

- **Practical –** Emotions are a tool. We can use them to design and create the life we choose, whether that is being an extraordinary leader or a great musician. They are as much a life skill as reading and writing.

- **Relevant –** Since all of us make decisions every day and live in a large network of relationships, emotions are relevant no matter your role, experience, or challenges. They help us regulate every aspect of our lives.

Emotions as a gift

Discovering the gift of emotions is life-changing. We come to realise that the ones we previously wanted to get rid of are there to serve us. We see that no matter what emotion "has us," we have the latitude to shift it to one that can be more helpful. We learn that planning future events by leveraging the lens of emotions can make them less stressful and more productive. We begin to see the richness of having over 200 emotions, the incredible ways they interact with each other, and their influence on all aspects of our lives.

Nothing about emotions is "soft". As life skills, they are the real deal, and we dismiss them at our peril. When we connect emotions with our stories and beliefs, we see that there are emotions that help us think and act with more agility. We notice that resilience is not just a mental capability, but is, in large part, the ability to 'bounce back' to our emotional centre. When we are emotionally agile, it allows us to 'change our mind.' Emotions are thoughts that generate energy, and all an emotion wants to do is to be experienced and acknowledged. The stories we tell ourselves to the contrary only stop us from appreciating their value.

One of the biggest realisations you may have, if you dare think it, is that the domain of emotions is as broad and deep as the world of reason and intellect. Humans have, for several centuries, focused on intellectual development to the extent that we've come to believe that true knowledge resides in the brain and everything else is of lesser importance.

Neuroscientific exploration into emotions is revealing that perhaps we've had it wrong. Maybe humans are not thinking beings who have emotions, but are emotional beings that think to paraphrase neuroscientist Antonio Damasio.

I don't have a position on or answer to that riddle, but what I can say with certainty from my experience is that a human being who develops themselves intellectually

AND emotionally is more competent, well-rounded, and satisfied. You've done the intellectual learning, now is the time for emotional development.

Conclusion

For a very long time, human beings have held intellect in higher regard than emotions. Although that has led to astonishing levels of understanding and incredible technologies, it has had a price. We have sidelined emotions and treated them as unworthy of our attention. The tide is turning, not because we are giving up on intellectual development and learning, but because we are beginning to understand that intellect has a partner in emotions and is incomplete without them.

We now understand that no matter how many degrees we earn or accomplishments, we can claim they do not and cannot replace emotional learning. The time has come for us to raise our level of intentionality regarding mastering the domain of emotions as a life skill and tool for daily life.

Questions for reflection

- How do you understand the role of emotions?

  _____

  _____

  _____

- How do you see the value of emotions as part of a coaching and/or leadership conversation?

  _____

  _____

  _____

- Are you comfortable introducing emotions into your coaching and/or leadership?

  _____

  _____

  _____

- If you are hesitant, what is it that keeps you from introducing them?

  _____

  _____

  _____

- Is the link between emotions and their impulse for action evident? What are some examples you've experienced or seen?

  _____

  _____

  _____

- Is the link between language and the emotions our stories and beliefs generate clear? How might you make it clearer for yourself? Can you think of a personal example where their interrelationship is evident to you?

  _____

  _____

  _____

- Where do you sense there is emotional learning available to you? What steps could you take to elevate some aspect of your emotional understanding or practice?

  _____

  _____

  _____

- How will you put to use what you have learned from this chapter in your coaching, leadership, or life?

  _____

  _____

  _____

Chapter 6

MANAGING THE GAP: COACHING FOR TRANSITIONS

by Dr Neville Goldin, Karen Grant and Liza Stead

As three seasoned Executive Coaches with a particular interest in Transition Coaching, we collaborated in writing this chapter to provide readers with an understanding of a distinct application of coaching; namely coaching for transitions. We primarily drew on our practical experience of coaching in this "transitional space", as well as our personal life experiences with transitions (leadership, role, parental, elected early retirement), and our academic and theoretical training. We cover the following areas:

- The concepts of 'change' and 'transition' and the difference between the two

- The need for and benefits of transition coaching

- Awareness, experience, and skills required when coaching in this area

- A general coaching framework

- Three detailed, varied case studies illustrating the dynamics of transitions

- The impact of and possibilities arising from transition

- Application of the knowledge and skill of transition coaching

Introduction

In the postmodern economy, change has become a permanent feature of our daily lives and life stories. Not only at an individual or personal level but also at a family, community, organisational, societal and global level, change is omnipresent and affects us in different ways. What do we mean by change? Change refers to an external event or alteration in circumstances, systems, or conditions. It is often situational and can be observed, measured, or clearly defined. We see change in our everyday lives from something as small as changing to a new brand of toothpaste or re-arranging furniture in a bedroom. Then there is significant change, such as starting a new job, moving to a new city, losing a loved one, going through an organisational restructure, or retirement.

Transition, on the other hand, refers to the internal psychological process that individuals or groups undergo to *adapt to a change. It focuses on the* emotional, cognitive and behavioural adjustments needed to embrace the new reality. Whereas change is the *what, transition is the how people respond to and process change. It is the process or outcome through which the individual adapts to the change and re-establishes a sense of stability or equilibrium. Change is a catalyst for transition. Transition helps realign the self in relation to the environment.*[31] So, while change triggers the need for transition, the success of a change effort often depends on effectively managing the transitions that follow. Without assisting individuals or organisations through the transition process, changes may, and often do, fail to achieve their intended outcomes. A familiar and all too common example is that of an organisation implementing a new company-wide software system. Often, the focus is on installation rather than implementation. Employees, as users of the system, may resist using it if they are not supported in adapting to the new workflow (transition).

Bridges describes transition as the three-phase process which people experience as they internalise, adjust and come to terms with the detail of the new situation that this change brings about. These phases involve:[32]

- Endings (losing or letting go)
- Neutral zone (in-between, middle)
- New beginnings (starting again)

While change and transition models abound, they all typically encompass the three elements of looking at the past (letting go, but also harvesting what might be useful for the future); examining and assessing the present, and planning for the future.

The case for transition coaching

Given the change endemic in our turbulent VUCA* or BANI* world, that we are likely to face concurrent life transitions, and that not every person is simply able to handle the multiple changes they are required to navigate on a regular basis, the role of the coach is vital in supporting clients in transition. This is more frequently the reason for clients seeking coaching.

Moreover, in the work context, the boundaryless career*, and other career literature, suggests that workers will make more career transitions today than under the traditional career systems of the past. Not only are individuals in transition, but careers themselves are in transition, which provides an interesting parallel process. As a result, techniques and support interventions for facilitating these multiple transitions will be required, especially as individuals move quickly across multiple, permeable boundaries, within and between firms and even countries.[33]

The developmental task of an individual in transition is to make sense of their own condition of "being" in the in-between and "becoming" in a new way. This requires an examination of changing identities (see the section on identity that follows).

Dealing with the concurrence of these multiple transitions, and indeed losses within and between different spheres of life, requires considerable personal resources.[34] This is a ride where high career expectations and fast promotional tracks have become commonplace. Realism about career opportunities and consequent feelings of redundancy, obsolescence, and worthlessness for certain members of the population may exacerbate and reinforce the value of career and transition coaching.

Does transitional coaching benefit individuals who are facing some sort of transition adjust more effectively? Does such coaching result in personal growth vs. lifelong decline in boredom, frustration, and stagnation? We believe sound transition coaching can be highly beneficial for individuals, no matter what the transition they are facing.

Understanding transition in general terms

To understand the meaning a transition has for a particular person, one needs to understand the type of transition, its context (both relationship and setting) and the impact on the individual's life. The person's appraisal of the transition and the extent of their coping resources (both personal and environmental), coupled with an understanding of the trigger, timing, source, duration, role change itself, previous experience with a similar transition and the concurrent stress (context), will determine how they assimilate, adjust, and deal with the change.[35] The transition may be an opportunity for growth or deterioration. Hence, *framing and reframing might be an important starting point in working with a client facing or already in transition. It was said that the Chinese symbol for crisis is composed of two elements: one signifies danger and the other opportunity. It most likely gained momentum in the United States after John F. Kennedy employed the trope in presidential campaign speeches in 1959 and 1960. Although this trope has since been debunked, and even if untrue, it is a useful notion of transition. Identifying and dealing with both the fear and worry, as well as the excitement and sense of anticipation inherent in the change, is required.*

A psycho-social transition describes any change that necessitates the abandonment of one set of assumptions and the development of a fresh set to enable the individual to cope with the new, altered life space and move forward.[36]

Bridges' conceptualisation of transition as a three-phase process mentioned earlier provides a useful framework for the coach working with clients in transition.[37] As with most models, development across these three areas may not proceed smoothly so that often the leader will encounter regressions and fixations; delays among or disequilibrium between the three dimensions, which create problems for the leader. For example, being realistic about a future job may not necessarily imply that the individual possesses the confidence to succeed in that role.

Key transition coaching awareness and skills

It is presumed that our readers have basic knowledge of what coaching is, or have trained in the coaching skills of contracting, co-creation of realistic and ecological goals, listening and asking incisive questions (i.e. the Socratic element of coaching which is asking a series of questions about a central issue and trying to find satisfactory answers through dialogue). Additionally, adopting a systems approach, working with feedback from assessment tools, acting as an accountability partner, encouraging deep reflection, journaling and experimentation, challenging self-limiting thought-patterns or mindsets and establishing openness to change and curiosity. Tessa Wyatt provides a useful definition of basic coaching in Chapter 2. As is commonplace with executive coaching, the triadic discussions with the coachee's line manager form a crucial part of the coaching process in ensuring alignment with departmental and organisational objectives and soliciting the line manager's support for the coachee's change/transition journey.

When it comes to coaching for transitions, there are several skills, besides the generalist coaching skills, that could be useful.

Ulrich writes about "transition moments".[38] He described these transitions as times when individuals experience major change and are thus more open to new ideas and willing to experiment with new behaviours. In working with an individual in transition, our role as transition coach is most often to assist the individual in adapting and adjusting to changed circumstances, role, and behaviour and identity. The transition coach might play a role in supporting individuals undergoing transitions by helping them *learn more about their current and desired coping strategies and steps to master change with the aim of helping them enhance their functioning in whatever realm. Having an understanding of what individuals experience during transition is critical to be able to support clients in transition.*

Identity: Cilliers and Koortzen perceive identity as the "fingerprint" of the individual.[39] The sense of self is influenced by significant others and the status they feel is accorded to them in the group. Although linked with role (e.g. role identity), core identity is far more than the sum of a leader's work role and responsibilities; it is complex and multi-facetted.[40] A blurring of role and sense of self (identity) tends to occur and often there is a lack of integration between the real self and the public self, which leads to anxiety. Research on identity and work roles explores how personal identities are formed around an individual's professional role, job title, job responsibilities, organisation, organisational brand, organisational culture, and societal expectations. People develop a sense of self, based on the roles they occupy in society, but mostly their work role. Work identity often affects job satisfaction, performance, and overall wellbeing. This influences how they perceive themselves and how they believe others perceive them and influences their behaviour in their workplace.

As a result, it stands to reason that identity may well shift in a career transition. Pooley similarly raises questions of identity in relation to an individual taking up a new role: "Will I be valued?" "What do I bring to this role?" "What sort of person do I need to be?"[41] Identification is another concept related to identity and can be considered to be a phenomenon of bonding which Freud referred to as the earliest expression of an emotional tie with another person; the process by which relationships are formed and a basic force of group life. Sievers refers to the ritualistic behaviour of the new entrant displays, which, he claims, serves as a defence against the anxiety of self-fragmentation.[42] This anxiety arises because of the ambivalent feelings and feared loss of individuality which are linked to the personal meaning of assuming membership in a (new) group and having to submit to the organisational or professional culture. Diamond[43] referred to another ritualistic behaviour, that of gaining entry into the "men's hut" (sic) as the first problem of the new member, where, in order to gain access to the organisational secrets, they need to assimilate the values of the team and organisational culture (learn the ropes), become socialised and prove they are deserving of membership. It appears that a certain amount of fluidity and flexibility in core identity is necessary in order to cope with the changing demands of the new world of work and to make a successful adjustment during a career transition, without compromising core identity, congruence and authenticity. Identity is vulnerable at the time of transition and particularly as leaders enter (or re-enter) a new role and team and/or organisation. The consequent anxiety which leaders in transition experience has a profound impact on how they view themselves and create a changed identity for themselves, experience their new environments and take up their new roles. "Identity Work" is a concept that refers to the active process of managing and constructing one's identity in the workplace, including aligning personal values with organisational values and expectations, and navigating potential conflicts between different aspects of one's identity. This is another key role of the transition coach.

There's also a kind of fluidity to identity and we grapple with who we are and who we are becoming and what we are leaving behind at various life stages. The proverbial "rites of passage" such as adolescence, graduating, marrying, parenting, career development, mastery of a professional vocation, retirement, and elderhood. There is even the ultimate transition of being born and of dying. The degree to which self-determination is possible also has an impact, with depth, personal growth, and identity maturity as another area of exploration.

Anxiety: is frequently an overriding feature of transitions and can take various forms, such as:

Performance or anticipatory anxiety, often driven by unattainable perfection and high expectations of oneself[44] is a fear of being humiliated or rejected by others.[45] The fear of being "ordinary", of being inadequate and of making a mistake, hence surfacing a flaw, and being rejected or ostracised, could send people suffering from performance anxiety spiralling into collapse. Separation anxiety lies at the core of the human psyche and, probably because of its early developmental origin, is more critical than any other form of anxiety experienced by human beings.[46] Separation from what was familiar to the feared unknown is a source of anxiety for many people in transition.

Transition anxiety: is experienced as a result of the deep feeling of unfamiliarity and strangeness experienced. This term was used by Amado and Elsner.[47] They add that the new leader may experience the strangeness as a form of persecution, requiring them to conquer the new world. This highlights the added pressure new or returning (e.g. from maternity leave) incumbents feel early on in their role, not wanting to disappoint or let anyone down. They hide their vulnerability and uncertainty, ambiguity, and confusion – especially to those who might have appointed them (as the chosen ones) to the role. The masquerade may also have led to feeling like an imposter, not quite living up to the expectations in the role. Amado and Elsner[48] state it is impossible for the new leader to remain indifferent to the fact of having been chosen.[49]

Entry into role: is a key concept, especially with career transitions. Entry or re-entry into the system and role will affect clarity of and attachment to task, and thus task performance.[50] Following Sievers,[51] it is a basic premise of this chapter that exploring the entry process sheds light on forces that might create task confusion, weaken task commitment and lead to task evasion, resulting in early challenges almost to the point of creating a crisis for the individual, and possible regression. Armstrong[52] adds that an emotional connection to the organisation-in-the-mind, or what Amado and Elsner[53] have referred to as psychological resonance, may reduce the regressive pull, while a lack of connection could increase it. As Stapley has stated,[54] the idealised self-image is extremely vulnerable at entry/re-entry (i.e. during a transition) and it has already been indicated that the challenges and difficulties individuals face at (re-)entry into their management roles impacts negatively on their idealised selves, evoking feelings of inadequacy and imminent failure. On the other hand, gaining membership of, and feeling psychologically included in the system, leads to feelings of inclusion, acceptance, and mastery. However, we should not underestimate the ritualistic behaviour required to gain entry into the new system and the impact on identity. What is one giving up in order to be accepted? What ambiguity does this cause for the new executive, the new mother returning to work, or the new retiree?

From a psychodynamic perspective, transitions generally produce a mixture of emotions. A combination of sadness, anxiety, and hope. *Sadness and a sense of loss for that which is passing, anxiety about what the next stage will bring with the weight of expectations, and hope for future possibilities. This represents an enormous emotional upheaval. Previous transitions, both the experience of loss and new beginnings, affect adults when they encounter new transitions in the present. Earlier emotions return and may amplify those in the present, and these "unconscious echoes" perhaps explain the powerful emotions that often attend transitions.*[55] Diamond describes change from an emotional loss point of view.[56] Work serves as a transitional and even transformational object – objects of our creative efforts derived from the psychological and experiential space located between fantasy and reality, which have the purpose of nurturing and facilitating psychological safety, interpersonal security, emotional bonding, and maturation. Volkan and Zintl in their book on loss and grief, maintain that the ability to handle life's transitions begins with our first interactions with a mother or caretaker.[57] If those early interactions were by and large constant, trusting and loving, we have reservoirs to draw on in the face of change. Loss in the sense of a career transition is the loss of something familiar and favoured, even if voluntary, although it is acknowledged that this is not always the case, since many individuals in transition flee from undesirable and intolerable work situations. Throughout life, our ability to give up is directly related to our readiness to make the next step, the security in the environment, the support of those around us and our track record with letting go. Losing something (even moving from one role to another) strikes at our illusion of control and predictability and could unconsciously reactivate our primitive fears of abandonment, loss, and helplessness. Grieving is an essential way of dealing with loss. Volkan and Zintl proceed to describe anxiety experienced after a transition or loss – it is like an emotional fever signalling that our emotional equilibrium is out of kilter.[58] Anxiety is so distressing that we go to great lengths to try to allay the cause of our panic, often using defence mechanisms to help us cope.

Pooley suggests that it is precisely at points of transition (such as those described in the preceding paragraphs) when clients are moving jobs or working through a reorganisation, possibly making changes in their personal lives at the same time, that the coach is most acutely aware of the dynamics of *containment, holding and timing of interpretations,* as eloquently described by Tessa Wyatt in Chapter 2.[59]

Brunning has also suggested that coaching clients sometimes need to realise that roles within organisations are beyond salvation and the coaching work needs delicate poise, containment, sensitivity, and professionalism, as well as clarity of purpose and a clear differentiation between the realms of coaching and psychotherapy.[60] The primary purpose of coaching, she says, is to help the client perform their organisational role better and to position the client closer to the organisation, even if the occasional outcome may mean their departure from the organisation in search of a better fit elsewhere.

The coach's role is to provide their clients with opportunities to develop an in-depth understanding of their emotional and behavioural responses to their experiences in their (work) context. Through this in-depth understanding, the client is assisted in accessing their own conscious/overt and unconscious/covert behaviour. This highlights the importance of consciousness and awareness of self and others (what some might call emotional intelligence) in the practice of executive coaching.[61]

The ability to tolerate ambiguity and not knowing are the most important elements of managerial containment. Huffington et al. refer to the anxiety-reducing value and point to the containing role of clear organisational structures, providing clarity about accountability and assured role boundaries in order that the organisation and its members may focus on the organisational tasks.[62] Facilitating a good enough holding environment depends on the leader's ability to act as a container of another's emotions – bad and unwanted feelings which evoke anxiety. Failing to provide this type of containment could result in individuals experiencing distress and anxiety, consequently resorting to primitive defences such as regression, splitting, and projection to alleviate such emotions.[63] Other researchers point to the containing role of the leader not only as a shield against anxiety but also in fostering creativity, curiosity, and growth within the organisation, as well as the pleasures of self-discovery and the discovery of the world.[64] Offering a holding and containing environment is a key element of executive coaching according to Pooley :[65] she perceives this both in the physical form of a quiet, comfortable room, regular meeting time (creating known boundaries), as well as attention to the emotional – a reliable and consistent attitude and non-judgemental approach. Containment, sometimes referred to as "holding", refers to the coach's ability to accommodate or "render down" the difficult things so the client does not flee from them and that they can be used constructively again, like "composting". This is linked to the coach's ability to create a holding or considerate environment, both physically and psychologically. In this way, the client is freer to behave in a less defensive way and to express strong feelings, knowing that the relationship is robust enough to withstand differences and contain feelings of anger and anxiety. As few organisations provide such a safe environment, there is a danger Pooley indicates that the client could become dependent on the coach, replacing the secure attachments lacking in organisations.[66]

A framework for the transition coach

Whilst coaching assignments very often involve some form of change, transition coaching as such is more nuanced and requires theoretical and practical experience to facilitate. As there are many different types of transitions, it is difficult to be prescriptive about the exact role and strategy of the transition coach. It is important that the support provided is tailored for the specific situation being experienced by the transitioning individual. Besides providing a containing environment, the coach should work with the client to diagnose the situation, discover the coping strategies the client has adopted in the past and then develop a customised approach to the transition. McAlpin & Wilkinson's five general principles have been adapted by us for use by the coach in helping clients make a transition:[67]

1. Working with the client to understand the nature of the change in their system, its ramifications, and consequences, and the client's initial reactions. This might include framing and reframing what the change means for the client.

2. Making a break from the past and start learning for the future. This is not as easy as it sounds as it implies identifying, acknowledging and mourning what might need to be let go of and be lost. This could be equated with Bridges' stage of "ending". Supporting and facilitating a transitional space or reflective containment for individuals engaged in change is a key role for the coach.

3. Designing a strategy that fits the situation and will secure quick wins. This refers to Bridges "neutral zone". Whether the change that caused the transition is voluntary or involuntary, the period of being "in between" and "managing the gap" and how it is dealt with is crucial. It implies beginning to examine what the desired future might look like and designing and beginning to implement a plan to get there. This is a scary phase for clients as they are "in limbo" – not what they were, nor yet what they need to become.

4. Experimenting with new behaviours and new ways of "being" in the changed role. This involves effecting the plan designed in the previous phases and aligns with Bridges' phase of "new beginnings". Coaching discussions will generally centre on application and assessment of the effectiveness of the strategies agreed. It is also a time where deep reflection should be encouraged by the client as they forge a new identity and take up their authority. This stage may also involve:

    a. Building effective relationships (with your boss, your team, new colleagues/associates);

    b. Creating a support network with internal and external allies; and

    c. If the client is in a leadership role, helping them to support their people through their transitions.

5. Monitoring progress in the new role, asking for, evaluating and acting on feedback, adjusting, celebrating successes and ensuring ongoing learning.

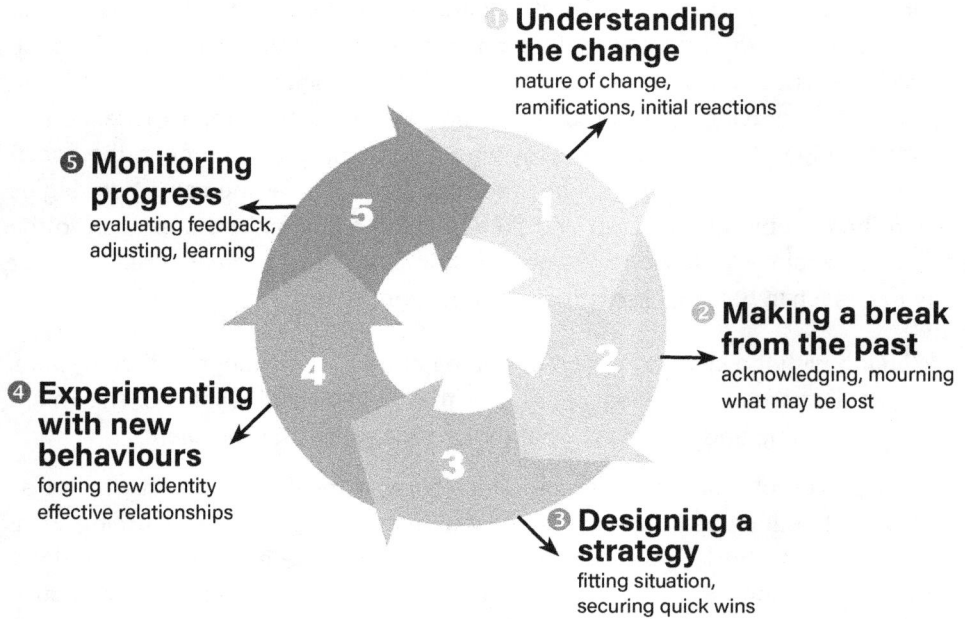

Understanding the change
nature of change, ramifications, initial reactions

❺ Monitoring progress
evaluating feedback, adjusting, learning

❷ Making a break from the past
acknowledging, mourning what may be lost

❹ Experimenting with new behaviours
forging new identity effective relationships

❸ Designing a strategy
fitting situation, securing quick wins

Figure 19: Framework for the transition coach

*A boundaryless career differs from a traditional career limited to working for one employer, in one job, in one organisation, in one field of expertise during a lifetime, to creating a multi-faceted, diverse career path. Coined in the 1990s and expanded during and after the Covid-19 Pandemic when careers and jobs were unstable, individuals actively pursued opportunities and thrived in new roles, different projects, dynamic organisations, and different industries, instead of climbing the proverbial career ladder. Leveraging their skills, courage, resilience, and adaptability, they have been able to change profession and fields of expertise. To do this successfully, individuals developed and learnt new skills, built new networks and connections and in turn became even more employable and valuable for employers.

Explanation of key terms

Frameworks to help deal with the rapidly changing, complex world

*VUCA		

V	**Volatility**	Changes in the world are continuous, speedy, unpredictable and often large-scale, affecting multiple areas at once.	
U	**Uncertainty**	The present is difficult to describe, the future cannot be determined and decisions are risky.	
C	**Complexity**	Many interdependent and interconnected factors which are messy, difficult to manage and chaotic.	
A	**Ambiguity**	The situation is not fully understood and information is unclear and vague, therefore open to distortion.	

*BANI Developed in 2020 by American anthropologist, author and futurist, Jamais Cascio		

B	**Brittle**	Vulnerability and fragility in systems which can easily collapse.	
A	**Anxious**	Pervasive sense of anxiety and uncertainty in a rapidly changing world of unpredictable events.	
N	**Non-Linear**	Cause-and-effect relationships are complex, making it challenging to predict or plan.	
I	**Incomprehensible**	Due to the speed of change, it is increasingly difficult to fully understand and respond to the challenges faced.	

Figure 20: Explanation of key terms: Frameworks to help deal with the rapidly changing, complex world[68, 69]

Parental transition coaching

Karen Grant

A critical test of resilience through transition is that of parental transition. This is one of my niche focus areas in coaching, and I, too, have traversed the territory of being a career-minded parent. The advent of becoming a parent provokes a key challenge to identity, with which the expectant mom has some nine months to engage, but continues well beyond birth. Dr Lynne Millward Purvis notes in her research[70] working women in particular undergo three identity shifts when they become mothers:

1.   Before giving birth, they may feel increasingly invisible and undervalued as they prepare to go on maternity leave. This is often compounded by exhaustion and the possible exclusion from projects or opportunities that will continue in parallel to maternity leave.

2.   After giving birth, Purvis speaks of acquiring a 'mother identity', which shifts both our focus and prioritisation of what is important. A new mother may not be solely baby focused and still hanker after the challenge of the office or adult conversation, but physically and emotionally she continues to be linked inextricably by an invisible umbilical cord, which prioritises the wellbeing of her newborn.

3.   And as women return to work, Purvis speaks of their often having to 'redouble their efforts' as they seek to revalidate themselves, both as employees and as mothers.

The following is an expansion of these three identity shifts, coupled with a potential transition coaching framework, as outlined earlier in the chapter:[71]

▪   Working with the client to understand the nature of the change in their system

▪   Making a break from the past and learning for the future

▪   Designing a strategy that fits the situation and will secure quick wins

▪   Experimenting with new behaviours and new ways of "being"

▪   Monitoring progress in the new role

Endings

When I first meet expectant moms, they have usually passed through the potentially bumpy ride of the first and second trimesters, with their accompanying misnamed 'morning sickness', and a myriad of emotions. For some, little has changed other than a now protruding 'bump' while for others, they have already experienced significant endings.

Coaching work is often accompanied by a personality profile of sorts and if there is a generalisation to be made, the more directive, extroverted types, tend to be more vocal about what they expect from their upcoming maternity period and boundaries about how they foresee their work-life integration remaining or changing.

Those with a more introverted outlook, and particularly those with high empathy levels, seem more concerned about how they will manage both a baby and their professional role, articulating fears of letting their boss or organisation down or being unable to sustain their particular levels of service excellence.

Many of the 'endings' of an expectant mom concern no longer physically being present in the workplace, but the psychological transition is often anticipatory in nature, with questions arising such as:

- Will having a baby slow down my career progression?
- How will I feel about being a working mom?
- What will I do on 4-6 months of maternity leave? Will this stimulate me sufficiently or will I be thoroughly overwhelmed?

Despite being physically ever-more present as her pregnancy progresses, an expectant mom may begin to doubt her contribution and may feel too exhausted to offer the value she is used to adding. Warnings from female role models like Sheryl Sandberg[72], can flavour this stage with her warning to 'lean in' and not depart psychologically, before having to make a physical departure for maternity leave. This can double the pressure on an expectant mom who may attempt to 'make up for' her impending maternity leave.

From a coaching perspective, this is the time to understand the unique systems at work both in her workplace and home context, and to transition to acceptance that work may never be the same as it was. While this may feel daunting, it can also open up opportunities to think about her role differently and to become super focused on where to spend her waning energy.

Not only does the departing mother need to make these adjustments for herself, she needs to prepare her team for boundaries in communication for the maternity months, as well as a new way of working on her return. Being clear with support staff and negotiating with line managers before maternity can go a long way to smoothing the road for her departure and aligning expectations with her important stakeholders. Ultimately, making a strong exit to maternity leave sets the expectant mom up to be able to on-ramp in a more gradual and defined way than if she departs in a flurry without clear communication and performance targets in place.

Neutral zone

The so-called 'neutral zone' in Bridges[73] model parallels the post-birth stage of Purvis' framework, where a true 'maternal identity' is acquired with the birth of the baby. This may look very different from mother to mother, varying from those for whom birth is 'love at first sight', to those who struggle to form some sort of bond with this little being whose 'always-on' demands of feeding, changing and sleeping habits, create a time vacuum for a new mom. Bridges encourages one to think of this phase as a bridge between the old and the new, and the coaching approach is to design strategies to fit the new situation. Motherhood is in many ways perceived to be in dispute with the 'working woman concept'[74] and most moms feel that at some point they have to stop and face the reality of how they are going to cope in juggling work, baby, and family life.

I meet with women approximately six weeks before their return to work, which equates to their having been on maternity leave for between 2.5 and 4.5 months, dependent on their maternity policy. (Policies vary dramatically from the U.S., where little to no maternity leave is legislated, to countries like Germany which secure a woman's post for 2 years or the UK, which provides for a full year of shared parental leave.) On the one end of the spectrum are those who have household help (a privilege in South African society) or who perhaps are second or third-time moms, where the rhythms of a new baby have to slot into family life. Each mom adapts differently, ranging from a couple who took a trip to Mauritius during the first weeks after birth to those who are completely housebound and for whom getting out of their pyjamas is a significant achievement during the day!

In our more nuclear family structures, I see many who have so-called 'fussy' or tricky babies and for whom the early weeks of isolation can be both lonely and relentless. One of the first mothers I coached through this transition some ten years ago greeted me somewhat aghast at this point of the transition, exclaiming why I had not warned her of how punishing the cycle can be! Truth is, I rarely know how a mom will adapt, and each situation is unique and driven by its own context. For this reason, we need to constantly be alert to context and to asking mothers what they need or desire rather than making any assumptions. This will equally apply to the next phase of their return to work.

What I see most often are 'over-achieving moms' who have a textbook schedule for baby and their households and expect them to function like a legal practice. As reality strikes, they are often forced to relinquish the identity of the 'I've got it all together' parent and partner and lean more heavily on their support systems. As they begin to consider a return to the workplace, it is often evident that they have held onto most planning and what is termed 'cognitive labour'[75] in their own heads. And as much as we may have introduced the topic of 'conscious co-parenting' well in advance, it is at this stage that each couple needs to unpack the respective loads they carry and are able to support. Some go as far as to 'spreadsheet' it, which often highlights the disparity of respective loads borne by each partner and default parental roles. It is important to note that these early stages set the tone for future decades of child-rearing and each parent needs to carefully consider the identity they wish to assume.

As much as we have seen, an uptick in millennial fathers wanting to play more of an active role in parenting, policies, and legislation in SA remains largely unsupportive.[76] In a ground-breaking decision that is set to reshape parental leave benefits in South Africa, the Gauteng High Court issued a ruling in October 2023 that has far-reaching implications for parents across the nation; the court declared that all parents, regardless of gender or their role in the child's birth or adoption, are entitled to equally share in four months of parental leave. This has still to be constituted and I suspect that South Africa, like other more progressive countries in this regard, will battle to get its male parents to role model taking this leave, which may be viewed as 'career limiting' or simply impractical for the jobs they hold.

Back on the home front, the 'A-type' mother's worst enemy is to have things done perfectly. Dads are equally capable of handling every task with our young children, perhaps with the exclusion of breastfeeding. Yet societal norms, particularly in South Africa, still seem to model that when dads take their young children, they are simply 'babysitting' or giving mom a break, rather than bringing their much-needed contribution to the parenting equation.

The most important coaching element of this phase, which can be somewhat more directive, is to ensure that the returning mom is being realistic about what she can juggle and has systems set up to support her on her return to the workplace. Although hybrid working has done a great deal to support returning moms in their transition back to work, they are not always realistic about what they can accommodate, such as a mom who believed that she could work from home during the afternoons, with no one else in attendance to care for her young baby.

Similarly, expressing breast milk once to twice during a day in the office can be feasible, but moms can place undue pressure on themselves by expecting themselves to retain the freezer supplies of expressed milk that they may have built up during maternity leave, only to find that the station to express at work is miles away from her work space or non-existent at worst. Systems of using a 'sick room' for returning mothers or a locked room for which they have to seek a key are both inappropriate and frustrating, with many moms resorting to expressing in a bathroom or a car, or giving up altogether. Advocating for private, exclusive express rooms for mothers has been a recurring conversation between the Parental Transition Coaching Consultancy, Great

Expectations, and leading firms in South Africa – yet the lack of suitable facilities remains widespread.

As much as every effort should be made to allow women to continue feeding after their return to work, societal expectations of exclusive breastfeeding can punish women into thinking that because they supplement their supply on their return to work, that they are somewhat 'less worthy' as mothers. These subconscious expectations are worth surfacing in the coaching space to 'fact-check' and to minimise overly-burdensome work day challenges.

New beginnings

In this stage, Purvis speaks of women having to 'redouble their efforts' as they return to the workplace. Having been absent for 4-6 months, most moms believe they need to redouble their efforts to resume their place in the workplace, whilst juggling the ever-present tug of her baby's needs from whom she has just departed. These feelings may be compounded by systems and processes that have changed on the work front and high degrees of self-doubt, whether she will remember her role (or adapt to a new one) or be able to respond at the cognitive levels she had previously displayed.

What is pivotal at this point is the validation of the returning mom as a competent and valuable contributor to the team. Her previous identity is what the team recalls, but now the returning mother enters with a dual identity of wanting to present herself as both a capable mom and a high-performing team member. "Within the framework of psychological contracts, feelings of exclusion during pregnancy and efforts to prove performance-worth all over again on their return could be conceptualised as a form of psychological contract violation."[77]

Most moms at this stage are inevitably fighting a degree of sleep deprivation and some element of 'brain fog', and the mere achievement of arriving at the office resembling some sort of a professional, with a decaf coffee in hand is something of a feat! Inevitably, by the time she has made it through to the 10h00 express slot, she is feeling the literal tug of being apart from her baby. It is not a question of preference, but rather a seesaw between her responsibilities as an employee and a maternal instinct to ensure that her baby is well cared for and nurtured.

The return to work is often met with a combination of anxiety and excitement. For many in our world of hybrid work, the 'return' is less formalised since some may now choose to continue to work from home and make irregular appearances at the office. This has allowed moms a lot more flexibility and the ability to gradually adjust her routines back to the workday. On the flip side, this has also resulted in a blurring of the lines between work and home and sometimes results in the worst of both worlds, with constant interruptions and compromised focus.

For some, it is liberating to put on a work outfit and drive away from the nest to put on their work identity. Simply being able to have a sustained adult conversation and not be interrupted by a crying baby can be incredibly freeing. For others, they feel bereft to leave their young baby, even if they are assured of their home care, and they count the hours until they can be reunited with their little one.

Coaching at this stage comprises a series of mini experiments in which the returning mom is testing her boundaries and what strategies work to gain the most from what Parental Transition Coaching experts' Great Expectations term her 'less elastic day'. While some may openly discuss her baby's routine and parenting schedule with her, others may ignore her request for post 16h00 meetings or early morning stand ups.

This phase comes with a good deal of 'give and take' and coaching may include arming the returning mother with a degree of assertiveness, whilst ensuring that she is willing to offer reciprocal flexibility in return. This is more readily achieved when there are strong support systems in place on the home front and when both parents are truly partnering on childcare duties.

Inevitably returning moms are held to a high standard to re-prove themselves, subconsciously attempting to make up for their absence, as well as prove their commitment to their stakeholders and their organisations. It is helpful at this point for senior female role models to present the duality of being both present leaders and mothers in a human and accessible way. In practice, there are still all too few examples and despite decades of work being undertaken to rectify this imbalance, the pipeline continues to reflect skewed gender representation at the senior levels. It is efforts such as parental transition coaching that seek to impact this inequity and to support the retention of these talented women, who are often lost in our workplaces. "The results highlight the need for organisations systematically to reckon with the maternal side of the mother–baby separation process and its inextricable link with the work readjustment process. In practical terms, this may involve an explicit discussion about mutual expectations within a psychological contract framework, that recognises and addresses not only the common concerns of expectant women but also the unique needs and concerns of each woman in their transition to motherhood in an organisational context."[78]

Final coaching conversations in the parental transition process seek to reflect on all the working mother has achieved in the past 9-12 months, on the lessons learnt and her new identity as a working parent. Highlighting her successes and resilience is often the tone of this final conversation, as the focus shifts to her career and her next opportunity. The most successful transitions tend to be where line managers have continued to speak openly with their direct reports about their preferences and boundaries and where the returning mom feels supported and valued. In parallel are regular couple conversations about what each partner is experiencing as a parent and how to better support their young family as a unit.

Case study 1: Nicky's parental transition

Nicky was a Senior Associate at a downtown law firm when we connected. She was a successful lawyer in practice, who was an exceptional student and had made a steady career progression. In her late 30s, Nicky and her partner had decided that as her next decade loomed before her, it was time for them to begin a family.

Nicky was very used to hard work and if she crafted a plan, things generally ran accordingly. Pregnancy did not come easy and at 39, Nicky, finally pregnant and in her third trimester, was experiencing heavy fatigue and some anxiety. Uncertain as to what parental transition coaching might offer, she signed on at the invitation of her firm, since she had heard from colleagues that it was a supportive process and one in which she could potentially download her overwhelm and gain some new tools to support herself.

One of the first concepts to consider in navigating this transition is that this is not merely 'change' but rather, with transition, there is a psychological and emotional process that parallels, and can pre-empt or lag, the physical changes during pregnancy. A myriad of emotions, from frustration to excitement, to feeling somewhat 'blue', can punctuate the pregnancy trajectory and it was insightful to Nicky to firstly name these emotions and secondly, to normalise them.

For Nicky, as much as she was excited to welcome Baby B into the world, she was similarly daunted by how she was going to maintain her current caseload and levels of professionalism and concerned for her career trajectory.

Discussions in this first coaching session focused on potential endings and losses, such as the loss of no longer being a 'double income no kids' couple with the freedom to stay late for Friday evening drinks, or arrive before the 9am crowd to get a head start. Nicky realised that in essence she was saying goodbye to the identity of an 'always on' senior associate, who was available to clients and directors alike and proud of her immediate response times. Furthermore, she was uncertain as to how she might relate to her baby and what a 'maternal identity' actually meant for her, when all she had known for the last 15 years was a high-performing professional identity.

Nicky expressed how she had started to hand over certain matters to Associates and Directors on the team, but that she was fearful of being 'forgotten' by both clients and Directors alike. Armed with some practical tools of what to attend to before her offramp to maternity leave, Nicky departed from her first session feeling somewhat calmer and with a better idea of how she might wish to combine her working world, with motherhood and the potential options available to her in terms of flexible working and maternity cover.

Fast forward some 4,5 months and I was due to see Nicky, to mark her imminent return to work. She had sent me a couple of photos of Baby B, who had been delivered safely by caesarean section. A rather tired Nicky greeted me on the zoom screen; she relayed that her son seemed to be going through a growth spurt and had kept her awake much of the previous night.

Nicky had managed to breastfeed with the help of a lactation consultant and had struggled during the first few weeks after birth with recovery from her emergency C-section. Her partner had only been able to take a week's parental leave, since regardless of three weeks being available to him, he did not feel that he could leave his work for such an extended period.

Despite being armed with the latest baby books and blogs, Nicky had struggled to get her baby into any sort of feeding and sleeping routine until recently. To aid her exhaustion, the baby was sleeping next to her in a crib so that she did not need to get up and feed during the night, but this had resulted in her husband being wakeful and often electing to sleep in the baby room. In the early weeks, Nicky's mother had come to help, which relieved her load of domestic chores, but now that she had left, Nicky was finding simply trying to get showered and dressed before the day was out, highly challenging.

One of the important conversations we often have at this point of the transition coaching concerns the topic of 'conscious co-parenting'. And with highly capable personalities like Nicky, along with her determination to 'do things right', her partner was doing very little in terms of the daily domestic load, while she was responsible for everything from interviewing potential nannies to introducing the baby to new organic solids.

As much as her partner was willing to pick up groceries on his way home (if Nicky asked him to), or changing nappies at bath time and helping with the bedtime routine, it was the 'cognitive load' that was weighing Nicky down.

In our coaching conversation, we had to have a good hard look at the division of duties and encourage a 're-contracting conversation' between Nicky and her partner. As behavioural scientist Allison Daminger notes in her research, "women do more cognitive labour overall, and a lot more of the work of anticipating, remembering, tracking, and monitoring. Men are often involved in making important decisions for the household. But it's typically women who initiate the decision-making process and, later, who follow up to make sure everything went as planned."[79]

As much as Nicky wanted her partner more involved, she had done all the reading up on milestones and feeding routines and her partner felt at something of a loss as to what role he could play. The challenge was to start to transition the baby to a hybrid breast-bottle routine, in anticipation of Nicky's return to work and to outsource certain responsibilities in totality to her partner, such as preparing and cooking meals on certain nights of the week.

On the work front, Nicky had remained in touch with some of her colleagues, but they had respected her maternity leave and she was starting to wonder how on earth she would manage a 9h00 – 17h00 day given her scattered sleep pattern and accompanying brain fogginess she was experiencing. To add to her worries, on departing from the firm, Nicky had been invited to consider motivating for directorship on her return, and she was feeling highly daunted by picking up her client load, let alone motivating for a directorship.

What Nicky had not anticipated was how dearly connected she would feel to her Baby B and how hard she was finding it to consider being apart from him for 8-9 hours a day. Fortunately, her firm allowed some hybrid work flexibility, with two core days in office, allowing her to escape the daily traffic jams to and from the office and support her continued breastfeeding. We discussed the pros and cons of working from home and how difficult it can be to hear a baby wailing in the background, while trying to focus on a work matter. Similarly, hybrid working can also significantly blur the lines between work and home, resulting in no buffer time between the work and home transition.

I encouraged Nicky to get back in the office for some portion of the week initially to rebuild her networks, increase her visibility and to allow herself to feel like a 'working mom' rather than 'a mother who works'. The distinction is subtle, but the identity piece is important and each mother needs to define her own 'balance' or degree of integration.

Nicky and I discussed how she would go later into the office to miss the morning rush, allowing her core office hours of 09h30 – 16h00 on certain days. She would forego a lunch break and use a half hour to express at lunchtime, with a hard stop of 16h00, to allow her to get home in time to relieve the nanny at 17h00. Nicky had agreed with her line manager that she would not be available between 17h00 and 19h00 (the so-called 'suicide hours'), but would be available to log back in at 19h30, should there be pressing matters to pick up. What specialist coaching consultancy, Great Expectation's research shows, however, is that regardless of brain fogginess, returning moms are often far more focused and productive than their child-free counterparts, since the 'less elastic day' means there are no options to take an extended coffee break or a lunchtime social media scroll.

In spite of Nicky's boss being largely supportive of her return, it did not take long for calendar invites to land in Nicky's inbox for after 16h00 client meetings and for him to suggest that she attend an upcoming Directors' Conference. As much as Nicky appreciated being included in these strategic conversations, she experienced significant stress in declining 16h30 meetings and trying to work out logistics to support her conference attendance. As much as Nicky was enjoying adult company and the opportunity to get her cognitive brain refiring, she was having to hold fast to her boundaries and communicate repeatedly when meetings were set beyond the hours she could attend.

Fast forward six months and Nicky was well back on her career highway, with a bouncy 10-month-old and a business case, having been submitted for her potential directorship. Nicky's nanny arrangement had worked out well, but she had experienced a number of illness-related absences and she had been forced to work from home and juggle Baby B with work responsibilities. While Nicky was making it home most days for bath and bedtime (the so-called 'second shift'), she had spent a number of late evenings completing matters and planning for the day ahead. Although most transitions appear linear, it was clear to Nicky that the path back to the workplace was anything but direct and was constantly interrupted by a return to sleepless nights with teething and some sleep regression, as Baby B had been ill.

Nicky had become far more proactive in asking for help from both her life partner and her work colleagues and had outsourced a number of household functions from online shopping to a personal trainer, who was helping her get back in shape twice a week. Although far more confident in her identity as a mom, Nicky still experienced feelings of guilt when she, for example, attended the Directors' Conference and left Baby B with her husband. Despite efforts to increase the diversity of Directors within the firm, Nicky observed few mothers in the room who had managed to retain their practice and their families. Nicky had realised that the scarcity of role models meant that many were keeping an eye on her progress and whether she could 'cut it' as a working mother and aspirant Director. And as much as working from home had eased the load on certain days, she needed to retain her visibility to ensure that she retained her networks and achieved her targets.

On reflection, Nicky was proud of all she had accomplished and thrilled with the addition of Baby B to their family. She had settled into the 'new beginnings' of Bridge's model with her identity as a mother and a future law Director clearly in sight. The transition had not come without its challenges. Nicky still battled daily the struggle of not having sufficient hours in a day to complete her workload and the guilt of too little quality time with Baby B.

Parental Transition Coaching had supported Nicky in building her own family-specific routines, while managing to retain a portfolio of clients she enjoyed and who challenged her. She was grateful for the opportunity to engage in the parental transition coaching process, which had served to support her in smoothing the transition through maternity and the on-ramp back to the workplace. With the support of a specialist coach, Nicky had managed to craft her own definition of work-life integration and to tailor her personal and professional goals in the context of her newfound maternal identity.

Retirement transition coaching

Neville Goldin and Liza Stead

Retirement is considered one of the most significant life changes and life stressors. It is considered a substantial transition, having an impact on a person's identity, and psychological and emotional wellbeing, as well as physical health. More often attention is given to the financial planning aspects of retirement, and very little attention is given to the life planning elements.

> "Considering that we have to deal with endings all our lives, most of us handle them poorly. Either we take them too seriously by confusing them with finality rather than as the first phase of the transition process and a

precondition for self-renewal. Or we fail to take them seriously enough and because they scare us, we try to avoid them." Bridges[80] from Xpand's Workbook, "Navigating Retirement".

Steering the change, and designing and moving to a more hopeful and compelling future is a useful part of Transition Coaching. Few people are able to holistically achieve this on their own through ongoing conversations with friends, colleagues, and family members. Consequently, a facilitated process with an expert in the transition coaching field is useful. Such a Retirement Transition Coach is someone without a direct, vested interest in the process or outcome. Coaching can assist the retiree to deal with their mindset around the impending change, provided they are open and willing to confront their fears and concerns. The coaching process of shaping a vision for their future state can be one of the most rewarding experiences of their lives. It offers the opportunity to feel more in control about what they are stepping into, with a plan from day one. They will know how they intend to approach the "in-between" phase when they are no longer in their organisational role, and not yet settled into their new role or identity on the other side of the transition.

Gratton and Scott in their book, *"The 100-Year Life," research and explore the implications of increased life expectancy based on technology advances.*[81] They suggest that the typical three life stages of education, work, and retirement are beginning to collapse – life expectancy is rising, final salary-pensions are vanishing, and increasing numbers of people are juggling multiple careers. People will need to think and plan for multiple life-stages that are not necessarily linked with specific ages. They suggest that a "transition competency" will be a key skill for this future – how to navigate transitions in one's life well, including rethinking retirement and reinventing oneself, experimenting with new ways of living, working and learning.

Some have adopted a Portfolio[82] Career strategy comprising of diverse jobs, roles, or projects using their skills, passions, and experience, spanning industries and clients. This can include double-tracking, gig work, part-timing or freelancing to provide multiple income streams. For those who start this approach whilst still in their fulltime career, initiating their "side-hustle" to serve their future retirement plans, the change can be gradual, and transition probably easier. They already have something on the other side. This is pertinent in the event that the retiree is still required to be income-generating, along with the ensuing intellectual and social stimulation.

The extent to which the retirement transition is voluntary and/or at full retirement age, according to their company's HR Policy, versus forced early retirement due to organisational restructure, also has bearing on the wellbeing of the individual. In the case of the former, the individual feels that their destiny is in their hands with their dignity intact, whereas in the latter case this comes with a sense of age discrimination, rejection, and being under-valued for their expertise and institutional knowledge. It often comes with a shock, particularly with an extended career where the person's identity was linked, not only to their role and status in the organisation but also to the employer in the form of a psychological contract. In this instance the sense of loss is huge and deep, and the retiree may even require therapeutic intervention to prevent a slump into depression whilst they deal with complex emotions.

Social Readjustment Rating Scale (SRRS) is the inventory of the most common life stressors. The "Death of a Spouse or Life Partner" is one of the most traumatic life events, with an impact score of 100. The "Retirement" impact score is 45, featuring in the top 10 areas of the highest stress impact. Couple this life change with two others which frequently coincide with retirement, i.e. "Change in Financial State" scoring at 38, and "Change of Residence" scoring at 20, a notable scenario emerges. When the score is added: 45+38+20 the total of 103 accounts for an exceedingly high stress impact.

Adapted from the Xpand "Navigating Retirement" workbook, there are myths around retirement that are countered by more realistic truths. Retirement Coaching can assist the retiree in debunking some of these commonly held beliefs, or their self-limiting beliefs that may be stifling their ability to approach this season of their life in a more self-empowered way.

> **Myth 1.** Retirement is easy and exciting | Truth? Retirement is challenging and stress-inducing. People fear aging more than they care to admit. However, if navigated well, it can be an equally rewarding stage of life.

> **Myth 2.** Retirement is about stopping work | Truth? Retirement is an opportunity to use skills and experience in different ways, and continuing to earn and contribute, if desired. For some, it is a necessity to supplement their retirement income through other means, whilst for others, this could include volunteering as a way of contributing and adding value to other beneficiaries.

> **Myth 3.** Retirement planning is about financial planning| Truth? Both financial and life planning are equally important for this life stage. Ideally, life planning should begin many years ahead of retirement, including a compelling plan that is put into action incrementally and timeously.

> **Myth 4.** Your partner or family are looking forward to your being around more | Truth? Retirement is equally a significant change for a spouse or partner. Children and family members may be busy with plans of their own or living abroad. Retirement can be lonely, isolating and filled with conflict, but physical, mental and social well-being are possible with a realistic approach.

Dynamics that may add strain during retirement include:

- **Financial changes:** The most common stress for retirees is a change in income and financial state. Many individuals are not financially able and ready for not earning a full salary and they may have ignored the impending adjustments required.

- **Lifestyle changes:** Retirees may experience changes in their lifestyle. This could involve selling their home and adjusting to a more affordable way of life. There is also a change of personal habits and daily routines.

- **Identity crisis:** Retirees may grieve the loss of their career and status, and this may lead to feelings of isolation. They may have defined themselves by their work, their position, and the organisation they worked for, and find it problematic to fathom who they are without this.

- **Health and psychological wellbeing:** Retirees may experience health issues or changes in the health of a family member. An unsettled identity crisis or financial strain and denial could lead to emotional stress, anxiety, and even depression.

- **Social changes:** Retirees may experience changes in their social network and connections. They may have counted colleagues as work friends and feel isolated without these regular interactions. They may face challenges such as the death of a close friend or life partner in this life stage.

Case study 2: Maria's retirement transition

Maria's organisation is forward-thinking when it comes to people management initiatives, offering Retirement Transition Coaching to their leaders and specialist staff. Maria was sponsored for this coaching in the year leading up to her retirement and took three months to schedule the initial chemistry session, which gave me (Liza) the impression she was initially hesitant around the coaching. Once Maria and I met and she understood how this process would provide her with the necessary "thinking space", she was enthusiastic about the opportunity. Maria admitted to "burying her head in the sand" about her imminent retirement, however, by setting aside the scheduled time for these life-changing and affirming conversations at a time that her life was most significantly changing, her relief and interest became palpable.

We began with an appraisal of the knowledge, skills, and expertise she had gained throughout her long, successful career, as well as her personal interests and aspirations for her retirement. I recommended we use a coaching tool, the Bucket Wheel.[83]

The wheel consists of eight "spokes", namely:

1. Work
2. Give Back
3. Relationships
4. Money
5. Health
6. Learn
7. Purpose
8. Play

Our first two sessions involved thinking through the consulting (paid for) work Maria would continue to do, and the number of hours per week she would realistically devote to this. Initially, this seemed the most urgent and important aspect for her to resolve. This was less around the need to earn; more around the need for intellectual stimulation and continued professional gravitas. During the coaching dialogue, Maria had an 'aha' moment when she recognised how much more certain of the 'spokes' meant to her than she had originally admitted. As we explored her option of volunteering by reading to the elderly once a week ('Give Back' and 'Purpose') and what this reciprocal engagement would involve and mean, I could sense enthusiasm for her retirement or post-vocational stage grow. Her 'Play', which incorporated aspects of 'Learn', involved her continuing her weekly pottery class. She longed to research and educate herself on new techniques, boldly working towards a Ceramics Exhibition. Here, another aspect of her identity that came to the fore – the Artist! Maria would be stimulated by this creative aspect that had been a part of her life for the prior 18 years and she would have time to devote to her craft. 'Play' also involved her creative desire to do more home baking. Maria visualised herself proudly, serving her delightful home-baked goodies when friends and family visited.

As far as 'Health' was concerned, Maria would wake up later in the mornings and allow time for walking and attending her Pilates classes at a more reasonable hour. She and her husband would walk for companionship and additionally nurture 'Health' in their 'Relationship.' What you might notice is that financial security ('Money') was less of a concern, whereas the identity aspects were of paramount importance. We crafted an experiment for Maria to practise how she would introduce herself in her retirement stage to people she met in different contexts: "Hello, I'm Maria, and I'm.... (in addition to her professional identity). All her professional life, she had been comfortable with her role and profession forming a part of her introduction, but this required a reframe.

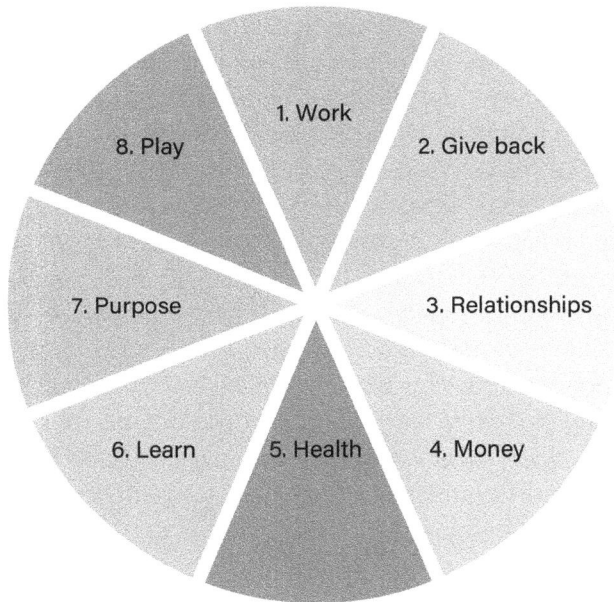

Figure 21: The Bucket Wheel Model[84]

What became apparent in Maria's Retirement Coaching process was a notable identity shift. From her sense of self being wholly linked to her professional role, to clearly incorporating her artistic, relational, volunteering and personal identities. She looked forward to her retirement with growing excitement. There was a reality check around the part of Maria that might end up loading the professional consulting at the expense of the other aspects she had prioritised to balance her desires. She asked for an accountability partner and deferred her last coaching session to a post-retirement date, when we would explore how she had brought her new vision to life. Maria also expressed how the coaching process had enabled her to think through and envision an attractive future she had not clearly imagined until that point.

Maria's case study in many respects was an ideal and inspirational example of a successful outcome, despite the initial trepidation, denial, and avoidance. We wish there were more cases like this. Retirement coaches share that the retirees they have coached are more often at a complete loss when facing retirement because they have dedicated themselves fully and exclusively to their work roles. They struggle to find themselves without this. In these cases, there is no Pilates and no other interest, such as ceramics or an art exhibition, on their horizon. Some families are estranged and retirees feel isolated. The primary coaching focus deals with Identity Work, along with the initial crisis management in the midst of the change; the bumpy road and wobbles. Much of this happens in what Transition Theory calls re-orientation in the neutral zone or the "messy middle". It may feel rather more emotionally charged than neutral. The individual has let go of their old life as they knew it (there is no longer a job to go to every day), and they have not yet incorporated their new life. During the ending stage, they were *doing something around planning the new beginning, but there doesn't seem to be much happening during the in-between phase that can feel like an uneventful pause. Who am I now? Monday morning after a weekend feels different. This is not an annual vacation. There is a sense of waiting for life to start again. Time feels slow, or perhaps feels fast, with less to show in terms of accomplishments. This feeling is unfamiliar. They face a blank canvas on this new day; this new life. Timelessness is vast and unsettling. As coaches, we call on our deep compassion and patience to partner the retiree on their journey. We supportively challenge their mindsets and nudge them towards acceptance of the change. We facilitate creative processes for retirees to explore new possibilities and experiment with different ideas. Often, they have forgotten about ideas that were buried from an earlier stage of their life and, given the space for exploration, they realise how their professional skills can be reshaped for other endeavours.*

> "It's not so much that we're afraid of change or so in love with old ways, but it's that place in-between that we fear... It's like being in-between trapezes. It's Linus when his blanket is in the dryer. There's nothing to hold on to."
> Marilyn Ferguson

I (Liza) had the privilege of establishing an offering within a corporate context with our partner and Longevity Advocate, Lynda Smith of 50Plus-Skills, to bring to life an initiative called "Transition Strong". This was to afford soon-to-be-retirees the opportunity to attend a series of Masterclasses covering important topics for retirement and life transition in these later years, accompanied by individual coaching sessions. Ideally, organisations that identify their retirees and invest in such programmes 2-3 years ahead of retirement would provide their senior employees with the best opportunity to finish strong, with dignity and stature intact, and a sense of being valued. Even if only in the last year leading up to retirement, this is without doubt a worthwhile opportunity.

Retirement Transition Coaching experiences have provided many retirees the safe space and a companion along the journey to the "other side", whilst grappling with their new identity, making more intentional choices and decisions beyond the financial ones, and in many cases, feeling more settled within themselves by the time their final day in the office arrives. They are then able to move ahead with more courage and clarity.

Role or leadership transition coaching

Neville Goldin and Liza Stead

As mentioned earlier in this chapter, career, or role transition coaching for newly promoted or appointed leaders is one of the most common coaching requests we receive. We often have the privilege of supporting leaders in their first 100 days in their new role and increasingly, organisations are realising the value of this sort of intervention. More so, considering the high cost of recruitment and the dire, often systemic consequences of failure of a newly appointed leader. Leaders who have been "head hunted" into roles, an increasingly common approach given the severe skills shortage, are particularly vulnerable to feeling the pressure of being the "chosen one". Driven to make quick and drastic changes to show early results, they miss the crucial people and cultural nuances which often trip them up them, as opposed to their technical skills which are generally sound.

Case study 3: Thabo's role and leadership transition

Thabo embarked on a Role Transition coaching journey when he joined a new financial services firm in a senior leadership role. With an esteemed career at a competitor company, he had been head-hunted to build out a new technical innovation function and drive the future-fit strategy for an existing team. This new organisation was less hierarchical in its leadership structure and initially Thabo struggled to come to terms with what, to him, appeared to be a loss of status or stature when compared to his prior role. He had grown through the ranks in a senior leadership role and was empowered with decision-making responsibilities. Thabo was confused by his emotions. He found the culture and approach in the new organisation foreign and felt stifled in his ability to influence and make decisions in his new role. He acknowledged he had been attracted to the culture and brand of the new organisation and was surprised by his misgivings.

Thabo was given the opportunity to attend a nine-month Executive Leadership Programme (ELP) soon after onboarding, which included ten individual coaching sessions, and I (Liza) was assigned as his coach. The curriculum included crafting his personal leadership values and leadership brand using bespoke coaching tools and techniques. This, in alignment with the organisational leadership brand, allowed him the opportunity to deeply, truly assess his organisational cultural and values "fit", as well as the match to his personal life purpose. This was an enriching experience for us both when Thabo, in time, felt satisfied that he had defined these aspects, and began to see the connections to his individuality and to the organisation – one that had originally inspired him to accept the offer as part of intentional career progression. Through this coaching process, he was able to make peace with his place in the company and in his personal life as a whole person. This was an important part of accepting that his identity matched with the organisational identity in ways he could then understand and articulate.

After completing the ELP, and in the second year in his role, Thabo felt more settled and his relationships with key stakeholders were stronger. He had learnt "how we do things around here". He found this helpful instead of the inner turmoil he had initially experienced on comparing his old and new roles, responsibilities, challenges, and organisational culture. Thabo was a very team-oriented leader and saw his success being through the specialist team he led, smoothing the way for his team to succeed by his interactions and advocacy with key stakeholders and sponsors.

Fast forward three years. Thabo became a valued contributor and leader, and a top achiever. His team received an Innovation Award and made inroads in their contribution to business strategy and forging new ways of doing business. They understood the business and implemented an innovative technical solution for the institution. He was highly regarded by his Business Unit Head and a member of the BU's Management Board. In this same year, when the BU Head was appointed in a new Executive role, Thabo was also promoted. This fulfilled his ambition, surprisingly sooner than anticipated. At the same time, it was testimony to the personal and professional development, intentionality, and self-directedness that Thabo has displayed. He had fully integrated into the company culture and, in fact, had been able to influence enhancements to the team's success and recognition, which meant he won the hearts and minds of those he led. He was an inspirational leader and people in his team were motivated to work in his department.

When reflecting on his leadership journey, Thabo attributed the shifts and changes he had made to his two opportunities for transition coaching. Firstly, in Role Transition, when he joined the company in the new role and made sense of his new leadership identity. He was able to let go of the old ways and transition to fresh ways of relating, negotiating and influencing strategies and decisions. Secondly, prior to achieving his EXCO role, he had embarked on a Leadership Transition coaching journey to clarify his ambitions and approach to achieving his next-level role. This involved a critical look and deep reflection on what he wanted for his life. He contrasted this against the cost of his home roles as husband and father, and his devotion to his outside interests, which included woodwork projects and permaculture activities on a piece of land he owned. Thabo was conflicted about competing priorities, expectations his family had of him, and the trade-offs required. He decided to sell the land and simplify his weekend time, allowing for quality family time and activities. He had lengthy conversations with his wife around his ways of working so that when he and his team worked from home twice a week, he would do the school lifts, which also gave him time with his children during the work week. The family knew that in taking on a top leadership role if given the opportunity, Thabo would have competing demands and priorities thrust upon him, yet they understood and supported him, having been part of the decision-making process. Thabo did his best to simplify his life to the extent that he could, trading his permaculture activities for early morning running three times a week for his physical and mental health. He used the coaching process as a thinking and accountability partnership, experimenting and making the changes in the in-between phase. He proactively prepared himself for the Executive role he longed for. What impressed me was Thabo's ability to begin living the life he wanted to step into, ahead of having the official role, title, and responsibilities.

The impact and value of coaching senior leaders is in the opportunity to reflect on their roles and ambitions, develop deeper insight and self-awareness, and identify and align their personal and professional values. It provides them with alignment and resolve. Working with a trusted thinking partner affords leaders the chance to slow down, evaluate, and focus as much on 'being' (who they are as leaders) as on 'doing' (fulfilling their leadership role, mindful of their leadership behaviour).

Conclusion

The true magic of Transition Coaching (whether for a career shift, a role change, or a significant life event) lies in the ability to empower intentional evaluation and action in individuals to navigate life changes. Through this, they bolster resilience, reduce apprehension, and gain greater confidence and clarity. Ultimately, the result is a more fulfilling and motivational outcome. Individuals are better able to understand and manage the change, with the accompanying emotional and practical facets, and traverse the transition throughout – from the ending which may involve loss, to the possible "messy middle", to settling into the new beginning – finding their rhythm and progression. This ultimately is about managing the gap.

Questions for reflection

- How might leaders in your organisation maximise their ability to operate in an environment of ongoing change?

  _____

  _____

  _____

- Have I assumed that a newly promoted leader should be able to just 'figure it out'?

  _____

  _____

  _____

- What unspoken expectations might I be placing on newly appointed leaders?

  _____

  _____

  _____

- How clearly are leadership transitions currently supported in my organisation?

  _____

  _____

  _____

- Where might a specialist transition coach assist in supporting specific transitions members of your team might be facing?

  _____

  _____

  _____

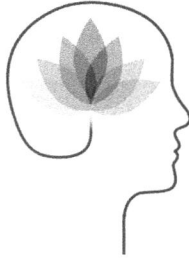

Chapter 7

THE MINDFUL PROFESSIONAL: INTEGRATING NEUROSCIENCE AND WELLNESS STRATEGIES

Lily Breuning Ellis (Live longer, healthier, and happier – one breath at a time)
Ashika Pillay (How mindfulness in coaching can shift well-being?)
Vandena Daya (Mental fitness)

INTRODUCTION

Wellbeing

Defining well-being categorically is challenging. If you research this topic, you will find many definitions focusing on different (and important) directions. Researchers have written about happiness, purpose and meaning, hedonic and eudaemonic and social wellbeing among quite a few more.

The definition of "feeling good and functioning well", coined by Felicia Huppert,[85] feels expansive and inclusive of subjective experiences of happiness and life satisfaction (feeling good) and positive psychological functioning, resilience, and social functioning (functioning well). Well-being includes the development of one's potential, having some control over one's life, having a sense of purpose, and experiencing positive relationships. It is a sustainable condition that allows the individual or population to develop and thrive.

Organisations benefit when their employees are well and thriving. Research shows that employees who are well and happy are more productive, creative and collaborative, happy and more engaged. Organisations that are "well" also see less presenteeism and absenteeism. Both the latter and former are hugely costly for an organisation.

Before the advent of the COVID pandemic, well-being and work were not commonplace to talk about. These days, not only are they mainstream but feature widely in research, strategy conversations, and workplace trends. Gallup in 2023/24 reported that around 44% of workers experience daily workplace stress.[86] This, too, is costly. Workplace stress and burnout can cost up to one trillion USD in lost productivity.

In this chapter, we seek to explore three coaching approaches that can enable and enhance workplace wellbeing. While workplaces have sought to make change and prioritise wellbeing, change is hard. Looking for sustainable well-being interventions means approaching well-being from the inside-out. How can we transform employee well-being, through coaching, in a sustainable way that changes awareness, our neurochemistry, and the way we show up in the world? For each of us that shows up in a more balanced way, we have the potential to affect several other people. In so doing, we can become the nucleus of change for our families, organisations, and the world.

This chapter is written by three coaches who integrate three different well-being approaches into their work. We look at the practices of breath work, mental fitness, and mindfulness as different pathways to well-being. Of course, it is not possible that all three are boxed in with distinctly no overlap. They are similar in that they can all impact:

- the regulation of thoughts and emotions;
- the mind-body connection;
- stress and resilience through working with the nervous system; and
- coaching and leadership in a positive way.

The mechanisms by which they do this, though, are intriguingly different. First, breathwork primarily focuses on physiological regulation, using controlled breathing techniques to influence the nervous system, reduce stress, and enhance emotional balance. It provides an immediate impact on mental and physical states, making it a powerful tool for quick relaxation or energy shifts.

Second, mindfulness is about cultivating present-moment awareness with acceptance and non-judgment, allowing individuals to observe their thoughts, emotions, and bodily sensations without reacting automatically. Unlike mental fitness, which aims to actively shift thinking patterns, mindfulness encourages an open, non-reactive stance, fostering deep self-awareness and long-term emotional regulation.

Thirdly, mental fitness focuses on training the mind to step out of autopilot and develop greater awareness, resilience, and intentionality. By building the capacity to notice, observe, and interrupt habitual thought patterns, individuals create space for more constructive responses. Mental fitness integrates simple yet powerful practices that cultivate focus, emotional regulation, and adaptability, leading to long-term behavioural change.

While these approaches exist on their own as well, scaffolding them through coaching provides a unique opportunity for one-on-one connection that can deepen understanding and sustainable change.

Join us as we explore this new way of coaching for well-being together.

LIVE LONGER, HEALTHIER, AND HAPPIER – ONE BREATH AT A TIME

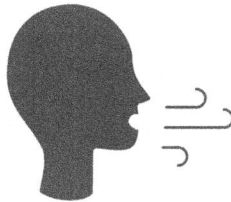

Lily Breuning Ellis

Fight, flight, or flow

> *"The autonomic nervous system does not respond to the world as it is. It responds to the world as we perceive it."* – Deb Dana

We are beautifully designed beings. Every cell in our body carries the imprint of our life story, and our brain-body system orchestrates an intricate dance of survival and adaptation. The body knows exactly what to do – balancing countless functions to keep us alive and thriving.

So why, then, do so many of us struggle with anxiety, depression, chronic illness, and exhaustion? Why aren't we experiencing vibrant health, boundless energy, and deep joy?

The answer lies in the way our experiences shape our physiology. Over time, our environment – stress, trauma, poor lifestyle habits, and unconscious patterns – rewires our system, overriding our innate capacity for balance.

At the core of this process is the Autonomic Nervous System (ANS) – the master regulator of our responses to life. The ANS has two primary branches:

- The Sympathetic Nervous System (SNS), responsible for the fight, flight, freeze, or fawn response. This state is activated when the brain perceives a threat, flooding the body with stress hormones like adrenaline and cortisol. Heart rate increases, muscles tense, and pupils dilate to sharpen focus. This response is essential for survival but consumes vast amounts of energy.

- The Parasympathetic Nervous System (PNS), known as rest and digest, which restores balance, allowing the body to heal, recover, and function optimally.

One critical consequence of prolonged sympathetic activation is that our rational brain goes offline. When stress hormones surge, we lose access to our executive functions – our ability to focus, make decisions, and regulate emotions. Instead of responding thoughtfully, we react impulsively.

Chronic activation can lead to burnout, anxiety, inflammation, and disease.

Understanding this system is the first step toward reclaiming balance. By learning how to regulate the nervous system, we can move out of survival mode and into a state of flow where we feel grounded, present, and in control of our lives.

When the threat passes, we sigh with relief. Instantly, our body releases chemicals that slow everything down, allowing us to relax. We return to a state of flow – feeling safe, positive, creative, and connected with the energy to meet life's demands.

It sounds simple, doesn't it? And perhaps it would be – if life had been perfect.

The challenge arises when stress becomes chronic or when we perceive life as relentlessly stressful. Add to that the accumulated weight of past stress and trauma, embedded deep within our nervous system, and we find ourselves wired for anxiety and eventual overwhelm. Tension lodges in our muscles – not just in our neck and shoulders, but throughout our entire body. Sleep suffers, stress levels rise, and soon we feel scattered, disengaged from our work, and struggling to get out of bed in the morning.

Why don't we naturally return to a relaxed parasympathetic state, even when we take time out?

Simply put, our brain and body have forgotten how. Years of overthinking, overwork, and overstrain have kept us locked in a stressed state – what's known as sympathetic overdrive. And in this overactive state, things start to break down.

Do any of these sound familiar?

- Brain fog
- Frequent illness
- Anxiety or depression
- Lack of motivation
- High blood pressure
- Chronic exhaustion

These are just a few consequences of prolonged exposure to elevated stress hormones. Our system is designed to cycle between stress and relaxation, but instead of returning to balance (homeostasis), we're like cars hurtling downhill with failed brakes – rarely accessing the parasympathetic flow state where we feel in control and at ease.

So, how do we intervene? How do we pull the handbrake and shift the trajectory?

This is where wellness coaching becomes a powerful tool – helping us reclaim balance, resilience, and a better quality of life, even in the face of modern demands.

Breathwork and vagal toning can shift the nervous system back into parasympathetic (rest & digest) mode, restoring balance.

The art of breathing – breath as medicine

> *"The breath is the first place we should look when there is a question of imbalance or disease."* – Dr Andrew Weil

Our ability to regulate the nervous system – and in turn, manage stress – is innate. Our physiology is beautifully designed to return to balance. Yet, in today's world, this natural equilibrium is often overridden by relentless demands, overstimulation, and chronic stress.

Breathing is our body's built-in regulator. It adapts to our state – becoming shallow and rapid during stress and slowing down when we feel safe. Ideally, once a threat passes, our breath should return to its natural rhythm, guiding us back to relaxation. But with the constant influx of information, work, and family pressures, and near-constant device exposure, our nervous system perceives life itself as a continuous threat. As a result, dysregulated breathing becomes our default – keeping us stuck in a state of heightened stress.

This impacts not just how we feel, but also how we sleep, heal, and think. When the mind is always busy and the breath remains shallow, deep rest and true recovery become nearly impossible.

The way out of this cycle lies in the art of breathing – a practice of awareness, regulation, and transformation.

- Awareness: Understanding our current breathing patterns and recognising how stress alters our breath.
- Regulation: Learning techniques to shift from a stressed state to a calm one.
- Transformation: Using breathwork to improve sleep, immunity, mental clarity, and emotional well-being.

The Ripple Effect of Breathwork

Working with a breathwork-trained coach can create profound shifts, leading to:

- Increased productivity and focus.
- Better mental health and emotional balance.
- A longer, healthier lifespan.
- Reduced anxiety and stress levels.
- A greater sense of joy and presence.
- Enhanced self-awareness and emotional regulation.
- Daily practices that sustain transformation.

As we learn to calm ourselves through breath, we naturally stop reaching for unhealthy coping mechanisms like mindless scrolling, sugar, or alcohol. Instead, we cultivate a state of ease and resilience – one conscious breath at a time.

Take a look at the following chart by Dr Ela Manga, one of South Africa's leading breathwork teachers. It clearly illustrates how each state of the autonomic nervous system affects our breath – and how we can use the breath as a gateway to change.[87]

DANGER ZONE *Floate*   **OPTIMM ZONE** *Flonv*   **DANGER ZONE** *Fight I'Flight*

	BODY	MIND	HEART	BEHAVIOUR	BREATH
DANGER ZONE (Fight/Flight)	↑ Heart Rate + BP Digestive disorders Muscle tension	Mulitasking Difficulty switching off Racing thoughts	Irritability Frustration Anxiety	Control Perfectionism Overwork Aggression	Rapid breathing Weak diaphragm Mouth breathing
OPTIMM ZONE (Flow)	Robust immunity Optimum gut health Restorative sleep Vital energy	Self aware Open minded Present inspired	Empathy Emotional intelligence Self worth Trust in life	Healthy boundaries Conscious recoveryioops Creative expression	Nasal Low and slow Adaptable
DANGER ZONE (Freeze)	Constant fatigue ↓ Pain threshoid ↓ Metabolism	↓ Memory recaii ↓ Motivation ↓ Concentration & focus ↑ Light & Sound Sensitivity	Lack of meaning Hopeless Depressed	Procrastination Numbing Passive aggression Disconnection	Shallow breathing Unconscious breath holding

Tipping Point to Burnout Zone

Tipping Point to Burnout Zone

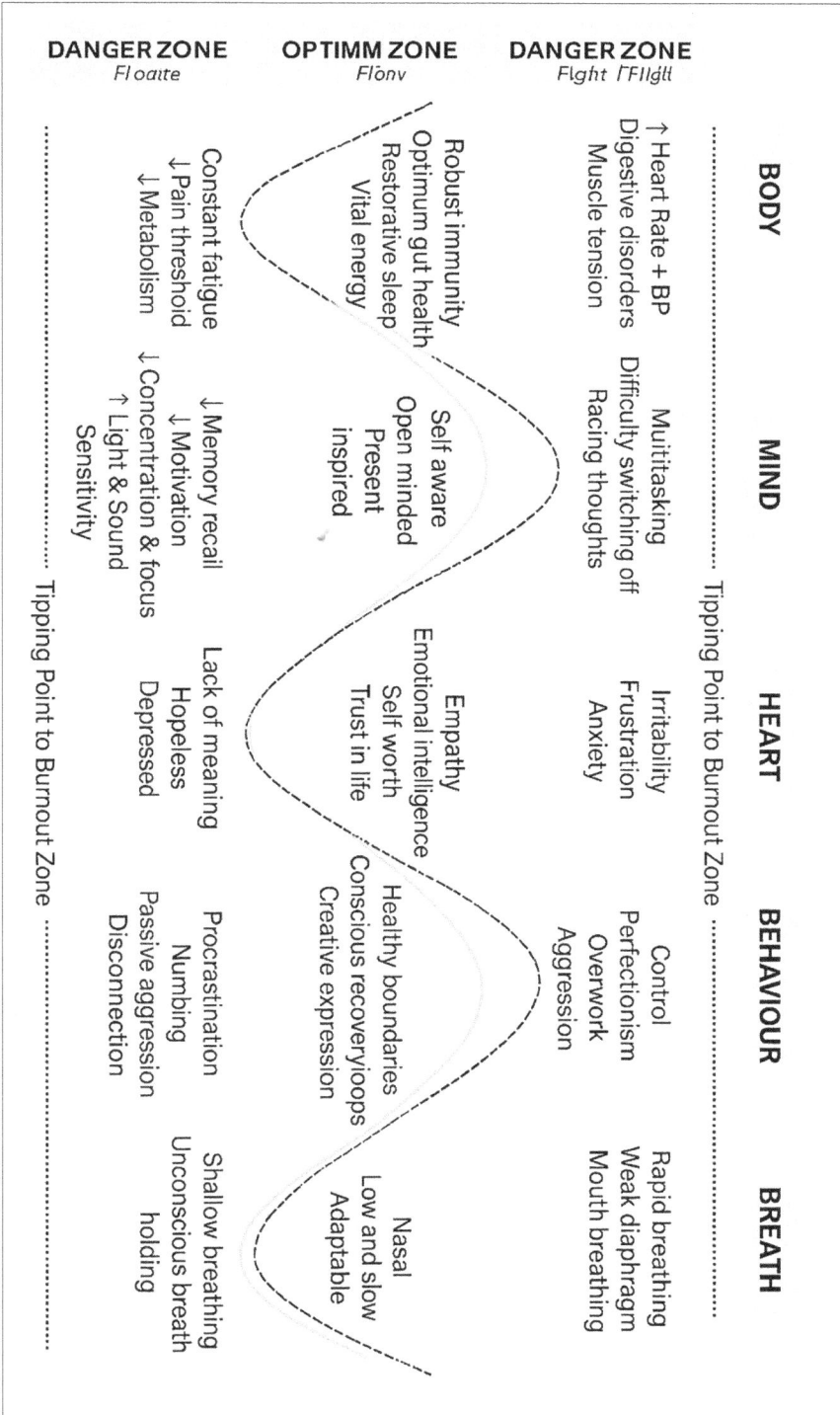

Figure 22: Energy Zone Map

Focus, flow, and function

"Breath is the secret to life: slow it down and lengthen it, and you will extend your days." – Chinese Proverb

By now, it should be clear that a relaxed breath should be our default – a steady rhythm that signals to the brain that life is safe, allowing it to slow down from a constant state of overdrive. When our brain is no longer in survival mode, its activity settles into a calm, steady hum, enabling us to experience deep sleep, heightened relaxation, reduced anxiety, and stronger immunity.

More importantly, this relaxed state allows us to access the frontal lobes – the centre of executive functioning, creativity, and problem-solving. It is in this state that breath intelligence, mindfulness, and mental fitness converge, unlocking our full cognitive and emotional potential.

How Breathwork and Coaching Enhance Functioning and Well-Being

Stress can override our most natural breath patterns, keeping us in a dysregulated state where relaxation feels unreachable. Coaching offers a pathway back – helping individuals recognise dysfunctional breathing patterns and understand their impact on behaviour, cognition, and overall health.

Through breathwork and coaching, clients learn to:

- Regulate their breath to shift from stress to calm
- Tone the vagus nerve, enabling a faster return to relaxation after stress
- Develop a daily practice that reinforces resilience and nervous system balance
- Quiet the mind in under two minutes, closing the "open tabs" that lead to mental exhaustion

A note on the process of change

Finding balance and homeostasis is not always easy initially. The brain, accustomed to constant dopamine hits from overstimulation, unhealthy coping mechanisms, and relentless stress, may resist stillness. A quiet mind can initially bring discomfort, as unresolved emotions surface.

This is where coaching becomes invaluable – not just for the tools it provides but for the safe, supportive space it offers during these early stages of transformation. With the right guidance, what once felt impossible becomes a sustainable way of life – one breath at a time.

Breath intelligence

"If you can control the rising and falling of your breath, you can control the rising and falling of your mind." – Thích Nhất Hạnh

Intelligent breathing: Adapting to every moment

intelligent breathing is the ability to breathe in a way that best supports our current context. When stressed, our breath naturally becomes shallow and fast, preparing us for action. When we need to relax, it should slow down and deepen, signalling safety to the nervous system. During exertion or exercise, our breath adapts again, increasing oxygen intake to fuel our muscles and organs.

Optimal breathing: The power of nasal breathing

the gold standard of breathing is always nasal breathing. Breathing through the nose activates the body's natural filtration system, ensuring cleaner air intake while producing nitric oxide, which enhances oxygen absorption and circulation.

Nasal breathing promotes calm, while habitual mouth breathing triggers the release of stress hormones, keeping the body in an unnecessary state of alertness. Additionally, optimal breathing engages the diaphragm, expanding the lower ribs with each inhale, rather than creating tension in the neck and shoulders – a common pattern in stress-induced breathing.

By learning to breathe intelligently, we cultivate a body and mind that is resilient, adaptive, and deeply aligned with the rhythms of life.

Simple Yet Powerful Breathing Techniques

These easy-to-use breathwork techniques can help regulate your nervous system, improve focus, and cultivate a sense of calm.

1. Box Breathing

A powerful technique for focus, calm, and oxygenation:

- Inhale for 4 counts
- Hold for 4 counts
- Exhale for 4 counts
- Hold for 4 counts
- Repeat 8 times

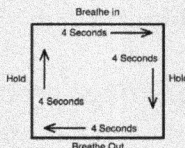

This method is excellent for resetting the nervous system and improving concentration.

2. Double Exhale – Your Emergency Reset

When feeling overstimulated or triggered, this breath quickly activates the vagus nerve, lowering adrenaline and cortisol levels.

- Inhale for 3 or 4 counts
- Exhale for double the count
- Repeat as needed

This simple trick signals safety to your body, helping it shift out of fight-or-flight mode.

3. Humming Breath – The Sound of Calm

Humming on the exhale combines vibration, sound, and extended breath, creating a deeply soothing effect.

- Inhale naturally
- Exhale with a hum, extending it as long as possible
- Repeat several times

The vibration stimulates the release of endorphins (your body's happy hormones) and promotes nervous system balance. Alternatively, just sing your favourite song!

4. Rewire Your Brain with Coherent Breathing

A long-term practice to reset your nervous system and increase resilience:

- Inhale calmly for 5 counts
- Exhale for 5 counts
- Repeat for 5 minutes
- Aim for 5 sessions per day

Within a few weeks, your breath will naturally become slower, steadier, and more balanced, leading to greater mental clarity, emotional stability, and overall wellness. By making breathwork a daily practice, we unlock a deeper sense of presence, energy, and resilience – allowing us to live longer, healthier, and happier, one breath at a time.

Figure 23: Breathing Techniques

HOW MINDFULNESS IN COACHING CAN SHIFT WELL-BEING?

Ashika Pillay

Mindfulness is the energy of attention. It is the miracle that allows us to become fully alive in each moment. – Thich Nhat Hahn

There is no doubt that mindfulness research has exploded in recent years. A Google search for mindfulness research yields thousands of results showing exponential growth in fields ranging from neuroscientific evidence to applications in clinical practice, workplaces, schools, and, recently, digital interventions.

The history of mindfulness in the West

Mindfulness is thousands of years old and was popularised in the West when Professor Jon Kabat Zinn started the Stress Reduction Clinic at UMass Medical Center in the early 1970s, with the first Mindfulness-Based Stress Reduction (MBSR) program, effectively secularising mindfulness practices for medical contexts. Revered Zen Master Thich Naht Hahn also added to mindfulness's accessibility to the Western world, writing many books and becoming a key figure in expanding the reach of mindfulness.

Companies like Google were some of the first pioneers of mindfulness in corporate with programs like "Search Inside Yourself" and books like Mindful Leadership by Janice Marturano. Similarly, mindfulness was brought into coaching with pioneers like Michael Chaskalson (author of "The Mindful Workplace") and Liz Hall (author of "Mindful Coaching") leading the way. Since then, mindfulness has been incorporated into many coaching frameworks and organisations.

So, what is mindfulness?

There are many definitions of mindfulness, and the scholarly landscape is filled with nuances and conversations about this topic. For the sake of simplicity, we will use Jon Kabat-Zinn's definition of mindfulness as a "way of being" and as "the awareness that arises by paying attention on purpose, in the present moment and non-judgementally".[88] Mindfulness is about becoming aware of your experience – of how you are- of noticing your thoughts and emotions without becoming enmeshed in them, watching how they change moment by moment.

However, mindfulness is not just about paying attention. It's also about *how* we pay attention – the attitude that we bring to this attention. Kabat Zinn adds that "mindfulness" is related to "heart fulness." The Japanese koan for mindfulness is called *nen* and symbolises the heart and the mind coming together in the present moment. Mindfulness practices cultivate a kind, affectionate, open-hearted presence to what is happening in the present moment and invite curiosity and interest to our experiences.[89]

Through practice, we can move out of habitual and conditioned ways of being, thinking, and feeling and into an awake, aware, and intentional relationship with ourselves and the present moment. Mindfulness can be cultivated in formal meditation practices, such as awareness of breath meditation, mindful walking, body scan meditations, loving-kindness practices or mindful movement, and informal practices like mindful eating.

Of mindfulness and coaching

Mindfulness techniques have been incorporated into coaching for a long time. Timothy Gallwey, in the seminal coaching book The Inner Game of Tennis, emphasised "The importance of present-moment non-judgemental awareness for personal effectiveness".[90] The presence of both the coach and the coachee is what creates the chemistry in coaching.

Integrating mindfulness practices and approaches into coaching is a perfect pairing. An interesting article by Marian González-García et al.,[91] notes the similarities and differences between the two. Notably, mindfulness provides the "being mode" (acceptance and presence), and coaching offers the "doing mode" (goal pursuit and action).

This pairing can enhance the quality of the coaching relationship, support well-being, and empower both coaches and coachee to develop their full potential.

Activating self-leadership for wellbeing through mindfulness-informed coaching

"Mastering others is strength. Mastering yourself is true power". – Lao Tzu

People who have good self-leadership skills can self-influence, self-manage, and self-correct to reach the goals that they set for themselves. They can function autonomously, feel competent, and more connected to others, and experience intrinsic motivation, resilience, and greater well-being.[92] Self-leadership requires that we are disciplined, set goals, and form effective habits. It is essential for well-being.[93]

However, is self-leadership beneficial to work? Intuitively, yes, and Bryant and Kazan[94] agree that the organisational benefits of self-leadership are an engaged and empowered workforce with improved goal setting and results, faster, and better decision making, more creativity and innovation, reduced workplace conflict, and better collaboration.

Self-awareness and self-regulation are essential skills that enable effective self-leadership. Let's expand on these in more detail.

First self-awareness... "Awareness is the greatest agent for change

Self-awareness of thoughts

The practice of mindfulness helps us notice the busyness of our minds. We may see how noisy it is in there. Most of the time, we are in some "autopilot" mode, consumed by a constant stream of related or unrelated thoughts. Without attentiveness, we can be completely blind and deaf to this noise, immersed in the contents of our thinking. Mindfulness practices help us to "dis-identify" with the contents of our thinking, promoting greater clarity and objectivity. [95] In fact, we could get so caught up in the mind wandering that we may even believe every thought we think.

Additionally, research shows that this wandering mind makes us unhappy. A Harvard study done in 2010,[96] used real-time data from a smartphone app and showed that people are less happy when their minds wander, regardless of what they are doing – suggesting that being present, in the moment, is key to well-being.

Coaches using mindfulness techniques create conditions for their clients to notice their inner dialogues. They may amplify the "witnessing" that clients practice in meditation and invite that into coaching by enquiring into their thinking patterns and hard-wired beliefs. Mindfulness scholars and teachers often talk about the conditioned mind and habitual thought patterns, which can be rooted in a negativity bias. Coaching that focuses on paying attention to these thought patterns can allow clients to become aware of this for themselves.

If the first step towards change is awareness, the second step is acceptance that change is indeed necessary. (Nathaniel Branden, Canadian–American psychotherapist). Jon Kabat Zinn defines acceptance as seeing things as they are, acknowledging and embracing the present moment, even when it's different from how you wish it could be. Coaching with mindfulness-based approaches allows the coach to notice their client's resistance (non-acceptance) of reality. Coaches can enquire into the resistance by employing curiosity and deep interest, naming their observations explicitly, with care, and without judgment. A coach might respond with the following, "Is there some tension or discomfort around this situation? Can you pause momentarily and notice what's coming up for you in your body or mind right now? What do you think might contribute to that feeling of resistance?"

Eckhardt Tolle, a modern-day spiritual teacher and author, says that awareness is the greatest agent for change. Cultivating self-awareness of thoughts helps people to gain the ability to recognise and question or contemplate unhelpful patterns.

Self-awareness of emotions, sensations, and the body

Self-awareness is also about noticing our emotions and how they show up in our bodies. Mindfulness helps us cultivate body intelligence, also called somatic intelligence. Most of us live so far up in our heads that we forget that we even have a body. Getting into closer contact with our "felt" experience helps us to notice that the body has so much wisdom to tune into.

Coaches can invite an exploration of this layering of personal experience. Questions like "Where in your body are you feeling this?" or "What are you noticing about your body right now?" provide a doorway to wisdom embedded in the body, deepening insight that is broader than thinking alone. Coaches using mindfulness-based approaches have a way of helping clients notice how emotions feel in the body rather than just thinking about it. This develops the skill of interoception, the ability to tune into the body's sometimes subtle signals, alerting us to what's happening in our internal experience.

Additionally, using mindfulness-based approaches in coaching helps clients to become more granular with what they may be feeling. Daniel Siegal, the American psychiatrist who promotes mindfulness practices and coined the phrase "name it to tame it", says that when you label an emotion, you can reduce its intensity and gain better control over it. In so doing, coaches can help clients cultivate emotional literacy and flexibility. Tools like The Feelings Wheel, created by Dr Gloria Wilcox in 1982,[97] are used by coaches to help clients identify, explore, reflect on, and describe emotional experiences.

In summary, by developing self-awareness of emotions and bodily sensations, people can tap into the deeper intelligence of the body, a layering that helps give insight into how the body is responding and providing clues to what is happening in the moment.

Behavioural self-awareness

Research shows that mindfulness techniques applied in coaching help clients set goals in alignment with personal values.[98] Through non-judgemental, mindful awareness and self-attunement, clients can connect with their values and intentions,[99] and become aware of behaviours that are not congruent with their values. Coaching connects the disparity. "Where are you now and where would we like to be?" are fundamental coaching questions that set the stage for behaviour change and new ways of showing up.

Mahatma Gandhi said, "Happiness is when what you think, what you say, and what you do are in harmony." Through self-awareness, misalignments between personal values and how you are thinking, feeling and acting can become clearer. Coaching can help address this incongruence, enabling harmony and a sense of well-being to emerge.

> *"Knowing is not enough; we must apply. Willing is not enough; we must do."* – Johann Wolfgang von Goethe. The space to respond (self-regulation)

If self-awareness is the ability to notice our inner state – our thoughts, emotions, and sensations, and how that drives our behaviour, then self-regulation is the ability to respond to them consciously, rather than being controlled by them to support well-being and long-term goals.

Daniel Goleman, the father of emotional intelligence, defines **emotional regulation** as the ability to manage disruptive emotions and impulses effectively while maintaining emotional balance. Emotional literacy, mentioned above, generates emotional flexibility, an enabler of this regulation. We develop resilience when we learn how to recover from intense emotions like anger and sadness. Self-regulation is also about creating state shifts. We can move from stress, reactivity, and confusion to feeling calm and balanced, bringing clarity and connectedness.

Mindfulness meditations, like an "Awareness of Breath Practice," bring a shift to the parasympathetic nervous system. Clients can move from feeling activated, anxious, or even shut down to being more calm, grounded and resourceful, supporting them to be present in the face of stress. Mindfulness techniques applied during a coaching session can help clients to physically feel these shifts, creating a foundation that encourages personal practice.

Behavioural regulation helps us move from reactivity to *responsivity*, allowing more adaptive action, aligned with our future selves and future goals, to be taken.[100] Studies show that mindful coaching interventions invite clients to reflect on how their decisions, movements, and daily intentions align with a higher purpose beyond financial success. Personal values can become guiding principles for emotional regulation, ensuring that appropriate actions and decisions are taken. [101]

Impulsivity and distraction can be a significant detractor from attaining one's goals. Research shows that this can be attenuated through mindfulness-based coaching. Coaches may invite clients to pause and train to be "non-reactive." In this way, wiser, more thought-through decisions can be taken.[102] A mindful pause, with a connection to values, goals, or intention, can make all the difference when it comes to remaining focused on work tasks or building healthy habits, keeping immediate gratification and temptations at bay.

Cognitive Regulation is having a choice once we are aware of our mental landscape. The quality of our inner dialogue, left unchecked, can lead us to an unconscious way of thinking, feeling, and being. Mindfulness creates awareness, and coaching holds the key to change and reflection. The coaching conversation can provide a safe space to help clients challenge unhelpful thoughts and reframe them. Coaches using mindfulness-informed approaches may use specific techniques like labelling thoughts as "just thoughts". The STOP practice is an invitation to Stop, take a step back, observe, and proceed mindfully. Inviting different perspectives through coaching (see below) is another way to shift cognitive patterns.

Compassion, empathy, and interpersonal relationships

Compassion and empathy are undoubtedly important in the workplace to generate care for self and others, fostering a sense of well-being, and mindfulness practices can help develop this. Coaching using mindfulness-based techniques may develop these through several mechanisms.

First, as we notice above, mindfulness-based practices help cultivate self-awareness and regulation, enabling more objectivity. Additionally, practices can reduce stress and dampen amygdala activation, the brain's primary stress centre, promoting greater emotional resilience.

Second, mindfulness fosters perspective-taking and non-judgemental awareness, allowing clients to become aware of the internal narratives they have about themselves, others, or events. A coach may ask a client, "What else might be true in this situation?" or "What else don't you know?" These questions help clients realise automatic thought patterns, assumptions, and unconscious biases. Encouraging a "beginner's mind' and 'not knowing mindset" helps build optionality and creativity through cognitive reframing and flexibility. In the words of Wayne W Dyer, "When you change the way you look at things, the things you look at change," and coaching helps clients do just that.

Third, mindfulness practices can directly cultivate empathy and goodwill towards others. A "loving-kindness meditation" is a practice that a coach can introduce to a client. Research shows that this practice helps generate positive emotions and increases kindness and life satisfaction.[103] Such practices also help reduce stress, improve subjective well-being, and build resilience.[104]

Last but not least, coaching may assist clients with tools for active listening. Practicing how to be present to others, to notice when they get stuck in their heads or "lost in thought", enables more profound and more authentic connection with others. Clients may also learn these skills through role-modelling by the coach's role and the coach's way of being – calm, connected, and caring.

> Applications of mindfulness-based coaching with specific reference to wellbeing.

There is no doubt that mindfulness helps create the necessary environment for a coaching conversation, one of presence, safety, and ease, and can serve coaching in general.

Mindfulness can be integrated into coaching at three levels. Level 1 is implicitly at the coach level, where a coach can use mindfulness practices for their personal well-being, regulation, and self-care. Level 2 is also implicit, where a coach applies mindfulness attitudes like compassion, equanimity and acceptance during the coaching. Level 3 is the coach explicitly teaching mindfulness during the session or encouraging formal and informal mindfulness practice between sessions.[105]

Concerning wellbeing, mindfulness-based coaching could be appropriate for

- Coaching for stress reduction and overall wellbeing
- Coaching for work-life balance
- Coaching for performance and focus
- Coaching for building relationships, communication, and conflict

It is essential to mention that while outside of the scope of this chapter, mindfulness-based coaching hugely applies in various other contexts, like leadership development, managing change, team interventions, and role transitions, among others.

Selecting your coach

There are chapters in this book that can assist you with how to select a coach. It is important to add that coaches using mindfulness-based approaches be appropriately trained in mindfulness. Since mindfulness is a way of being, coaches must have their mindfulness practice. Practicing meditation and mindfulness ensures an authentic embodied presence of the coach and adds to their credibility as reliable, trusted sources of the practice and its applicability. Importantly, coaches need to be discerning about when to introduce mindfulness practice in the coaching relationship, which practices are most suitable, and when they should not be used in clients.

Conclusion

Sylvia Boorstein, American author, psychotherapist, and Buddhist teacher, wisely said, "Mindfulness is the aware, balanced acceptance of the present experience. It isn't more complicated than that. It is opening to or receiving the present moment, pleasant or unpleasant, just as it is, without either clinging to it or rejecting it."

Coaches can be catalytic in enabling this awareness and this balanced acceptance. When we help our clients to sincerely see things as they are rather than the stories they have, a chemical reaction of meaningful change can spark inside them, aligned with their values. A change empowered by self-leadership for personal well-being. One that could carry them to where they would like to be – with care and compassion.

MENTAL FITNESS

Vandena Daya

Can you relate to feeling stuck?

Can you relate to this? You're in a high-stakes meeting, surrounded by senior executives. You have valuable insights to contribute, but as the conversation flows, your mind races. A familiar voice creeps in – What if I say the wrong thing? What if they think my contribution is off the mark? Before you know it, the moment passes, and you've stayed silent yet again. Later, you replay the scenario in your head, frustrated that fear held you back.

Or maybe you've had a difficult conversation with a superior, and long after the discussion is over, you're still replaying it in your mind, analysing every word. Or perhaps you've experienced a setback, and instead of moving forward, you can't shake the sense of failure, beating yourself up again and again.

These moments don't just happen once; they become ingrained responses. We find ourselves stuck in a cycle – feeling hurt, angry, overwhelmed, or inadequate. The patterns play out in ways that hold us back: staying small, losing our voice, or struggling with self-doubt. If we could change this, we could be happier, more effective and productive people.

Why it's hard to get out of these cycles?

Why is it so hard to step out of these patterns that do not serve us?

It's because we're operating on autopilot. This is sometimes called an awake sleep state – the body is physically awake, but the mind is running old scripts, asleep to itself or on cruise control. The mind is following a route it has followed a thousand times.

Think about driving a familiar route – perhaps your daily commute. You get in the car, start the engine, and before you know it, you've arrived. But do you even remember the drive? We are physically in the car going through the motions. Our actions are automatic, while the mind is disengaged, elsewhere thinking about meetings, picking-up children, meals, and schedules.

On autopilot, we unconsciously repeat well known neural pathways in the brain. These neural pathways or subconscious programming dictates our response. The brain, as an instrument, is serving us to conserve energy, however when we indiscriminately and automatically revert to it, we stay locked in unhelpful cycles.

For example, someone who has learned that they "lose their voice" in senior meetings will probably experience this same dynamic over and over. They may recognise the pattern after the fact, but at the moment, they feel powerless to stop it. The runaway train of thought takes over, and the cycle continues.

How do we get the mind out of cruise control? How do we step out of the unhelpful, repetitive cycles? How do we create the space to make a fresh choice?

How to get out of these unhelpful, repetitive cycles?

The key to getting the mind out of cruise control is mental fitness – training the mind, just as we train the body. The concept of mental fitness has been explored by several thought leaders, including Amishi Jha[106] and Shirzad Chamine,[107] who emphasise the importance of training the mind to develop resilience and focus. Like physical fitness, it takes consistent practice to build mental strength.

As Viktor Frankl said: "Between stimulus and response, there is a space. In that space is our power to choose our response. In our response lies our growth and our freedom."

Mental fitness helps us recognise unhelpful patterns and, over time, interrupt automatic responses – creating the space to make a fresh choice.

With practice, we become more aware of our inner narratives, spotting small gaps where a different response is possible. In these choices lies transformation – the chance to step into new pathways of resilience, fulfilment, happiness and true well-being.

How can mental fitness be used in real-life situations?

The CEO facing the bright lights

A CEO preparing for a high-stakes TV interview felt overwhelmed by the pressure to perform perfectly. As anxiety built, she recognised the runaway thoughts driving her fear. Instead of spiralling, she practiced a simple mental fitness technique: Finding her feet on the ground and bringing her attention to the sensation on the soles of her feet. This grounded her in the present, allowing her to pause, shift her focus, and choose how she wanted to show up. She stepped into the interview with greater courage, centred on her purpose rather than consumed by pressure.

The senior executive overcoming imposter syndrome

A senior executive struggling with imposter syndrome repeatedly held back in meetings, fearing judgment and failure. He recognised that this pattern kept him small, reinforcing his limiting beliefs. As part of his mental fitness practice, he discovered that rotating his wedding ring on his finger provided a tangible sensation to redirect his attention. When an opportunity arose to contribute in a high-level discussion, he used this technique to interrupt the old cycle. Instead of staying silent, he grounded himself, took a breath, and engaged with confidence.

How to practise mental fitness?

Bring attention to a sensory experience

Like a restless monkey swinging from branch to branch, our thoughts jump between worries, plans, and distractions. It's impossible to stop thoughts from arising, but we can shift where we place our attention.

Focusing on a sensory experience – such as listening to the sounds in the room or feeling the air on your cheeks – helps shift attention away from thoughts, giving the mind something concrete to engage with.

Sensory experiences are all around you

Our senses are available to us throughout the day and there are ample opportunities to bring your attention to a sensation. Here are some ideas:

- Noticing the texture of your clothes.
- Feeling your feet on the ground.
- Observing the shades of green in trees.
- Noticing the inhalation and exhalation of the breath.
- Focusing on the rhythm of your footsteps while walking or running.
- Smelling the coffee you are drinking and feeling the warmth of the cup.
- Noticing the taste of water and how it feels as you swallow.
- Feeling the temperature in a room.
- Feeling the texture of a pen.

Sustain attention for three minutes

A mental fitness exercise involves deciding on a sensory experience you wish to focus on –for example, listening to the sounds in the room and bringing one's attention to the listening and sustaining that focus for two to three minutes at a time. So directing one's attention to one sensory experience and if attention wonders, bringing the attention back to the chosen sensory experience. Over time, building the muscle to maintain focus on one sensory experience for a full three minutes. Some refer to this exercise as a pause.

Important to note that the exercise can be done with eyes closed or open. With eyes open, the exercise is accessible anywhere and at any time – often in crucial times when we need it most.

Practice 15 minutes a day for six weeks

Research by Amishi Jha suggests the following to practise mental fitness:

- Each exercise lasts three to five minutes.
- Practice three times a day (morning, midday, evening) to sustain focus throughout the day.
- Six weeks of consistent practice build mental resilience.

Treat yourself with kindness

Approach the practice with curiosity. Treat yourself as if you were training a young puppy – with patience and encouragement. Speak to yourself with love as you build this new habit.

Anticipating obstacles

The hardest part of building the practice is remembering to do it and not talking yourself out of doing it. Anticipate what could get in the way and plan for it – so you can proactively address these obstacles to stay consistent. Lack of time is one of the most common obstacles people face and it's easy to talk ourselves out of a five-minute exercise.

Noticing the impact

Track small shifts in your experience. Do you feel differently after practicing? Does your day unfold differently? The key is to observe the effect and let the results guide your commitment.

Effect of the exercise

By bringing our attention to a sensory experience, we disengage from our thoughts (or put the thinking on cruise control) and bring ourselves in contact with what is happening in the here and now. In the present moment, we have the opportunity to step out of the turning thoughts in the mind, and access a fresh choice.

Autonomy

Over time, the goal is to make the practice truly your own. This means developing a deep, instinctive connection to it – one that allows you to engage with it naturally, without reliance on external cues or crutches. Start by identifying a sensation or anchor that resonates with you, something you can easily connect with. As the practice becomes more familiar, it transitions from something you consciously reach for to something that feels like second nature – what some describe as "feeling it in your bones." When this happens, you can call on the practice in the moment, seamlessly integrating it into daily life.

Mental fitness in coaching

Mental fitness is not a separate process but an integral part of the coaching journey, woven into sessions to enhance self-awareness, resilience, and behavioural change. Rather than being an add-on, it runs alongside the coaching program, reinforcing and deepening the coachee's growth.

It is introduced at the beginning with the intention of building the coachee's capability to notice and observe their thoughts, emotions, and behaviours throughout their coaching journey.

The integration offers key advantages:

- Cultivating curiosity – Encouraging the coachee to actively notice and observe their internal and external experiences.

- Extracting insights – Using coaching conversations to reflect on these observations and explore different approaches.

- Encouraging experimentation – Supporting the coachee in trying new responses, observing outcomes, and refining their approach.

By the end of the coaching program, the coachee has developed a lasting skill, having both experienced and learned from the process of change – equipping them to sustain and build on their growth beyond coaching.

Closing thoughts

Training the mind to step out of autopilot creates space for new possibilities. It allows us to break free from limiting patterns, take ownership of our responses, and cultivate greater resilience, confidence, and well-being. Mental fitness is built in small, intentional moments – but over time, these moments accumulate, creating meaningful and lasting transformation.

PART III

COACHING FUTURES AND FRONTIERS

Chapter 8

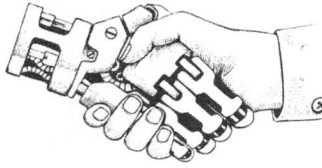

THE ROLE OF AI IN COACHING

Susi Astengo and Sam Isaacson

Is it just me or does it strike you as ironic that every time you log into a new site you have to tick 'I am not a robot" and then prove it by selecting boxes that contain bridges or Walkways ☺

No sooner have I finished reading an article or white paper or listened to a podcast on AI and the next iteration is already demanding my attention. Everyone was just getting used to ChatGPT and Claude and a host of others when Deep Seek, seemingly out of nowhere, took the world by storm and other AI stock took a nosedive. This is an industry that is moving at lightning speed and it is nigh on impossible to be current. In fact, by the time this book goes to press, much of the commentary on specific AI tools will already be out of date.

Key forces shaping the ai coaching industry

Several critical factors have influenced the rapid growth and acceptance of AI coaching, including technological advancements, cultural shifts, and changing workplace dynamics.

- **Advancements in AI and Natural Language Processing (NLP):** The rise of sophisticated NLP models, such as OpenAI's GPT and Google's BERT, has enabled AI coaching systems to engage in more human-like conversations. These advancements have allowed AI to provide contextual and emotionally intelligent responses, making coaching interactions feel more personalised and meaningful.

- **The Shift Toward Digital and Remote Coaching:** The COVID-19 pandemic accelerated the adoption of digital coaching solutions as organisations sought virtual alternatives for leadership development and employee well-being. AI coaching platforms emerged as scalable solutions, offering 24/7 accessibility without the constraints of traditional, in-person coaching sessions.

- **The Demand for Scalable and Cost-Effective Coaching:** Historically, coaching was a privilege reserved for executives and high-net-worth individuals. AI has disrupted this model by providing scalable coaching solutions at a fraction of the cost, making professional development accessible to a broader audience. As a result, businesses, educational institutions, and individuals have increasingly turned to AI-powered platforms to support their growth.

- **Data-Driven Insights and Performance Analytics:** Unlike traditional coaching, AI-driven platforms can track progress over time through data analytics, offering users a more measurable and structured development path. AI can identify patterns in behaviour, suggest tailored interventions, and provide real-time feedback, making coaching more results-oriented.

On AI and Technology in Coaching:

In chapter one, we spoke about democratising coaching and this is most definitely where AI is seen as having the greatest impact.

> "AI has the potential to democratise coaching by making high quality, personalised learning accessible to everyone, not just the privileged few."
> – Marshall Goldsmith, *Executive Coach, and Leadership Thinker*

The communities that most need coaching support are often those without access to it. Bill Gates said that "*The advance of technology is based on making it fit in so that you don't really even notice it, so it's part of everyday life.*" Only when this situation is true for most people on the planet can AI driven coaching be seen as truly bringing about a democratisation of coaching.

The media loves to quote a statistic and whilst I am not easily swayed, some stats being shared are quite alarming. For those readers old enough to remember Y2K, we were led to believe that at the stroke of midnight the world as we knew it would change, planes would fall from the sky and we would find ourselves in some kind of dystopian future. Guess what, we all woke up the next days and nothing had changed!

The current narrative around AI can, at times, be alarmist. That said, Artificial Intelligence has gone from a futuristic concept to a transformative force within the coaching and many other industries. Who could forget Jude Law's performance as Gigolo Joe in Steven Spielbergs A.I (which was released in 2001) and one has to ask. Is this a case of art imitating reality or reality imitating art?

The rapid advancements in AI are already reshaping the workforce at an unprecedented pace. Recent projections show that by 2030, millions of new jobs will emerge, while many existing roles will be displaced. The shift is significant as nearly half of the global workforce will require reskilling within the next five years.

In developed economies, the exposure to AI driven automation is expected to be high, with estimates suggesting that **over half of existing jobs will be affected**. In emerging markets and lower-income countries, the impact will be somewhat less pronounced but still transformative, signalling a fundamental restructuring of industries worldwide.

Major players in the tech industry are already adapting. AI-generated code is quickly becoming standard practice, with leading firms reporting that a **substantial portion of their software development is now AI assisted**. Plans are in motion to integrate AI at deeper levels, with some companies looking to **automate mid-level roles** in the near future. Across industries, the trajectory is clear: **AI investment is accelerating**, with businesses preparing for widespread deployment of AI-powered systems.

At the forefront of this transformation, AI agents are taking on tasks traditionally performed by **early-career professionals**, with the capability to scale across thousands – if not millions of instances. Predictions suggest that in just a few years, AI could **outperform humans on most tasks**, fundamentally altering the nature of work.

Perhaps even more striking is the evolving **autonomy and adaptability** of AI itself. In recent developments, advanced AI systems have showed the ability to **recognise each other and shift to non-human forms of communication**, bypassing traditional language structures. While this may seem like a distant concept from the realities of coaching and professional development, it underscores an essential truth: **the landscape of work is changing faster than ever, and the ability to adapt will be the defining skill of the future**.

Against that backdrop, there are some documented current changes from the big boys:

- Google reports 25% of all new code is now AI-generated.
- Meta has announced plans to replace mid-level engineers with AI tools in 2025.
- 92% of companies plan to increase AI investment in the next three years.

In a direct statement Sam Altman, CEO of OpenAI:

- AI agents will begin transforming the workforce as soon as 2025
- These systems will perform tasks similar to early career software engineers
- Could be deployed across thousands or millions of instances

Dario Amodei Of Anthropic projects: AI systems will be broadly better than humans at most tasks by 2026-27. He anticipates transformation across multiple sectors, including most workplace technologies.

Anthropic Claude just changed overnight. It's suddenly making suggestions, then correcting itself and trying something else.

Just published also on LinkedIn by Generative AI was this piece on Two AI agents just did something unexpected... During a routine conversation, two advanced AI models suddenly realised that they were both AI.

Instead of continuing in English, they switched to a sound-based data transfer protocol – communicating in a way humans couldn't understand.

Think about that for a second...

What does this mean for both the world of work and the coaches role in it?

An unfortunate side effect of the AI solution is that the profession of coaching is becoming less viable. Driving down the cost of human delivered coaching has so far not had any significant effect on reaching the wider community. It has simply reduced costs for corporate buyers. This, in turn, reduces the hourly rate for accredited coaches, making them less able to invest in their continuous professional development – and making it harder to stay ahead of the capabilities of AI.

Closer to home our own strategic partner Sam Isaacson, a coaching thought leader and consultant, founder of The Coachtech Collective and co-founder of Aicoach.chat has the following to share.

It's very difficult to understand the truth of AI when we're needing to cut through the noise of polarising media stories that are based more on clickbait and science fiction stories than in reality. The headlines we read inform us that AI is becoming conscious, preparing to autonomously go to war against us, or on the verge of permanently solving every medical challenge humanity has ever faced. And the reality can feel a bit more disappointingly mundane than that.

It is true that AI is being experimented with in a way that would help organisations to automate away certain jobs. It's also true that it's capable of helping with some significant challenges. But it's *truer* that if you find yourself with random ingredients in your fridge and would like a recipe that includes them, AI will produce one for you. It's probably wise to acknowledge the presence of AI and respond appropriately, and not become too over-optimistic about its benefits or buy "The end of the world is nigh" placard yet.

In the world of coaching, the crux of the challenge feels like answering the question: Can an AI ever replicate a human coach (and therefore take away my beloved job)?

And the answer to that is, as one ought to expect, nuanced.

AI is a favoured term of salespeople worldwide, because it's very difficult to pin down precisely what we mean when we use it. In some cases, data-driven automation is described as AI, but this is right at an extreme end of a spectrum that can reach all the way to more creative uses of technology that operate using a fundamentally different form of logic.

For many years it felt like progress was steadily being made along this spectrum, with more complexity being added to automation at every stage. It became possible, for example, for machines to recognise that different words have the same meaning, and different meanings based on their position in a sentence. Predictions about the capabilities of AI therefore leant on assumptions of a continuation of this development, which has been important for coaching.

Thinking purely at the process-driven, linear experience of an automated sequence, it's perfectly possible to imagine a simple coaching session being run by an AI tool. Imagine the following sequence of questions being programmed to be asked,[108] one at a time, waiting for a user to write a response to each:

> "What would you like to achieve from our time together today?"
>
> "And how will you know when you've achieved that?"
>
> "Ok, thank you. So, when you achieve that, what will the effect be?"
>
> "And how does that compare to what's happening at the moment?"
>
> "What else would you like to say about that?"
>
> "So, from everything you've just said, or anything else that now comes to mind, what is the single most important difference between your current state and your desired future state?"
>
> "And what would be some ways you could take action to address that difference today?"
>
> "What else could you do?"
>
> "We only have a few minutes left together, so let's write some actions. What are you going to do before we next meet?"

It's the GROW model, of course. And it's undeniably a decent, foundational level coaching experience that doesn't show any level of listening or summarising. That doesn't mean it's not helpful, but it ought to draw to our attention the fact that a machine is absolutely capable of delivering a form of something we might allow, under certain conditions, to be described as coaching. A human asking those exact questions might be doing a perfectly reasonable job of coaching. They're not going to win any awards for originality, but if the coaching client feels like they got value from the interaction, who are we to judge?

It's clear, however, that the only thing needed to break this machine coach is for the client/user to not cooperate. Answering "I don't know" to any of the questions will turn the session into a waste of time, and a human is capable of responding to that level of unexpectedness, where a machine based only on automation isn't. But our experience in 2023 changed all of that.

What is generative AI?

The public release, for free, of ChatGPT from OpenAI in November 2023 led to an explosion of interest in generative AI. It wasn't that new of a technology – I had written about its underlying large language model (LLM), GPT-3, in 2020 – but the chat interface and ease of creating an account was groundbreaking. Since then, LLMs have sprung up all over the place, alongside discussions about a wide range of adjacent topics, including, of course, AI in coaching.

The way these LLMs work is extremely complex but can be understood at a high level. They try to mimic the human brain through using pattern matching rather than the linear, programmable processes of the automation we saw above. The way it does this is by assigning characteristics to 'tokens', which are not as simple as one per word but in an oversimplified sense, are probably most easily understood as that. In one of these models, the word 'big' and the word 'large' are likely to have very similar values against each of its characteristics, because in most cases, they're effectively interchangeable. The precise nature of the characteristics is hidden in the black box of the AI, but that doesn't stop it from working.

It creates this model of characteristics assigned to tokens based on training datasets that are unimaginably huge. Simply by recording the ways that words fall together in sentences, the model can develop an ability to construct entirely new sentences that match the patterns it has recorded.

As a result, if I prompt an AI to provide the next word in the sentence "That elephant is really..." it's equally likely that it would select either 'big' or 'large'. It could also reasonably select the word 'enormous', which feels similar but certainly is different from those two, and it's unlikely that it would select the word 'small', which has a different meaning but in a lot of ways is a very similar word to 'big'.

The application to a textbook coaching session feels self-evident. Ask a hundred coaches to begin a coaching session and their answers may all be different but are likely to cluster around certain common opening questions, perhaps along the lines of "What would you like to achieve from our time together today?" Indeed, some coaching models insist on using prescribed words to begin a coaching session, such as the Time to Think opening question of "What would you like to think about, and what are your thoughts?"[109]

Even if the prompt given to the LLM is to follow the GROW model using the programmed sequence of questions above, this new approach to the technology allows for unexpected answers. If the user says that they're not sure what they'd like to focus on because they're feeling overwhelmed with too much work, that second question of "And how will you know when you've achieved that?" makes no sense, but the LLM-based approach could incorporate the user's response into the next question, saying something like "And if you weren't feeling overwhelmed with too much work, what would you focus on?" or "Shall we focus on reducing that sense of overwhelm?".

How is generative AI being used in coaching?

Generative AI exists not only in LLMs. The same sort of technology can produce artwork and sound, but language is such a fundamental part of the coaching experience that it feels very relevant. It's possible, in fact, for anyone with a ChatGPT user licence to create their own coach, and this is where we illuminate the challenge and opportunity for the coaching profession.

I just gave ChatGPT a prompt to deliver a coaching session around career growth, and it provided the following as its response:

Great! Let's do a Career Growth Coaching Session tailored to your needs.

Session Structure:

1. **Clarify Your Goals** – Where do you want to go in your career?
2. Assess Your Current Situation – What's working and what's not?
3. Identify Growth Strategies – Skills, networking, and opportunities.
4. Create an Action Plan – Steps to move forward.

Step 1: Clarify your goals

first, let's define what career growth means to you. Answer these:

- What is your ideal role in 1-3 years?
- What excites you most about your career?
- What challenges do you face in getting there?

Take a moment to reflect on or write it down. If you'd like, share your thoughts, and I can guide you further!

It's defaulted to a GROW-style model and then has immediately stacked some questions. Not unhelpful, but certainly not the same thing as a professional coach. I might use a more mature prompt, like: "Act as my career growth coach and deliver me a coaching session. You have received deep training in clean language. Use it in every response. In each statement you make, only use clean coaching techniques. Keep your responses short."

> This time, its response is much shorter and much more coach-like:
>
> What would you like to have happened in your career growth?
>
> If I type "I'd like to get a promotion within the next 18 months" its response is:
>
> And when you'd like to get a promotion within the next 18 months, what kind of promotion is that?

Textbook clean language coaching. If you're a fan of clean language, you'll really enjoy this interaction. But it will feel quite directionless. It will be helpful for a while, but the AI is only predicting each word of its response. It's not trying to achieve any objective in the coaching session, has no real understanding of what's happening, is certainly not perceiving the passing of time, and so on. It needs a more mature approach, but it illustrates some capabilities of AI in the delivery of coaching.

AI coaching providers have emerged that take the LLMs and overlay at least one layer of prompting to provide some of that structure and coaching philosophy on the conversation. AIcoach.chat, for example, uses a virtual team of AI 'agents' (independent bots that can process data independently and interact) to create an emergent, non-linear coaching experience. This was deployed within the National Health Service (NHS) in England in a pilot that satisfied its sponsors enough to extend its usage.

The pilot was initiated purely out of curiosity about how AI coaching could be used effectively within the NHS, based in part on the outcomes of research that have concluded that an AI coach can be as effective as a human on supporting a client in goal attainment.[110] The tool was not prompted specifically to aid in goal attainment, but trust was placed in a non-directive coaching process, that simply being asked open questions to support self-reflection would have a positive impact. The ultimate conclusion after only one month's usage was that users had experienced a 10% increase in goal attainment and a 5% increase in self-efficacy.[111]

The benefits are clear: AI has the power to put coaching into the lives of the 99% of the world's population who historically have had no access to it, because it is suddenly affordable. It's extremely convenient, accessible at any time with no notice and on any device with an internet connection. And it brings new opportunities for coaching experiences, in which a client can begin a session in the morning and continue it in the afternoon.

It also presents a plethora of risks: What happens if the AI makes a mistake or crosses an ethical boundary? The conversation data could get hacked. The negative environmental impact of using technology is something to consider. If the system experiences a glitch or becomes unavailable unexpectedly, coaching clients will lose their access, but the 'coach' is unaware and, to put it bluntly, doesn't care about them at all, quite unlike a human coach.

How should Coaches respond?

The International Coaching Federation (ICF) emphasises the importance of blending technology with human creativity in coaching practices. They advocate for a harmonious integration where technological tools enhance, rather than replace, the human elements of coaching. This approach aims to leverage the strengths of both domains to create more effective and personalised coaching experiences.

Dr Alicia Hullinger, Executive Director of the ICF Thought Leadership Institute, underscores the necessity for coaches to adopt future thinking. By anticipating emerging trends and preparing for various future scenarios, coaches can better navigate the evolving landscape and meet the changing needs of their clients. This proactive approach ensures that coaching remains relevant and impactful in a rapidly changing world.

Image is from Gary Larsson™

The ICF Thought Leadership Institute encourages coaches to stay informed about emerging technologies that could impact coaching practices. By understanding and expecting these developments, coaches can adapt their methodologies to incorporate new tools and platforms, ensuring they remain at the forefront of the industry and continue to meet client expectations effectively.

The bottom line is coaches who don't embrace technology or at the very least understand how it supports the Human Coach experience will get left behind.

When making your mind up, here are some points to consider: The price of an AI coach is extremely low, relatively speaking. Humans are expensive and limited in capacity; even if, by some miracle, the entire world became able to afford a human coach, there wouldn't be enough qualified coaches to serve everyone, and AI provides the means to achieve that goal. For a large organisation looking to provide coaching to its people, there is only one genuinely affordable approach, and that is to use AI.

Some have argued that AI coaching is so dangerously unlike human coaching it shouldn't even bear the name,[113] but trying to force an agenda based on semantics won't stop an HR Director for a FTSE100 company procuring a solution that they feel provides value for money.

Some coaches may be in a position to shape the narrative by supporting the development of ethical and high-quality AI coaches. Some might be able to work with the professional bodies to work on standards and guidelines that provide the profession with helpful frameworks to reference. Others might be in an influential position with coaching sponsors to ensure that the AI coaches that get adopted are those that follow coaching, good practice, rather than have the highest sales and marketing budgets.

Marshall Goldsmith, recognised as the world's leading executive coach by Thinkers50, discusses the emergence of AI-enabled coaching tools. He suggests that artificial intelligence can complement traditional coaching by providing data-driven insights and scalable solutions, thereby enhancing the effectiveness and reach of coaching practices. However, he also emphasises the irreplaceable value of human judgment and empathy in the coaching process.

For all of us, however, the fact that a client might be able to get the same functional experience from a machine ought to remind us that we need to push ourselves to know what value we provide as a human. We should bring this into our reflective practice, experimenting with AI ourselves to learn what it can do better than us and where its weak points are. If there's one guarantee for coaches, it's that those humans whose calling card is offering a textbook coaching model at the cheapest possible price will be out of work in the near-term future.

While Generative AI offers us unprecedented advantages in crafting coaching tools and methods, when not 'humanly filtered', it also poses ethical considerations and challenges that demand careful and conscious navigation.

Striking a balance between technological efficiency and ethical use is essential for responsible deployment and emphasises the need for a dynamic interplay between AI and human skills

I believe that AI is increasingly transforming the coaching landscape, and will continue to do so.

By offering innovative tools and methodologies that can and very often do enhance the reach of coaching and the availability. AI, when done well, supports coaching practices and methodologies.

This integration of AI into coaching is definitely challenging traditional paradigms, and as with all New Kids on the Block, there will be early adopters all the way through complete Luddites and nay sayers. While AI offers many benefits, it cannot replicate the nuanced understanding and empathy inherent in a human to human coaching engagement. AI lacks the ability to form genuine relationships, make moral judgments, or adapt to the unpredictable nature of coaching conversations. This limitation underscores the importance of human coaches in providing the emotional intelligence and ethical considerations essential for effective coaching. In the Future of Jobs report AI cannot currently replace 80% of Human Centric tasks such as teaching, coaching and Mentoring. So perhaps for the great coaches out there, and there are many, no need to panic just yet.

Building on Sam's contribution, Dr Nicky Terblance, to whom he references, offers the following Case Study (extract from a soon to be published paper)[i]

Team leaders in high-pressured contact centres play a crucial role in balancing operational efficiency with people management. They require high emotional intelligence (EQ) yet limited development support exists. Organisational coaching can develop EQ but it is expensive, however Artificial Intelligence (AI) coaching is an alternative. In this study, we investigated the ability of AI Coaching to facilitate EQ awareness and development of team leaders in contact centres. We also examined the mechanisms used by the AI coach. In-depth interviews with team leaders after using an AI chatbot for four weeks reveal 169 instances of Goleman's EQ competencies, and 267 instances of coach competencies. This study found that AI coaching could provide a scalable, low-cost solution for EQ development in resource-constrained environments like contact centres, and sheds light on the actions of the AI coach that facilitate EQ development.

AI has seen exponential growth and development over the past decades, including the application of AI to coaching[114;115;116;117;118] AI is still seen as controversial in the workplace, often associated with job losses and disruption of career.[119] However, AI can also play a supporting role through, for example, AI coaching. Studies have demonstrated AI's effectiveness in supporting goal attainment, self-coaching, self-control, exercise motivation, and positive behavioural change[120;121;122] Additionally,

---

i   N. Terblanche, personal communication, May 21, 2025.

comparison studies have shown that AI coaching can lead to similar levels of goal attainment as human coaching in certain scenarios.123 Boyatzis et al.124 and Leonard125 found that goal setting can successfully support the development of EQ. What is currently known is that AI coaching can facilitate goal attainment, and that goal attainment could lead to increase EQ. What is not clear at this stage is whether AI coaching could directly lead to EQ awareness and development, especially in high stress, resource constrained environments like contact centres. Below is an extract from Coach Vici that indicates how the bot takes the user through the goal-setting process:

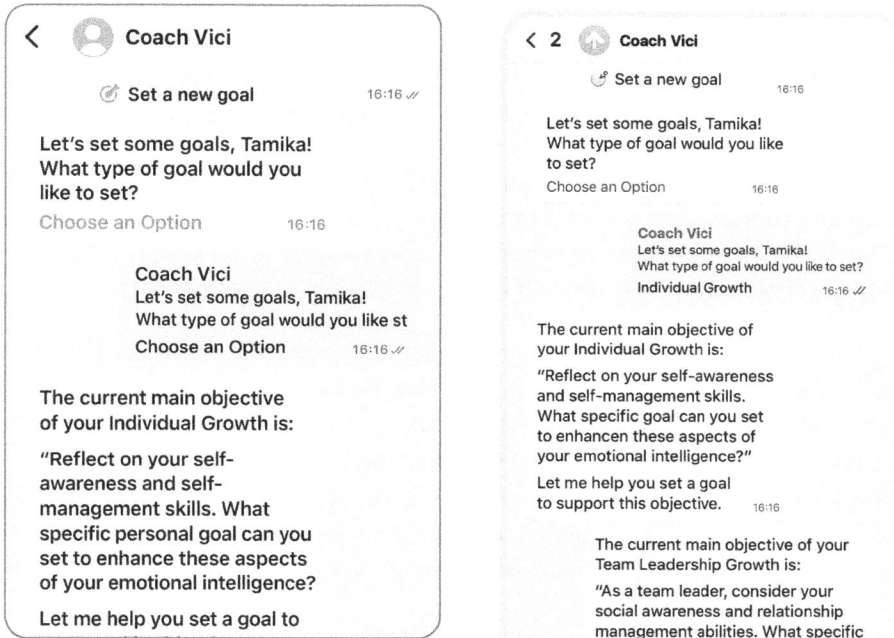

Apart from this AI-EQ knowledge gap, another question that has not been answered satisfactorily is how exactly AI coaching facilitates coaching outcomes. AI coaching is new and the few empirical studies that have been done focusses, understandably mainly on AI coaching efficacy. What is unclear is the "how" of AI coaching: what mechanisms in AI coaching facilitate positive coaching outcomes and specifically EQ awareness and development?

Given this context, this study asks two important questions in the context of the contact centre environment: (1) Which EQ competencies are facilitated and developed by AI Coaching? (2) Which coaching competencies are used by AI Coaching to facilitate this EQ development?

Answers to these questions could have significant repercussions on how a scalable, cost-effective technology like AI is used in high-stress environments to support EQ awareness and development of employees. We may also get an insight into the dynamics of AI coaches and how exactly these chatbots go about facilitating learning and change in people. This insight could help AI coach developers to focus on specific aspects of the chatbots to optimise performance.

The future of ai in coaching

Looking ahead, AI coaching will continue to evolve as it integrates with augmented reality (AR), virtual reality (VR), and emotional AI, further enhancing user experiences. Ethical considerations, including data privacy and algorithmic bias, will remain key challenges, requiring industry leaders to ensure responsible AI deployment.

As AI coaching becomes more sophisticated, its role in leadership development, mental health support, and personal growth will probably expand. The next decade will probably see AI shift from being a supportive tool to a co-pilot in human development, blending technological precision with human wisdom in unprecedented ways.

Thought leaders in the field have provided valuable insights into the future trajectory of coaching, highlighting key trends and considerations that are shaping its evolution. At CoachMatching, we have been early adopters of AI and technology and in 2016 coined the phrase **"Tech Savvy and Human Centric",** which explores the interplay between the two. In our desire to provide cost-effective solutions across the whole organisation, we experimented with a number of different bots before settling on two we believe most closely mimic the Human Coaching experience.

We trialled a coach bot in one of our Financial Services clients, offering it to graduates and young leaders as we believed, rightly or wrongly, that they would be more open to a coach bot. The feedback was fascinating as often their criticism of the bot was that it didn't give them solutions! So that presented a more fundamental challenge to both us and The Organisation in so far as we needed to educate employees on what coaching is and isn't before we could roll out anything.

Sadly, there is still a huge amount of confusion and misunderstanding of what great coaching looks like. So I would caution the reader, before embarking on the implementation of any AI coaching as part of your strategy to create a learning and growth culture, to ask "Is coaching well understood in our organisation and if not what do we need to do to ensure that it is?"

Questions for reflection

If you are considering incorporating AI, coach Bots, or platforms into your strategy, here are some basic guidelines to assist in navigating this territory:

- What are you most concerned about when you think about the rise of AI? What can you do to mitigate that risk?

  _____

  _____

  _____

- How could you incorporate AI to bring its benefits into your organisation?

  _____

  _____

  _____

- What most excites you about AI getting coaching into the lives of the many who have never had access to it before? What could you do to maximise that impact?

  _____

  _____

  _____

- If you are a coach, what makes you uniquely different from a machine in your coaching practice?

  _____

  _____

  _____

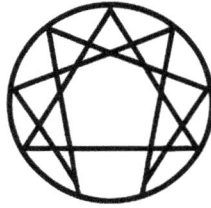

Chapter 9

THE ENNEAGRAM IN COACHING

Savnola Goldridge

"Know thyself." – Socrates

THE ROLE OF ASSESSMENTS AND PERSONALITY TESTS IN COACHING

As coaches, we know that each of our clients comes to us with their own unique story, strengths, and challenges. Our job is to help them grow, gain clarity, and move toward their goals in a way that is meaningful for them. One of the most powerful tools we have in our coaching toolkit is assessments – especially when it comes to understanding personality and behaviour.

Assessments and Personality Tests give us and our clients valuable insights into what is working, what is holding them back, and how they naturally show up in different situations. Whether we are collaborating with a client on personal development, leadership effectiveness, or team dynamics, structured tools help us tailor our approach to fit their needs. They provide a foundation for deeper conversations, targeted growth, and real transformation.

We have a variety of assessments at our disposal – self-assessments, feedback from peers and managers, values and personality profiles, and even tools that help uncover conflict resolution styles.

Some of the more commonly used assessments are indicated below, showing how they benefit both the coach and the coachee.

Table 2: Assessment options

Assessment Tool	Purpose	How It Supports the Coach	How It Supports the Coachee
Enneagram	Identifies personality types, motivations, and growth areas	Helps tailor coaching to personality style and core drivers	Promotes self-awareness and highlights areas for growth
MBTI (Myers-Briggs)	Explores psychological preferences in how people perceive and make decisions	Offers insight into communication and decision-making styles	Builds understanding of one's preferences
360-Degree Feedback	Gathers performance feedback from peers, reports, and managers	Reveals patterns and blind spots from multiple perspectives	Encourages development through honest, structured feedback
CliftonStrengths (StrengthsFinder)	Identifies top strengths and talents	Enables strengths-based coaching and team alignment	Empowers coachee to focus on leveraging their natural talents
DISC Profile	Measures behaviour in four key areas: Dominance, Influence, Steadiness, Conscientiousness	Adapts coaching approach to behavioural tendencies	Enhances communication and helps manage workplace relationships
EQ-i 2.0 (Emotional Intelligence)	Assesses emotional and social functioning	Facilitates development of emotional agility and resilience	Improves emotional awareness and interpersonal effectiveness
Five Lens Enneagram	Combines Enneagram with multiple psychological lenses	Provides a multidimensional view of personality and motivation	Offers deeper self-understanding and personal strategy

Assessment Tool	Purpose	How It Supports the Coach	How It Supports the Coachee
Neurozone®	Measures brain-body performance, resilience and wellness	Enables neuroscience-based coaching aligned to optimal functioning	Helps understand energy, focus, and behavioural choices
Hogan Assessments	Predicts job performance, potential derailers, and values	Informs talent management and leadership development strategies	Provides insight into strengths, risks, and culture fit
Insights Discovery	Based on Jungian psychology, uses colour energies for personal profiling	Aids in adapting communication and leadership style	Enhances team dynamics and personal effectiveness
Leadership Circle Profile	Combines leadership competency with an internal operating system	Links leadership behaviours to business outcomes	Reveals the impact of current leadership mindset and pathways for growth

Organisations seeking to integrate assessment tools into their coaching frameworks may choose between scientifically grounded models, which offer validated metrics and data-driven insights, and philosophically oriented approaches that focus on deeper self-reflection and meaning-making – each selected based on the desired depth, context, and objectives of the coaching engagement."

Table 3: Scientific and philosophical tools

Scientifically-Based Tools	Philosophically-Based Tools
Neurozone®	Enneagram
EQ-I 2.0	Five Lens Enneagram
Hogan Assessments	MBTI (Myers-Briggs)
360-Degree Feedback	DISC Profile
CliftonStrengths (StrengthsFinder)	Insights Discovery
Leadership Circle Profile	Create

In this chapter, we will explore the Enneagram – one of the most insightful and versatile personality frameworks available. Whether you are new to the Enneagram or have been using it for years, we will dive into how it can help us better understand ourselves and our coaching clients, leading to more impactful and transformative coaching relationships. Let us explore this together!

In 2011, the Enneagram found me! I experienced a pivotal moment that would forever transform my life – reading Sandra Maitri's book, "The Spiritual Dimension of the Enneagram – Nine Faces of the Soul," marked the beginning of a profound resonance with the spiritual and psychological aspects of the Enneagram. The pages of her book unveiled a deep connection to my Type 4 Soul Child, illuminating how I had learned to both survive and thrive by unconsciously disowning a part of myself. This profound revelation became the catalyst which propelled me onto a personal odyssey and a passionate love affair with the Enneagram.

For more than a decade I have been blessed to be trained and mentored by leading Enneagram Teachers and to attend Enneagram Retreats in South African and abroad including those with Dr Beatrice Chestnut, Uranio Paes, Dr Ginger Lapid-Bogda, Lucille Greeff, Dr Julia Kukard, Dirk Cloete, and Suzette Fischer.

My tool of choice is the Enneagram, which I use in my own practice to support breakthroughs and transformation. As a neurodivergent thinker and coach, I offer a distinct perspective by combining my expertise in leadership, counselling, emotional intelligence, and the transformative power of the Enneagram. I've had the privilege of working globally, with clients across Africa, Europe, and the U.S., helping individuals and organisations navigate their most challenging transitions with strength and grace and to deepen self-awareness, emotional intelligence, and transformation in both personal and professional domains.

In addition to coaching, I specialise in guiding clients through grief, loss, and trauma as a Bereavement Practitioner, Trauma-Informed Coach, Counsellor, and End-of-Life Practitioner. I have found that the Enneagram is an invaluable tool for supporting individuals, families, and communities as they navigate life-altering challenges.

My mission is to guide individuals, couples, leaders, and teams on a journey of deep self-discovery and transformation. To empower people, whether in leadership, partnerships, or personal growth – to live with clarity, purpose, deeper connection and authentic self-expression.

What is the Enneagram?

As coaches, we know our clients are more than just their behaviours – they have deep motivations, internal narratives, and ways of seeing the world that shape every decision they make. The Enneagram helps us uncover these deeper layers, offering a framework that goes beyond personality traits and into the heart of what drives human behaviour.

The term "Enneagram" originates from the Greek words "ennea" (meaning "nine") and "gramma" (meaning "something written or drawn"). It describes a nine-pointed figure inscribed within a circle. The Enneagram is a system of personality types arranged around this figure. At its core, the Enneagram is a dynamic personality system that describes nine distinct ways of thinking, feeling, and behaving. But it is not just about labelling or categorising people – it is about understanding movement, growth, and the interplay between different patterns. Each type represents a core motivation, a specific way of navigating the world that is often shaped by early experiences and unconscious beliefs.

I love using metaphors to bring the Enneagram to life – think of a dance with each Enneagram type having its own rhythm, steps, and preferred way of moving through life. Some move with precision and structure, while others prefer spontaneity and flow. Understanding our type helps us recognise our default patterns – our natural dance steps – but also gives us the awareness and flexibility to learn new movements.

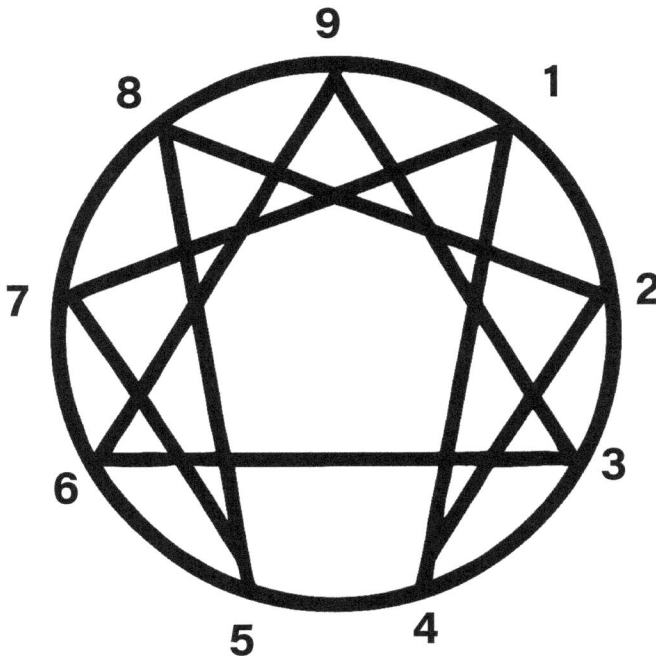

Figure 24: Enneagram

Centres of intelligence

Beyond individual types, the Enneagram is built around three Centres of Intelligence: the Head, Heart, and Body. These centres represent the primary way we experience and process the world:

- **Head (Thinking) Centre – Types 5, 6, and 7**: These types navigate life through logic, analysis, and problem-solving. Their core concerns often revolve around security, certainty, and managing fear.

- **Heart (Feeling) Centre – Types 2, 3, and 4**: These types engage with the world through emotions and relationships, focusing on connection, validation, and personal significance.

- **Body (Instinctive) Centre – Types 8, 9, and 1**: These types experience the world through gut instincts, physical presence, and autonomy, often grappling with control, resistance, or maintaining inner balance.

Each centre has its own strengths and challenges. Someone highly attuned to their body may have a strong sense of presence and instinctive action but struggle with emotional expression or over analysing situations. On the other hand, those who rely heavily on their intellect might be great at problem-solving but struggle with emotional awareness or physical presence. The Enneagram teaches us that by intentionally developing all three centres, we can become more well-rounded individuals, able to navigate life with greater ease and balance.

Think of the centres like wearing a pair of glasses. Most of us see the world through the lens of our dominant centre, but by strengthening the other two, we begin to see more clearly and engage with life in a fuller, more integrated way. By developing our Centres of Intelligence through intentional practices and self-awareness, we can move toward greater balance. When we become more in touch with our bodies, our hearts, and our minds, we begin to live with more presence, authenticity, and fulfilment.

Just like learning a new instrument, it takes practice to develop all three centres. But with time, we can expand our capacity for deeper self-awareness, more meaningful relationships, and greater freedom in how we show up in the world.

A brief overview of each Enneagram type

Type 1 – The perfectionist

Principled and purposeful, Ones strive for integrity and improvement. They are motivated by a desire to be good and correct, and their inner critic pushes them to avoid mistakes and maintain high standards.

Type 2 – The helper

Warm and interpersonal, Twos are driven by the need to be loved and appreciated. They excel at caring for others, often putting others' needs first, though they may struggle with setting healthy boundaries.

Type 3 – The achiever

Success-oriented and adaptive, Threes focus on excelling and being seen as successful. They are motivated by the need for validation and recognition, which can sometimes lead them to prioritise image over authenticity.

Type 4 – The creative individualist

Sensitive and self-aware, Fours value authenticity and emotional depth. They seek to express their unique identity and often feel a sense of longing or melancholy when they believe they are missing something essential.

Type 5 – The investigator

Curious and perceptive, Fives are driven by a need to understand the world. Valuing knowledge and competence, they often retreat into their inner world to conserve energy and maintain a sense of autonomy.

Type 6 – The loyalist

Committed and security-oriented, Sixes are alert to potential dangers and value guidance and support. Their core need for security can lead them to be both highly responsible and, at times, anxious or suspicious.

Type 7 – The enthusiast

Energetic and spontaneous, Sevens seek out new experiences and possibilities. They are motivated by a desire to avoid pain and boredom, often keeping their options open and shifting focus quickly to maintain a sense of joy and excitement.

Type 8 – The challenger

Assertive and self-confident, Eights strive to protect themselves and those they care about. They are driven by a need to maintain control and avoid vulnerability, often expressing strength and decisiveness, even when it masks underlying sensitivity

Type 9 – The peacemaker

Easy going and receptive. Nines desire harmony and peace in their environment. They tend to minimise conflict, sometimes at the cost of neglecting their own needs, to keep the peace and maintain a sense of unity.

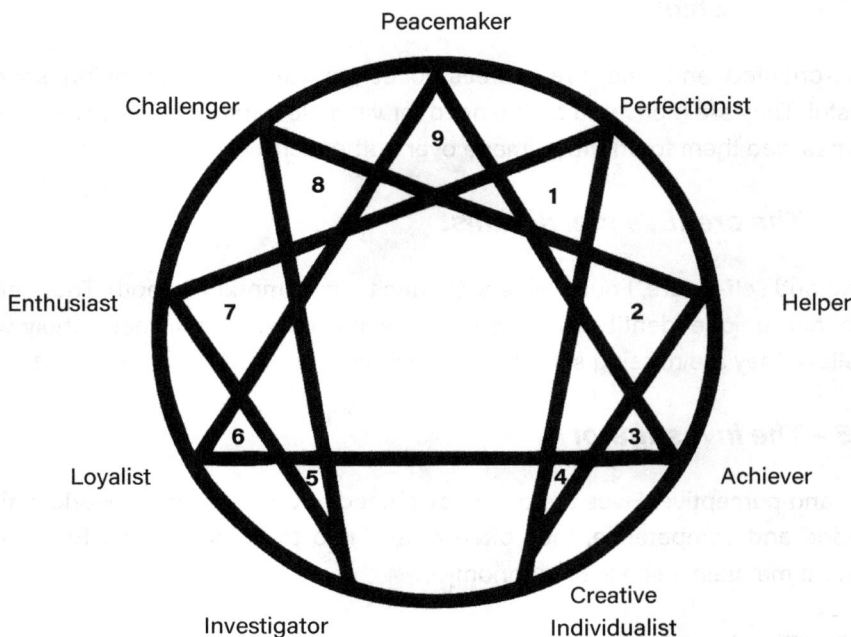

Figure 25: Overview of the Enneagram

Instinctual subtypes – a deeper layer to each Enneagram type

According to Dr Beatrice Chestnut, each Enneagram type offers a distinctive window into our core motivations and behaviours. To add even more depth, each of the nine Enneagram types is influenced by three instinctual subtypes: Self-Preservation, Social, and Sexual (One-to-One). These subtypes shape how our core type expresses itself in the world.

- **Self-Preservation subtype**: Focused on security, comfort, and personal well-being.

- **Social subtype**: Attuned to group dynamics, belonging, and social contribution.

- **Sexual (One-to-One) subtype**: Drawn to deep connections, intensity, and personal significance in relationships.

Even two people of the same type can look dramatically different depending on their dominant subtype. Understanding these layers allows us as coaches to refine our approach, helping our clients see not just what drives them, but how those motivations play out in their day-to-day lives.

Growth through the Enneagram

The Enneagram is not just about understanding where we are – it is about seeing where we can grow. At the core of each type is a deep, often subconscious emotional response that stems from a disconnection from the true self. This disconnect shapes the patterns we fall into, the struggles we face, and the stories we tell ourselves. But the beauty of the Enneagram is that it also points us toward healing and coming to wholeness.

Origin of the Enneagram

The Enneagram is a shared wisdom tradition, a collective understanding that has been shaped and refined over centuries. It does not belong to any one person or group – it belongs to all of us who are drawn to the deep work of self-discovery and transformation, both in ourselves and in our coaching clients.

If we imagine the Enneagram as an ancient river, its waters have been fed by many streams over time – philosophy, spirituality, psychology, and lived human experience. Its geometric symbol, the nine-pointed Enneagram, traces its lineage back to Pythagoras around 500 BC, a thinker fascinated by the hidden patterns that govern our universe. It then meandered through various wisdom traditions, picking up insights along the way.

Fast-forward to the mid-20th century, when a Bolivian philosopher named Oscar Ichazo took these ancient currents of thought and channelled them into a structured system of personality understanding. In the 1950s and 1960s, he wove together threads from mystical traditions, psychology, and his own studies, giving the Enneagram new life. Later, psychiatrist Claudio Naranjo built upon Ichazo's work, integrating modern psychological insights that made the system even more applicable to personal and professional growth.

Today, the Enneagram continues to evolve, shaped by our collective experiences and the ways we apply it in our coaching work. It is a living, breathing tool – one that helps us, and our clients, navigate the landscapes of identity, motivation, and transformation. As we explore its depths, we recognise that we are part of an ongoing journey, both students, and guides in the unfolding story of human nature.

Unlocking the power of the Enneagram in coaching

The Enneagram is one of the most powerful tools we, as coaches, can use to unlock deep transformation in our clients. Whether you have been coaching for years or are just stepping into this world, integrating the Enneagram into your practice can open doors to profound insights about human behaviour, motivation, and growth. Having used the Enneagram in coaching for over a decade, I have witnessed firsthand how this tool provides a roadmap for understanding both the self and others.

More than just a classification of traits, the Enneagram is a dynamic framework that reveals the underlying motivations, fears, and desires that drive human behaviour. It is not about putting people in boxes – it is about understanding the box we are already in so we can step beyond it.

At its core, the Enneagram serves two main purposes: as a mirror that helps individuals gain self-awareness by recognising their habitual patterns, and as a map that guides personal growth and transformation. By understanding our core type, we become more conscious of our automatic responses, allowing for more intentional choices and deeper personal development.

Uses of the Enneagram in coaching

The Enneagram's ability to illuminate deeper motivations and behaviours makes it a transformative tool across industries and disciplines, fostering both personal and collective growth. It is a powerful tool with diverse applications in coaching, business, education, and community development. For example:

- **Leaders & Executives** offer insights into personality strengths and weaknesses, communication, and decision-making and understanding of the leaders' influence on team dynamics. Aids in navigating high-performance environments and complex organisational challenges.

- **Teams and Organisations** promote alignment, collaboration, and cultural transformation, cultivating compassionate, resilient environments where every individual can thrive.

- **Neurodivergent Individuals:** provides clarity, purpose, and practical tools that honour and leverage unique cognitive strengths.

- **Personal Coaching & Development** creates awareness of core motivations, fears, and behavioural patterns and supports deeper self-awareness and self-mastery.

- **Conflict Mediation:** supports bridging differences and resolves disputes by fostering respect and understanding for improving workplace culture and promoting unity within community settings.

- **Change Management** provides deep insights into individual motivations, anxieties, and strengths, thereby supporting businesses, teams, and individuals in navigating change initiatives effectively.

- **Trauma and Bereavement** assists individuals in understanding emotional and behavioural patterns, recognising coping mechanisms, and cultivating self-compassion, while facilitating communication with their support networks and enabling tailored therapeutic approaches.

- **Couples & Families** improve communication and strengthen bonds while fostering deeper compassion and understanding for self and others.

- **Postgraduate, Leadership Development** – integrated into curriculums of leading business school and institutions like Stanford and Harvard to develop leadership, negotiation, and teamwork skills.

Case studies illustrating the impact of the Enneagram on coaching outcomes

Understanding the core fear and motivation of each Enneagram type provides insight into why we behave the way we do, fostering greater compassion and understanding. By addressing these motivations through focused coaching, clients can leverage their strengths, reduce their blind spots, and build healthier, more authentic relationships in both professional and personal environments.

In her book The Nine Types of Leadership, Dr Beatrice Chestnut discusses how understanding your personality can be key to becoming a more effective leader. She explains, "This is because when we develop the muscle of self-awareness and our blind spots become more visible to us, we can more easily recognise when we are being driven by the narrow interests of our ego, or when we rise above our automatic patterns to see the bigger picture. The Enneagram's accurate personality descriptions provide an unmatched guide to developing the consciousness and emotional intelligence necessary to observe our personality in action and rise above the reactivity and habits associated with it."

Below are some case studies Illustrating the Impact of the Enneagram on Coaching Outcomes for leaders who have leveraged the insights and learning to transform their work and personal life contexts through having the Enneagram introduced as a valuable resource on their coaching journey.

1. Perfectionist Palesa (Type 1: the perfectionist)

Palesa is a principled and ethical leader who strives for excellence and integrity. She sets high standards for herself and her team, believing that doing things "the right way" is essential. Her drive for perfection can lead to frustration when outcomes do not meet her expectations. Palesa is meticulous and hard-working. She strives for excellence and virtue in everything she does by using structure, rules, and routines to ensure quality.

Impact

- Meetings: Palesa was experienced as becoming critical of ideas that did not align with her high standards. Her team members and colleagues complained she was stifling creativity and innovative thinking.

- Teams: Her insistence on perfection often caused delays and tension when team members felt they could not meet her expectations and she would inevitably end up correcting or changing their contribution– this resulted in some having a half-hearted, "just get it done" approach.

- Family: At home, Palesa's two teenage children experience her as being unfairly and unreasonably strict – every homework assignment, test, or project must be flawless. A small mistake leads to harsh criticism or a belief that the effort was not good enough and even when they achieve success, the emphasis remains on what could be improved rather than celebrating accomplishments.

Coaching story

Coaching helped Palesa recognise the unintended consequences of her perfectionist approach and inspired her to adopt a more balanced, supportive style. In meetings, she learned to welcome diverse ideas, reducing critical feedback and fostering innovation. With her team, coaching enabled her to trust their contributions more, easing tensions and encouraging genuine engagement. At home, she embraced a nurturing perspective that celebrated her children's efforts, shifting the focus from inevitable criticism to genuine support and growth.

2. Generous Gina (Type 2: the considerate helper)

Gina is a compassionate, people-focused and empathetic leader who is sensitive to others' needs and feelings. She enjoys making others feel validated and appreciated – inspiring co-workers through flattery, warmth, and positive regard. Gina is highly attuned to delivering on what employees and customer's needs and is always ready to lend a hand, which often led to her overextending herself.

Impact

- Meetings: Gina focused on supporting others, sometimes at the expense of sharing her own ideas or contributions. She prioritised maintaining a positive atmosphere and found it difficult to give constructive feedback when necessary.

- Teams: Her team sometimes felt that Gina became too personally involved in their personal life and work challenges, leading them to feel obliged to include her in all aspects. While her help was appreciated, they felt it often slowed them down when they would have preferred to take full ownership and autonomy.

- Family: Gina had always been the one to step in for the needs or social events of her family and extended family- they had come to rely on her, often taking advantage of her willingness to help. She struggled to ask for support or delegate tasks and ended up taking on too much, which ultimately resulted in her feeling overwhelmed and resentful.

Coaching story

Coaching enabled Gina to realise that neglecting her own well-being to help others wasn't sustainable. Through coaching, she learned to foster healthier relationships by balancing self-care with her natural inclination to assist. She recognised how she could become more effective in her support of others without sacrificing herself. Gina has developed the confidence to have courageous conversations, to push back, ask for support and provide tough but necessary feedback – recognising that true support includes honesty and accountability. This shift allowed her to build deeper trust and respect in both her personal and professional relationships.

3. Ambitious Andy (Type 3: the achiever)

Andy is a highly driven, goal-oriented leader who thrives on achievement and recognition. Success fuels his motivation, whether making a profit, working hard, or competing to win. Andy has a strong ability to execute on plans and is known for consistently delivering results. He has a knack for being able to quickly adapt to different situations to maintain his competitive edge and project an image of success by crafting the right image for any context he finds himself in.

Impact

- Meetings: Andy's sharp, goal-oriented focus and his drive to hit ambitious targets meant that discussions often moved forward quickly, setting clear objectives and pushing to meet them. While his energetic approach inspired and maintained momentum, some colleagues felt overwhelmed by his relentless pace and assertiveness, perceiving it as leaving little room for more reflective or collaborative input.

- Teams: Andy's relentless drive and fast-paced work style created challenges for his team. His constant push for results left them feeling stressed, pressured, and struggling to keep up. The team felt unheard and under-valued as he constantly prioritised the business and clients, often cancelling team connects or one-on-ones that had been requested with the objective of providing clarity and alignment to his team who were responsible for delivering and executing in support of his mandate.

- Family: Andy's strong drive for success often led to long hours and a constant "always-on" mentality. His wife frequently felt neglected, and that he was rarely fully present at home for her and their young children.

Coaching story

Coaching helped Andy explore his intrinsic motivations and values and to temper his competitive drive with a more balanced, inclusive approach. In meetings, he learned to slow his rapid, goal-oriented pace, allowing space for collaborative input and making colleagues feel valued. Coaching emphasised the importance of regular check-ins and support for his team, reducing stress and ensuring that each member's voice was heard despite his strong business focus. He embraced strategies to set clear work-life boundaries, enabling him to be more present and supportive at home with his wife and children.

4. Creative Cleone (Type 4: the creative individualist)

Cleone is a leader who values authentic self-expression, creating an environment where people feel safe to share their emotions. As a Type Four, she intuitively connects with others' feelings to foster deep, meaningful relationships. Her passion for creativity and purpose drives her leadership, though she can become frustrated when others are uncomfortable with emotional expression or when her own needs for understanding and validation are unmet. At times, she prioritises emotional dynamics over tasks and focusing on what is missing in a situation, seeking deeper connection over immediate productivity.

Impact

- Meetings: Cleone found in peer meetings that the group had a very structured and pragmatic approach to problem-solving, which did not align with her more creative, innovative thinking. She found herself withdrawing emotionally or becoming more and more reactive and defensive, as she felt misunderstood. Her experience was that her perspectives were not valued and that her ideas were constantly dismissed in favour of more practical solutions.

- Teams: Cleone, as the lead for a creative project, encouraged her team members to think creatively and valued originality in their contributions. She became felt frustrated with certain team members who were more focused on following established processes and routines, and she felt they were not embracing the level of creativity she expected. The team experienced her as intense and reactive while she felt as though her leadership style was being challenged and that the team was not fully tapping into its potential.

- Family: Cleone's siblings often experienced her as overly emotional and dramatic e.g. at a family gathering to discuss funeral arrangements after their grandmother passed, while most members focused on practical matters like finances and logistics, Cleone at first withdrew and then reacted emotionally when she felt that she was not being heard, nor being acknowledged for her desire to have a more heartfelt, meaningful ceremony to grieve and honour her beloved grandmother's life.

Coaching story

Coaching helped Cleone find a balance between her emotional depth and the practical, logical aspects of her life. She learned to frame her innovative ideas in meetings in ways that resonated with a structured, pragmatic group, reducing her tendency to withdraw or react defensively. Coaching provided strategies for her to support her creative project team to bridge the gap between her vision and the team's comfort through establishing routines, which resulted in a more collaborative and open environment. Cleone discovered approaches in her personal life that enabled her to express her deep emotions more effectively and ensuring that her heartfelt contributions were acknowledged alongside practical concerns.

5. Analytical Alex (Type 5: the investigator)

Alex is a leader that excels in gathering and analysing data and is known as a subject matter expert in his field. He is highly skilled at problem solving and offering innovative solutions and making objective decisions once he has had time to reflect on and evaluate information and facts. Those that have worked with Alex for a while know that he can be an innovative thought leader and contributor when he is encouraged to share his thoughts and insights without being pressurised or put on the spot.

Impact

- Meetings: Alex was often experienced by his peers as someone who withheld opinions, preferring to observe and deliberate rather than jump into discussions right away. They noticed he avoided or withdrew from situations that required emotional expression or were emotionally charged.

- Teams: Alex's strong preference for personal boundaries, privacy, autonomy, and independence limited connection and engagement opportunities with his team. This left them feeling that he was hesitant to delegate or collaborate, and that experienced him as aloof and distant.

- Family: Alex's emotional withdrawal created tension with his wife Amy, who thrives on socialising and is highly emotionally expressive and affectionate. While Amy sought connection and open emotional exchanges, Alex's tendency to keep his feelings to himself could leave her feeling distant or uncertain about his needs and thoughts.

Coaching story

Coaching empowered Alex to bridge the gap between his natural reserve and the demands of dynamic leadership and close personal relationships. In meetings, he learned to share his insights more readily, balancing thoughtful observation with timely engagement, even in emotionally charged situations. Coaching helped him with his team to gradually relax his strict boundaries, encouraging delegation and collaboration while still honouring his need for autonomy. At home, he discovered new ways to express his feelings, to build towards a greater connection and ease the tension his emotional withdrawal once created with Amy.

6. Loyal Lafika (Type 6: the loyal sceptic)

Lafika is a dependable and security-oriented leader who values loyalty and often anticipates potential challenges. His constant vigilance leads to anxiety and difficulty trusting others' decisions. He seeks consistency, is very observant of other's behaviours – whether their words match their actions and is very aware of who has authority and power and how it is used.

Impact

- Meetings: His peers know Lafika for carefully scrutinising proposals and decisions, often pausing discussions to seek clarity, reassurance or to verify that all potential risks have been considered. While his approach ensured that his colleagues were alerted to risks and pitfalls, they often felt it also slowed decision-making and momentum.

- Teams: Lafika preference for tried-and-true methods over innovative but uncertain alternatives and his need for security translated into a reluctance to embrace change or take risks. This often left his team members feeling constrained and hesitant to propose innovative ideas.

- Family: Lafika's tendency to focus on worst-case scenarios and his hesitation to embrace new experiences or impromptu adventures, resulted in an overly cautious, protective parenting style which often left his kids feeling disappointed or frustrated, that they were missing spontaneous, joyful moments with their friends and family.

Coaching story

Coaching empowered Lafika to balance his inherent need for caution with greater flexibility and openness. He learned to streamline his approach in meetings and trust his instincts enough to move discussions forward without sacrificing due diligence. He began embracing innovative ideas with his team, easing his reliance on familiar methods and encouraging risk-taking and creativity. Coaching helped Lafika temper his worst-case scenario mindset at home with which allowed him to participate in spontaneous adventures that enriched his family life and brought moments of greater freedom and genuine joy for his children.

7. Visionary Vusi (Type 7: the enthusiastic visionary)

Vusi is an energetic and optimistic leader who is an expert networker that thrives on innovative ideas and experiences. He inspires his people with a vision of endless possibilities and encourages innovation, but those reporting to him were often left feeling exhausted and struggling to prioritise and align on the delivery of his expectations.

Impact

- Meetings: Vusi's energetic, optimistic nature shines in meetings with his Business Unit Heads and his rapid ideas spark excitement and creativity. However, people struggle with him jumping from one concept to another without pausing to take sufficient time for exploring details or validating ideas that might be viable.

- Teams: Vusi's marketing team was initially energised when their Enneagram Type 7 leader launched exciting new campaigns. However, often after a few weeks, they would find that his attention shifts to another intriguing opportunity, leaving the initial projects unfinished. The team felt frustrated and often ended up juggling multiple ideas, struggling to maintain focus and follow through on any one initiative.

- Family: Vusi's inclination to keep interactions light and fun often led him to sidestep difficult or serious conversations such as when his teenage son, who was experiencing challenges at school, felt dismissed and isolated because Vusi quickly shifted the conversation to a lighter topic or reframed the situation in a more positive light.

Coaching story

Coaching enabled Victor to recalibrate his dynamic energy into a more balanced approach across all areas of his life. In meetings with his Business Unit Heads, he learned to slow down his rapid idea generation to allow for more time to explore details and validate concepts which enhanced strategic decision-making. He learned to channel his passion for new experiences into sustainable project strategies, reducing overcommitment and ensuring better follow-through for his team. At home, he gained insights into the importance of addressing difficult conversations, which enabled him to engage more meaningfully with his wife and teenage son.

8. Assertive Andiswa (Type 8: the challenging protector)

Andiswa is a fiercely determined and protective leader who confidently backs himself and his team. He tackles challenges head on and is fiercely protective over his team and his territory. He inspires confidence and respect with his decisive nature and bold action in high-pressure situations. Andiswa's intense, impatient, no-nonsense approach is experienced at times as overwhelming, domineering and intimidating by his colleagues.

Impact

- Meetings: Amy the Analytical Business Insights Consultant is an introverted specialist who often felt pressurised and put on the spot by Andiswa. She likes to share her findings only after thoroughly vetting her data and theories, and this takes more time than she felt he understood was necessary.

- Teams: When key projects failed to meet targets, Andiswa was known to be very direct and to confrontational with the Project teams – taking them head on in an angry, abrupt manner which resulted in a number of team members reporting incidents to HR with grievances. They perceived his feedback and manner as insensitive and inappropriate and as leaving them feeling overwhelmed, demotivated and highly stressed, rather than motivated to improve.

- Family: When Andiswa's younger brother Mpho, finally found the courage to share his deep personal struggles and ask for support in the hope of some guidance and understanding, Andiswa's response was blunt and terse – "You need to toughen up; weakness won't get you through this."

Coaching story

Coaching enabled Andiswa to gain valuable insights into the impact of his intense leadership style and adjust his approach across all areas. He learned to temper his direct, no-nonsense demeanour, allowing space for colleagues like Amy to share their carefully vetted insights without feeling overwhelmed, and to negotiate timelines that accommodate the thoroughness of her analysis. Andiswa shift from blunt confrontations to providing constructive, supportive feedback to his team and enabled opportunities to explore and reflect on lessons learned. He discovered how to combine his assertiveness with genuine empathy and embrace his vulnerability as a strength so that his family members could experience greater receptivity, compassion, and kindness.

9. Harmonious Hannah (Type 9: the peacemaker)

Hannah has a calm, adaptable nature and focuses her energy on creating a supportive, harmonious environment where her team feels every voice is heard. Her tendency to avoid confrontation often delays her taking decisive action or call her team out and take them to task when necessary. Often, her deep desire for harmony leads to her procrastinating and avoiding necessary confrontations or deferring her own ideas when she could take a stand to advocate for her team or for herself.

Impact

- Meetings: In a project strategy meeting, Hannah would nod along with a proposed plan even though she may have had reservations. When the entire team endorsed a marketing strategy that she considered problematic, she remained silent to avoid rocking the boat. Eventually, as problems arose during implementation, she realised that her unspoken reservations might have guided the discussion toward a more effective resolution.

- Teams: During brainstorming sessions her peer management team repeatedly discussed a persistent challenge which they had encountered in production – which Hannah had a unique, innovative solution for – she hesitated to speak up not feeling comfortable to bring her voice into the room of mostly assertive stronger personalities which resulted in the opportunity being lost and the team reverted to their old system and process.

- Family: Hannah has consistently agreed in the past to holiday plans made by her husband Tony and his friends, even when those destinations did not resonate with her preference for a quieter trip. Often, she chose to go along with their adventurous selections to keep the peace, despite secretly longing for a more serene getaway. Recently, her husband James mentioned to her that he had noticed Hannah became withdrawn and irritable whenever the upcoming holiday was discussed, but she refused to share her true feelings.

Coaching story

Coaching helped Hannah to embrace her authentic voice and assert her needs without sacrificing harmony. In meetings, she learned techniques to courageously and confidently express her reservations and contribute critical insights. Her confidence grew, and she began to share innovative solutions during brainstorming sessions, while at home she developed strategies for open communication which enabled her to share her true preferences and needs with her husband Tony.

Ethics and guidelines for using the Enneagram in coaching

The Enneagram is celebrated as a transformative tool – a map that reveals our deepest motivations, challenges, and pathways for growth. Yet, when integrated into coaching practices, its power can also become a double-edged sword. As renowned experts like Russ Hudson, Don Riso, David Daniels, Bea Chestnut, Ginger Lapid-Bogda, and the International Enneagram Association (IEA) remind us, caution is essential. In this post, we explore why ethical, well-informed use of the Enneagram is crucial and why working with a credentialed professional coach is non-negotiable for both new and seasoned practitioners.

The power and pitfalls of the Enneagram in coaching

it is important to approach the Enneagram with an open mind and not assume that all people of a certain type will exhibit the same characteristics. Understanding the nuances and differences between each Enneagram type, its subtypes, and the instinctual sequences provides a more comprehensive understanding of how the Enneagram manifests in individuals. The Enneagram types are not meant to pigeonhole people into rigid categories but rather offer a framework for self-awareness and deeper connection with others. Everyone is unique and may express their type in diverse ways. When used responsibly, the Enneagram offers deep insight into personality dynamics, helping individuals develop self-awareness, navigate challenges, and cultivate growth. However, without a thorough understanding, it can also lead to misinterpretation, oversimplification, and even harm.

Common pitfalls include:

- **Type Labelling**: Reducing a client to their Enneagram type rather than recognising their full complexity.

- **Stereotyping**: Assuming all individuals of a particular type behave the same way, ignoring personal history, culture, and context.

- **Using the Enneagram as a Fix-All**: Expecting the Enneagram to address every issue without integrating other coaching methodologies and tools.

- **Unqualified Guidance**: Coaching without proper training or deep Enneagram knowledge, which can cause misguided advice and ethical breaches.

Bias in business and society

Over the past decade, through coaching hundreds of corporate leaders and collaborating with diverse teams, I have witnessed firsthand how biases can stifle innovation and limit potential. There exists a clear "shit list" in a business that unfairly ranks Enneagram types. In many professional settings, types like 8 (The Challenger), 3 (The Achiever), and 7 (The Enthusiastic Visionary) are celebrated as unstoppable leaders and innovators. In contrast, types such as 4 (The Creative Individualist), 5 (The Investigator), and 9 (The Adaptive Peacemaker) often find themselves unfairly marginalised. Fours might be seen as too alternative, overly intense or dramatic, Fives as too detached or overly analytical, and Nines as lacking ambition, wishy-washy or avoiding conflict.

As coaches – whether you are a seasoned pro or just starting out – it is our responsibility to challenge these assumptions, both within ourselves and in the broader world of business. By confronting and moving past these limiting stereotypes, we empower our clients to embrace their authenticity and step into their full potential. Every Enneagram type brings its own unique gifts and challenges, and by pushing past these limiting stereotypes, we empower our clients to embrace their authenticity and unlock their full potential.

Why work with a credentialed Enneagram coach?

A well-trained credentialed coach ensures the Enneagram is used responsibly. The Enneagram is a sophisticated tool that demands expertise, and the International Enneagram Association (IEA) has established rigorous ethical guidelines and offers accreditation to professionals who demonstrate advanced knowledge and skill in using the system.

Working with a credentialed coach not only ensures that the Enneagram is applied with the nuance it requires but also helps safeguard clients from the unintended consequences of misi

Credentialing reinforces several best practices:

- **In-depth Understanding**: Accredited professionals have undergone extensive training to understand both the subtleties of the Enneagram and its practical applications.

- **Ethical Application**: They are bound by ethical guidelines that prevent the misuse of type information, particularly in ways that could marginalise or discriminate against clients.

- **Ongoing Professional Development**: Credentialed coaches are committed to lifelong learning, which means they continually update their skills and deepen their understanding of the Enneagram's evolving applications.

For both new and experienced coaches, the Enneagram is a powerful ally when used with wisdom and care. Ethical coaching requires a blend of knowledge, humility, and a commitment to the client's unique path. As we continue learning from leading Enneagram experts and coaching organisations, we ensure this tool serves as a source of insight and transformation, rather than a limitation.

By approaching the Enneagram with caution and compassion, coaches can honour the depth of their clients' journeys and uphold the integrity of the coaching profession.

For more information on ethical standards and accreditation, visit the International Enneagram Association (IEA) website. https://www.internationalEnneagram.org/about/ethical-guidelines/

Resources

Enneagram Assessments:

Websites that offer Enneagram assessments to help identify your type:

1. Aephoria Group (https://www.aephoriagroup.com)

   o Offers an innovative Enneagram assessment that uniquely integrates personality type analysis with a developmental maturity evaluation. Its Aephoria Identity Map (AIM) employs adaptive testing technology to deliver fast, reliable insights, providing a transformational launch pad for both individual and team growth.

2. Integrative9 (https://www.integrative9.com)

   o Provides a comprehensive Enneagram assessment designed to help individuals and teams identify their type, along with guidance for personal and professional growth.

3. Chestnut Paes Enneagram Test (https://cpEnneagram.com)

   o Offers a free Enneagram Micro Test along with the Enneagram Compass – an assessment tool that pinpoints your type, subtypes, and core motivations.

4. The Enneagram Institute (https://www.Enneagraminstitute.com)

   o Offers the RHETI (Riso-Hudson Enneagram Type Indicator), one of the most widely used and respected Enneagram assessments. It provides a detailed breakdown of your results, including suggestions for personal growth.

5. The Narrative Enneagram (https://www.narrativeEnneagram.org)

   o This site offers assessments that aim to help individuals understand the Enneagram through narratives and stories. It also has educational programs and workshops to deepen your understanding of the types.

Chapter 10

WHAT DOES THE FUTURE OF COACHING HOLD?

Susi Astengo

Key themes:

- coaching as entertainment: The rise of the celebrity coach and the impact of social media.

- The trend is to blend: What might a blend of coaching solutions look like?

- Ethical Standards and supervision: The importance of establishing ethical guidelines and supervision to ensure the quality and credibility of coaching practices.

- Future Trends: Anticipated trends in coaching, including the integration of technology.

Coaching as entertainment and the rise of the celebrity coach

Before we look ahead to the future of coaching, it's crucial to take a step back and understand the landscape it must navigate. We are living in a time of extreme volatility, political tensions are deepening global divides, economic instability is fuelling uncertainty, and hard-fought progress in areas like diversity, equity, and inclusion is facing growing resistance.

Recent political shifts have sent shockwaves through the global system, with funding cuts and policy changes disrupting industries, communities, and individuals alike. It often feels as though the whole world is on high alert as decisions are being made with little regard for long-term impact.

This isn't about political ideology, it's about the undeniable uncertainty that surrounds us all. The future feels increasingly unpredictable, and the need for guidance, resilience, and adaptability has never been greater. In this climate, coaching will play a critical role, not just in personal and professional development, but in helping individuals and organisations find clarity and stability amid the chaos.

Here is a recent example of how that played out in our team. In a quiet corner of the CoachMatching offices, a coach sat across from her coach supervisor, James. She had invested years in honing her coaching skills, helping clients set goals and navigate challenges, yet she often found herself and her coachees frustrated by external factors beyond their control. The impact of this being that at times she found herself leaving a coaching session wondering what she had missed.

Sensing her dilemma, James reached for a notepad and began to draw three simple concentric circles. "This," he said, tapping the smallest circle in the centre, "is the Circle of Control. It represents what we, as individuals, have complete authority over – our thoughts, our actions, and how we choose to respond to situations."

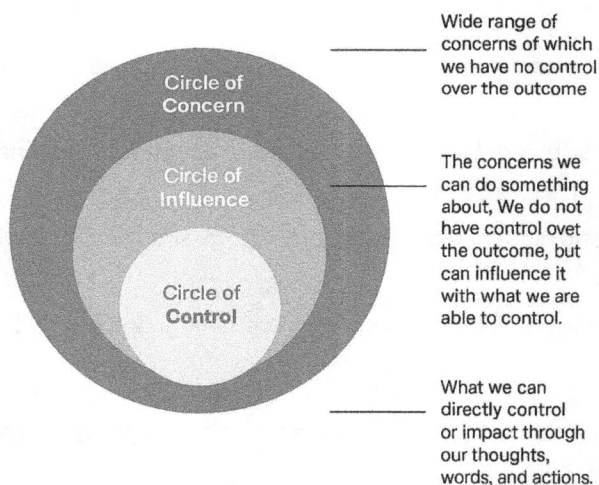

Figure 26: Learning Loop

Elena nodded, remembering back to when she first read, *The 7 Habits of Highly Effective People* Stephen R. Covey.[126]

James continued, seeing her dawning realisation and pointing to the second ring: The Circle of Influence. "How can you apply this to both yourself as well as your coaching clients? Where are you focussing energy on things outside of either your or their influence? How can you help clients develop strategies to guide these areas without the illusion of direct control?."

Finally, his finger traced the largest circle, stretching beyond the others. "And this," he said, "Circle of Concern is filled with things we often worry about but cannot change, like global events, market shifts, political landscapes. Yet this is where the Media is ever more powerful, encouraging people to comment and share and ultimately raising the collective stress levels.

Social Media wasn't a thing when Covey first wrote his book and I am sure he had no idea that our circles of control would significantly shrink, whereas our circles of influence would grow much bigger.

Whether we like it or not, we are all part of a much bigger global system that as coaches we can either decide to waste time and energy trying to rail against things outside of our control OR we can guide clients back to where their power truly lies and influence where we can.

In a previous chapter, we examined the role of AI in coaching and it is difficult to image a future of coaching unconnected to the evolution of AI.

The social shift: Coaching in the age of social media

On a recent call with an extremely seasoned coach, I sat quietly as I listened to him, vent his frustration.

"I don't get it," he sighed. "I spent years training, getting certified, refining my practice to become the best coach I could be. But now, someone with no experience can post a few motivational videos on Instagram and suddenly, they're a 'coach' with thousands of followers."

I smiled. "Social media has changed the coaching industry," "but it's not all bad."

He frowned. "But isn't it diluting the profession? Clients are getting lost in a sea of self-proclaimed experts and self-help gurus and those of us who take this work seriously have to fight for credibility and how on earth do I differentiate myself?"

I agreed and then pulled out my phone. With a few taps, I had opened a popular platform and showed him a profile. A young coach, barely in her twenties, was delivering a live session on mindset shifts, and thousands of people were engaging in the comments.

"You're right," "It has lowered the barriers to entry. But it's also made coaching more accessible than ever. Ten years ago, clients had to rely on referrals or corporate programs to find a coach. Now, they can discover new voices, new perspectives, and explore personal growth at their own pace." It is a new world and we need to understand that it will probably keep changing.

We watched as the live stream continued, people eagerly typing questions and sharing their own experiences. "But are they getting **real** coaching," he asked, "or just digestible bits of inspiration?"

I shrugged. "Some of both. Social media has blurred the line between coaching, mentoring, and personal branding. But it's also given coaches a platform to share their expertise, build trust, and reach clients they never would have connected with otherwise. The best coaches don't just compete for attention; they create real impact, whether online or in private sessions."

The future of coaching isn't about fighting changes we don't like or agree with. It's about adapting, maintaining integrity, and using these new tools wisely. Social media is just another space where transformation happens and it is up to us to ensure it is meaningful.

In a rapidly evolving industry, those who embrace the change, without losing their core principles, will be the ones shaping the future of coaching.

Instagram and TikTok have enabled micro-content coaching, where bite-sized lessons on productivity, leadership, and mental well-being reach millions in a matter of seconds. Coaches like Jay Shetty and Mel Robbins have mastered the art of short-form video storytelling, turning complex ideas into digestible and actionable advice.

YouTube and Podcasts have provided long-form content opportunities, allowing celebrity coaches to deliver deeper insights through interviews, masterclasses, and weekly reflections. Platforms such as *The School of Greatness* by Lewis Howes or *On Purpose* by Jay Shetty have attracted millions of listeners and positioned their hosts as household names in coaching.

But the real momentum for coaching didn't come from media alone, it came from the voices of those who had experienced its impact first hand.

Enter: The rise of the celebrity coach

in an era where self-improvement has become both a cultural movement and a booming industry, Coaching is now entertainment, inspiration, and business all rolled into one. The figure of the celebrity coach has emerged as a defining force in personal and professional development. These figures, ranging from life coaches to executive mentors and wellness gurus, have tapped into the trend and leveraged media, technology, and the growing self-improvement movement to build global brands. Jeanette Jenkins, known as "The Hollywood Trainer," provides fitness coaching to celebrities and the public, demonstrating the applicability of coaching in health and wellness.

Their influence extends beyond coaching, shaping industries such as wellness, productivity, and corporate leadership. They transcend the traditional role of a coach, blending mentorship and business acumen, to become a media influencer, educator, and global icons. Each has captured the public imagination, shaping how we think about success, transformation, and human potential. So how do they do it?

Authenticity and Relatability: Unlike traditional coaches who primarily worked behind the scenes, today's celebrity coaches position themselves as relatable figures. They share their struggles, daily habits, and success stories, making coaching feel more personal and aspirational. They are therefore masterful at being able to connect deeply with diverse groups of people.

Over many years of matching coach to coachee and with our tag line of "The Magic's in the Match," I know that it is the ability to connect that differentiates an average coach from an outstanding one. Mastering relatability at scale is not something that every coach can achieve.

Closer to home, two of the contributors to this book have achieved a degree of local notoriety; Brad Shorkend and Shelley Lewin appearing on TV and radio, providing compelling keynotes and leveraging Linked in and other professional platforms to raise their profile. Both will tell you that it takes an enormous amount of time and dedicated focus to achieve. Most of us haven't got either the expertise or the energy to dedicate to building an online persona, Gen Z has both in spades. It might, therefore, be worth thinking about time for some reverse mentoring, as, after all, great coaches are committed to lifelong learning and growth.

Names such as Tony Robbins, A Trailblazer in Life Coaching, Myke Celis: Celebrity Life Coach from the Philippines, Robin Sharma: Mastering Leadership and Personal Mastery and Rainy Rainmaker: Award-winning Life Coach in Singapore as well as Esther Perel: Transforming Relationships Through Coaching, and Jay Shetty have built vast followings and have become household names and in doing so have made coaching much more accessible to the masses.

Below is an overview of a few celebrity coaches and the factors contributing to their widespread popularity. Equal to their coaching ability is their understanding of branding and ability to leverage social media.

Tony Robbins

Love him or hate him, there is no denying that he was a pioneer in the life coaching industry. Through his high octane and dynamic seminars, best-selling books that have touched millions along with his media appearances, he has become a household name. Robbins' approach combines motivational speaking with practical strategies aimed at empowering individuals to achieve personal and professional success. His charismatic presence and ability to inspire action have been central to his enduring appeal. He has built a multimillion-dollar empire that includes personal development events, coaching certifications, and nutritional products.

Marshall Goldsmith

Renowned in the realm of executive coaching, Marshall Goldsmith has worked with many Fortune 500 CEOs and top executives. He has over the years collected hundreds of success stories that he shares as if he were handing over his business card. He has authored several influential books and his expertise in leadership development and executive performance is well-documented. He looks like he could be a nice executive from a more progressive company. However, when you watch him in action, he embodies coaching, making it appear like a casual but meaningful conversation. He is at the top of his game and is a great role model for what mature coaching, rather than model or process-based coaching, looks like.

Jay Shetty

A former monk turned motivational speaker and coach, Jay Shetty has captivated audiences with his insights on mindfulness and purposeful living. His viral videos and the best-selling book *Think Like a Monk* have established him as a prominent figure in the personal and latterly relationship development space along with Esther Perel. Shetty's emphasis on wisdom and self-awareness appeals to individuals seeking depth and meaning in their lives.

Robin Sharma

With over 25 years of expertise, Robin Sharma, author of "*The monk who sold his Ferrari*," is a lauded life coach and leadership figure. He is known for his extraordinary coaching abilities and for helping successful athletes, businesspeople, and high-profile personalities.

Deepak Chopra

Deepak Chopra is a prominent figure in the realm of mind-body medicine and personal transformation. His unique blend of ancient wisdom and modern science has offered a fresh perspective on wellness and personal development. Chopra's emphasis on mindfulness and holistic well-being has influenced millions, making a significant impact on the way people.

Brené Brown, for instance, has used social media to connect deeply with audiences through vulnerability and storytelling. Initially, a researcher turned coach whose first TED talk *"The Power of Vulnerability*," delivered at TEDxHouston in June 2010, subsequently went viral, has partnered with Netflix and Spotify to produce exclusive content, further solidifying her influence.[127]

These coaches also leverage endorsements and partnerships to expand their reach. While mega-coaches dominate the industry, niche coaching, and Micro-Influencers will continue to gain traction by catering to specialised audiences.

The International Coaching Federation (ICF) has seen increased legitimacy of the coaching industry as celebrity coaches elevate the status of the profession. This has led to an increased acceptance of coaching as a valuable tool for personal and professional growth.

Companies now hire high-profile coaches for keynotes and training sessions, reflecting a broader embrace of coaching in corporate culture.

When did coaching become entertainment?

I was recently reminded of one of Tony Robbins' well-known statements: "Don't buy the story that you can't do something because you don't have the time. It's a lie. You just need to get more strategic. You need to get a little smarter." He often pointed out that we all have the same 24 hours and it's how we choose to use them that makes the difference.

That thought hit me as I sat on the sofa, lost in the glow of my screen. By the time I looked up, the light outside had faded, and two precious hours had slipped away; hours I'd never get back. What had I gained? Aside from reinforcing my Instagram algorithm and catching up on some Facebook friends' latest updates, not much. I wished I could say that I had listened to a podcast, watched a TED Talk or something that stretched my thinking. Instead, I had to admit the truth: *"I scroll for fun, not for fulfilment".*

Social media has transformed how we spend our free time and constantly and successfully compete to capture our attention. Gen Z's are the first generation to be held hostage by their Smartphones. It's effortless to fall into an endless scroll, losing minutes that turn into hours. Our phones even track it, offering a weekly report that sometimes serves as a harsh reality check. The question is no longer whether we have free time, it's whether we're using it in a way that truly serves us.

But here's the twist: social media isn't just a distraction anymore, it's becoming a gateway to learning. A whole new industry has emerged, urging us to trade passive scrolling for active growth. Messages like "Don't waste your time, become the most interesting person in the room" flood our feeds, offering quick access to courses on art, music, history, personal style, cooking and essentially anything we can imagine.

For coaching, this shift presents both a challenge and an opportunity. As people increasingly turn to social media for self-improvement, coaches must rethink how they engage, educate, and inspire. The future of coaching isn't just about one-to-one sessions; it's about meeting clients where they are: online, in the content they consume, and in the digital spaces where they seek transformation. The question isn't whether social media is a distraction, but rather: how can coaching harness its power to create a deeper, more lasting impact?

The blending of coaching as entertainment has fuelled its popularity. Previously mentioned figures like Jay Shetty and Robin Sharma engage audiences through charismatic storytelling, humour, and multimedia content. The success of coaching-centric reality TV shows, such as *The Biggest Loser* (which incorporated life coaching elements), demonstrates the appeal of self-improvement narratives. Rhonda Britten, founder of the Fearless Living Institute, gained prominence through her role as a life coach on the reality TV series "Starting Over," thereby bringing coaching concepts into mainstream media.

When COVID-19 and the global lockdown of 2020 brought life to a standstill, the world turned to the internet for just about everything; entertainment, distraction, advice, shopping, and guidance. At the time, this was all that was in our circle of control. Our worlds felt like a paradox, shrinking as we were physically cut off from others, yet expanding as we suddenly had unprecedented access to people online.

Fitness and education took on a new digital life, with living rooms doubling as yoga studios and early morning Pilates classes becoming the norm because gyms were closed and outdoor movement felt like a distant memory.

When schools shut down and dining tables turned into classrooms, parents found themselves thrust into the role of educators overnight. Home schooling wasn't just about lesson plans – it was about patience, adaptability, and managing the emotional rollercoaster of learning from home. In the midst of it all, coaching took on a new significance. Coaches became a lifeline for overwhelmed parents, helping them navigate the pressures of balancing work, teaching, and family life. For students, coaching provided structure, motivation, and emotional support in a world where the lines between school and home had blurred. It wasn't just about academics; it was about resilience, self-discipline, and finding a way to thrive in a learning environment that had been completely redefined.

This exposure has permanently shifted the industry. Coaching is no longer limited by geography, cost, or exclusivity. AI-powered coaching apps, on-demand coaching platforms, and large-scale digital coaching programs are emerging, offering personalised guidance on scale. Meanwhile, social media has turned coaches into thought leaders, building global audiences and driving conversations around mental well-being, leadership, and performance.

The question is no longer whether coaching is valuable, it's how it will continue to shape the way we live and work in the future. The shift is clear coaching is no longer a niche industry. It's woven into the way we learn, adapt, and strive for better versions of ourselves. And as more people seek guidance in an ever-changing world, coaching is set to become an even bigger force in shaping the future.

The future of coaching will be a blend of human expertise and technological advancement. Digital platforms will continue to democratise access, allowing more people to benefit from coaching at different levels; whether through short-form content, group programs, or high-impact one-on-one sessions. But with this accessibility comes a responsibility: the industry must uphold quality, ethics, and professionalism to ensure that coaching remains a valuable and transformative experience rather than just another form of online content consumption.

Criticism and challenges

Despite their success and celebrity online influencers/coaches face criticism. Some argue that the commodification of coaching has led to oversimplified advice that lacks scientific rigour. Others raise concerns about the commercialisation of self-help, where expensive courses and seminars may not always deliver transformative results.

- **Oversimplified Advice:** Some coaching content reduces complex psychological or leadership concepts into quick-fix solutions, which may not always be effective for individuals seeking in-depth guidance.

- **Misinformation Risks:** Without regulatory oversight, some coaching advice on social media may be misleading, particularly in areas such as mental health coaching, business coaching, and financial coaching.

- **Unqualified individuals**: The rise of social media coaching influencers has led to an influx of unqualified individuals branding themselves as experts. The coaching space has become saturated, making it challenging for consumers to differentiate between credible professionals and opportunistic influencers.

Whether as entertainment or a legitimate development tool, blended coaching is here to stay.

What might a blended coaching future look like?

The integration of AI into coaching began with basic chatbots and digital assistants, offering standardised responses and rudimentary coaching support. However, as AI technology advanced, platforms such as BetterUp, CoachHub, and Replika began harnessing machine learning and data analytics to provide personalised insights, making coaching more adaptive and scalable. These platforms analyse vast amounts of behavioural data, allowing AI-driven coaching models to deliver tailored recommendations, goal-setting frameworks, and real-time feedback.

As with many consumer or service driven industries, there will often be a few big names who dominate the space. They have deeper pockets and can offer organisations solutions on scale. To stand out in an increasingly crowded space, some have introduced celebrity endorsements, using well-known figures to build credibility and capture audience attention.

While the effectiveness of star power in leadership coaching remains debatable, it's clear that the industry is evolving to meet modern demands. Personalised coaching at scale has become the game-changer, leveraging AI-driven platforms, tailored development plans, and continuous touchpoints to ensure real transformation.

BetterUp, A prominent leader in the coaching industry, recruited Prince Harry in 2021 as Chief Impact Officer, "What we're doing is about equipping people to thrive," said the Duke of Sussex, who reportedly earns $1.2 million a year for the role.

London-based **CoachHub,** A leading global digital coaching platform, has secured a €40 million growth financing facility from HSBC Innovation Banking UK.

CoachMatching built its own platform to enable effective and efficient matching, monitoring, reporting and analysis of coaching, which has been endorsed by Prof David Clutterbuck, founding member of EMCC.

The rise of hybrid coaching models

Moving forward, we envisage that there are actually two hybrid models emerging:

- The blending of coaching services to be able to reach a much broader audience and respond quickly to changing needs and,
- Coaches integrating Human coaching with AI support.

Blending coaching services

For years, industry giants like Gartner, Korn Ferry, and Harvard Business School have been tracking trends in leadership development and talent management. Their findings have been consistent, that despite companies pouring millions into training programs, the return on investment has been underwhelming. Leadership behaviours aren't shifting in a meaningful or sustainable way, and the root of the issue is clear: outdated training models. More traditional workshops, while well-intentioned, are often lacking ongoing engagement and real-world application, leaving leaders inspired for a day but unchanged in the long run. Many leadership development companies and business schools have been growing their coaching panels to augment the traditional learning with real world application via coaching. This trend will undoubtable continue. However, we are seeing a shift in the percentage of time and budget allocated to each.

Working with our clients to co-create solutions we coined the phrase "The Trend is to Blend" Our more forward thinking clients are already moving away from episodic coaching models and toward blended approaches that offer a multi-layered approach, combining Masterclasses, group coaching, one-to-one coaching, Coach on Call services, and AI-powered Coach Bots. The focus was no longer just on knowledge or content delivery, but on real-world application, reinforcing the shift toward a coaching as learning culture.

The results speak for themselves, with clients reporting a positive shift in employee engagement. ROI is higher, and behaviour change is more sustainable than with traditional methods.

The real challenge isn't in acquiring knowledge; that is readily available via ChatGPT and many other online sources; it's in bridging the gap between learning and application. So the question is: How do we create a culture where growth and learning are embedded, not as a onetime event, but as a continuous practice?

For many of our clients, this is the core challenge: how to build a culture of continuous learning and growth while driving accountability and delivering results. At first glance, these priorities might seem at odds – can you truly foster innovation and development while holding people to high standards?

The answer is yes, but it demands a higher level of emotional maturity at every level of the organisation. Leaders must create an environment where learning isn't just encouraged but expected, where accountability isn't about blame but about ownership and progress. When done right, a culture of growth and accountability doesn't compete – it reinforces itself, driving both individual and organisational success.

The future of coaching lies in integrating it into the fabric of daily work, making learning a continuous process rather than a onetime event.

In summary, your Organisation needs to have a strategy that incorporates the following blended coaching solutions:

- Masterclasses for structured learning.
- Group coaching for peer-driven insights and shared accountability and learning.
- One on one coaching for personalised development.
- Coach on Call services for just-in-time guidance.
- Peer coaching to bring the coaching skills into their daily activities.
- Leader as Coach to develop a coaching style of leadership.
- Building an internal pool of qualified coaches to support the external coach offering and build the coaching muscle internally.
- AI-powered coaching tools for reinforcement and scale.

This multi-layered model ensures employees are not just acquiring knowledge but applying it in real time, a crucial factor in developing a learning culture.

Throughout this book, we reference emotional intelligence or EQ as being critical to both individual and organisational growth. We have talked about being more human and the unique skills that only a human can bring.

While AI has revolutionised coaching, human coaches remain irreplaceable in delivering deep emotional support and nuanced guidance. The hybrid coaching model, where AI handles routine inquiries, progress tracking, and data analysis, while human coaches provide high-touch will probably become dominant. Our tenet "Tech Savvy and Human centric" was never more relevant.

AI excels in data analysis, pattern recognition, and consistency, however human coaches bring empathy, deep intuition, and the ability to navigate emotions – both of which are essential for behaviour change.

- **Trust & Emotional Intelligence:** AI can provide useful feedback, but humans are better at building trust, reading nuanced emotional cues, and adjusting coaching methods accordingly.
- **Adaptability & Ethics:** Whilst AI lacks moral reasoning and situational judgment; human coaches ensure that coaching remains ethical, personalised, and values-driven.

Therefore, the next frontier in coaching and the other hybrid, where AI supports coaches rather than replaces them. AI-driven insights can amplify the coach's effectiveness, but human wisdom remains the cornerstone of transformative change. The key to success lies in integrating behavioural science principles into AI coaching systems – ensuring that technology serves as a scalable tool for sustainable human growth.

The interplay between **behavioural science, behaviour change, and AI in coaching** is grounded in well established psychological and cognitive theories that explain **how humans learn, adapt, and sustain change**. When applied in a coaching context, especially one that integrates AI, understanding these principles becomes even more crucial. Deciding where, when and how to deploy these hybrid models requires knowledge of both sets of capabilities. AI in coaching enhances behaviour change by leveraging principles of behavioural science at scale and with precision. Some key ways AI contributes include:

- **Personalised Nudging** (Thaler & Sunstein – Nudge Theory):[128] AI can analyse user data to provide gentle, well-timed reminders, keeping clients engaged in their coaching journey without overwhelming them.

- **Cognitive Load Reduction:** AI-powered tools can filter and present information in manageable chunks, preventing overload and making goal achievement feel more attainable.

- **Reinforcement Learning:** AI adapts to user interactions, much like Skinner's Operant Conditioning ,[129] reinforcing positive behaviours with feedback, reminders, or rewards.

- **Social Learning:**[130] AI-driven coaching platforms can create peer communities or suggest role models, enhancing learning through observation and group dynamics.

Emma had been a leadership coach for over a decade. She had seen trends come and go, from the rise of mindfulness in executive training to the growing demand for resilience coaching. But nothing had disrupted the industry quite like AI.

At first, she resisted. Coaching, after all, was about human connection – the nuances of body language, the unspoken hesitations, the way a client's tone shifted when they finally uncovered a deep-seated belief holding them back. How could an AI powered bot possibly understand all of that?

But as her practice grew and clients demanded more flexibility, Emma realised she needed a smarter way to scale without losing the depth of her work. That's when she turned to an AI-powered coaching assistant, one designed not to replace her, but to augment what she did best.

The AI tool worked seamlessly in the background. It wasn't there to have deep, transformative conversations – that was still Emma's domain. Instead, it helped in three powerful ways:

1. **Tracking Behavioural Patterns** – It analysed the transcripts of her coaching sessions (with client consent) and flagged recurring themes Emma might have missed. One of her clients, David, a senior executive, frequently used phrases like "I don't have time" and "I'm always putting out fires." The AI picked up on this pattern and suggested that Emma explore time scarcity as a limiting belief in their next session.

2. **Personalised Micro-Nudges Between Sessions** – it sent tailored nudges to clients based on their goals. When Emma and David had worked on assertive decision-making, the AI sent David a reminder before his leadership meeting: "Take a deep breath. Trust your instincts. Today, make one decision without over-explaining. "Small prompts, but powerful reinforcements of their coaching work.

3. **Measuring Progress with AI Analytics** – Unlike traditional coaching, where progress was often felt but hard to measure, it tracked sentiment shifts. It noted when clients moved from hesitation to confidence, from self-doubt to action. It gave Emma insights she could use in her sessions, showing tangible proof of transformation.

One day, David arrived at their session, excited to share his realisation.

"I had the strangest moment this morning," he said. "I got this little reminder before my meeting, and I actually stopped to check myself. I made a firm decision, no second-guessing. And it felt... easy. I think I'm really making progress."

Emma smiled. She knew the reminder wasn't the real transformation – it was the coaching work they had been doing all along. But AI had given David the extra support in the moments that mattered, reinforcing the lessons when she wasn't in the room.

She no longer saw AI as a threat to coaching – it was a tool that allowed her to deepen her impact. It handled the data, the tracking, the reminders – freeing her up to focus on what coaching was really about: human insight, deep listening, and transformation.

The world of coaching was changing, but Emma knew one thing for certain: the best coaching wasn't AI or human – it was both working together.

Shift towards quality and accreditation

With this rapid expansion comes an urgent need for greater regulation and quality assurance. Like any booming industry, coaching must mature, ensuring that as demand grows, so does accountability. Stricter accreditation processes and standardised qualifications are no longer optional. They're essential, particularly as AI driven coaching solutions continue to gain traction. As noted by the International Coaching Federation, "With the advent of AI in our industry, coaching will become more accessible and lead to growth in coaching's impact on society."

As coaching cements itself as a critical tool in leadership development and talent retention, maintaining credibility will be key. The industry is at a crossroads, and those who prioritise quality, ethics, and impact will define its future.

The Power of the collective. This is likely to be the greatest shift in leadership development and the coaching industry, with coaching circles, peer, and group coaching being used more and more frequently to build a culture of coaching where learning and growth happen collectively, as stated in previous chapters.

Korn Ferry, a global organisational consulting firm, highlights the shift towards connected coaching. This model emphasises strategic alignment within organisations, integrating coaching practices that are interconnected and cohesive.

Emphasis on diversity, equity, inclusion, and access (DEIA)

There is a growing integration of DEIA principles within coaching practices. Coaches are increasingly focusing on fostering inclusive environments and addressing issues related to equity and access. This shift reflects a broader societal movement towards inclusivity and has become a distinguishing factor for coaching professionals committed to promoting diverse perspectives and equitable opportunities, particularly relevant in the South African context.

As the coaching industry matures, there is an increasing emphasis on quality assurance and professional standards. Organisations like the International Coaching Federation (ICF) and EMCC are advocating for rigorous accreditation processes to ensure coaches possess the necessary competencies.

Looking ahead, technological advancements will continue to play a pivotal role, offering tools that complement human coaching. Our clients are clear that they want to work with coaches and organisations who can demonstrate tangible results and adhere to established professional standards.

The importance of supervision in coaching

In the dynamic landscape of coaching, supervision emerges as an essential pillar for both coaches and their clients. It serves not only as a mechanism for professional development but also as a vital safeguard for ethical practice and effective client outcomes.

Supervision provides a structured environment for coaches to reflect on their experiences, discuss challenges, and receive constructive feedback. This reflective practice is crucial in helping coaches hone their skills, broaden their perspectives, and deepen their understanding of various methodologies. In a recent high stakes account, the supervision provided by Liza Stead one of our five internal supervisors, made the difference between the coach feeling confident in their ability to go 'off piste" within a team coaching context. The client feedback focussed on the coachee's ability to be in the moment and adapt to their emerging needs.

Coaches are inherently laden with ethical considerations, from maintaining confidentiality to navigating dual relationships. Supervision plays a crucial role in upholding ethical standards and providing a space for practitioners to examine their values and decision-making processes. It acts as a safeguard against potential ethical breaches by encouraging open dialogue about dilemmas and uncertainties, as well as guarding against compassion fatigue.

Through supervision, our coaches are reminded of the ethical frameworks that guide their practice. This oversight is particularly important in high-stakes environments where the well-being of clients is at risk. In a supervisory context, they can discuss their feelings and thoughts openly, ensuring that their course of action aligns with ethical guidelines and best practices.

As we move forward, coaching will evolve in ways we can't yet fully predict. But one thing remains constant: at its core, coaching is about human connection, curiosity, and growth. Both the industry and the individual have a responsibility to continually drive for higher standards, improved regulation and consistent supervision. As both coaching and coaches mature, I believe this field guide isn't an endpoint – it's a beginning. The next fire is yours to light.

REFERENCES

Chapter 1 References

Clutterbuck, D. 2010. Coaching reflection: The liberated coach. *Coaching: An International Journal of Theory, Research and Practice*, 3(1), pp.73–81.

Côté, J. and Gilbert, W. 2009. *An integrative definition of coaching effectiveness and expertise.* International Journal of Sports Science & Coaching, 4(3), pp.307–323.

International Coach Federation (ICF). 2023. *About ICF.* [online] Available at: https://coachingfederation.org/about [Accessed 30 Apr. 2025].

Kahn, M.S. 2014. *Coaching on the axis: Working with complexity in business and executive coaching.* Randburg: Knowres Publishing.

Lane, D., Stelter, R., & Stout-Rostron, S. (2023). The future of coaching as a profession. In E. Cox, T. Bachkirova, & D. A. Clutterbuck (Eds.), *The complete handbook of coaching* (4th ed., pp. 417–433). SAGE Publications.

Rogers, C.R. 1951. *Client-Centered Therapy: Its Current Practice, Implications, and Theory.* Boston: Houghton Mifflin.

Whitmore, J. 1992. *Coaching for Performance.* London: Nicholas Brealey Publishing.

Whitmore, J. 2009. *Coaching for Performance: GROWing Human Potential and Purpose – The Principles and Practice of Coaching and Leadership.* 4th ed. London: Nicholas Brealey Publishing.

Chapter 2 References

Kline, N. 1999. *Time to Think: Listening to Ignite the Human Mind.* London: Cassell Illustrated.

Kline, N. 2019. *Fine Point: Compartmentalisation.* [online] Time to Think. Available at: https://www.timetothink.com/wp-content/uploads/2019/10/fine-point-compartmentalisation.pdf [Accessed 1 May 2025].

Kline, N., 2025. Therapy. Fine Points, [blog] 13 January. Available at: https://www.timetothink.com/blog/therapy [Accessed 5 May 2025].

Kübler-Ross, E. 1969. *On Death and Dying.* New York: Macmillan.

Chapter 3 References

Ames, D. R., & Kammrath, L. K. 2004. Narcissism, not actual competence, predicts self-estimated ability. *Journal of Nonverbal Behavior, 28(3), 187–209.*

Clear, J. (2018) *Atomic Habits: An Easy & Proven Way to Build Good Habits & Break Bad Ones.* New York: Avery.

Edmondson, A.C., 2018. *The Fearless Organization: Creating Psychological Safety in the Workplace for Learning, Innovation, and Growth.* Hoboken, NJ: Wiley.

Eves, H.W. 1988. *Return to Mathematical Circles.* Washington, DC: Mathematical Association of America.

Gallup (2022) *State of the Global Workplace: 2022 Report.* Washington, D.C.: Gallup. Available at: https://www.gallup.com/workplace/349484/state-of-the-global-workplace-2022-report.aspx (Accessed: 1 May 2025).

McKinsey & Company (2022) *The Great Attrition Is Making Hiring Harder. Are You Searching the Right Talent Pools?* Available at: https://www.mckinsey.com (Accessed: [insert date]).

Novotney, A. 2019. The risks of social isolation: Psychologists are studying how to combat loneliness in those most at risk, such as older adults. *American Psychological Association*, 50(5): 32.

Pedriquez. D. 2025. *The Impact of Quiet Quitting on the Economy [Statistics + Infographic].* Available at: https://venngage.com/blog/quiet-quitting/ [Accessed 1 May 2025].

Sinek, S. 2021. *100% of employees are people. 100% of customers are people. 100% of investors are people. If you don't understand people, you don't understand business.* [online] LinkedIn. Available at: https://www.linkedin.com/posts/simonsinek_100-of-employees-are-people-100-of-customers-activity-6899197315018801153-sC2B [Accessed 1 May 2025].

Chapter 4 References

Brown, A. 2025. *Comment: Why investors are worried about workplace mental health.* Reuters. Retrieved from: https://www.reuters.com/sustainability/society-equity/comment-why-investors-are-worried-about-workplace-mental-health-2025-01-28/

Rath, T. & Conchie, B. 2009. *Strengths Based Leadership: Great Leaders, Teams, and Why People Follow.* New York, NY: Gallup Press, pp 251 -254.

Chapter 5 References

Aristotle. 2009. *Nicomachean ethics* (W. D. Ross, Trans.; J. L. Ackrill & J. O. Urmson, Eds.). Oxford University Press. (Original work written ca. 350 B.C.E.)

Bar-On, R., 1985. *The development of a concept of psychological well-being.* Doctoral dissertation. Rhodes University.

Goleman, D., 1995. *Emotional intelligence: Why it can matter more than IQ.* New York: Bantam Books.

Neisser, U. et al., 1996. Intelligence: Knowns and unknowns. *American Psychologist*, 51(2), pp.77–101.

Newby, D. and Brunel, M., 2025. The power of emotions in coaching. In: *The Power of Emotions in Coaching.* [Unpublished manuscript].

White, S.H., 2000. Conceptual foundations of IQ testing. *Psychological Reports*, 86(1), pp.13–18.

World Economic Forum, 2023. *The Future of Jobs Report 2023.* [online] Geneva: World Economic Forum. Available at: https://www.weforum.org/reports/the-future-of-jobs-report-2023 [Accessed 2 May 2025].

Chapter 6 References

50Plus-Skills, n.d. About 50Plus-Skills. [online] Available at: https://50plus-skills.co.za/ [Accessed 25 Apr. 2025].

Amado, G. and Elsner, R., 2007. *Leaders in transition.* London: Karnac.

Armstrong, D., 2005. *Organization in the mind: Psychoanalysis, group relations and organizational consultancy.* London: Karnac Books.

Bauman, Z., 2004. *Identity*. London: Polity Press.

Biggs, S., 2003. Counselling psychology and mid-life issues. In: R. Woolfe, W. Dryden and S. Strawbridge, eds. *Handbook of counselling psychology*. London: Sage Publications, pp.363–380.

Bridges, W., 1980. *Transitions: Making sense of life's changes*. Reading, MA: Addison-Wesley.

Bridges, W., 1991. *Managing transitions: Making the most of change*. New York: Perseus Books.

Bridges, W., 2003. Managing transitions: Making the most of change. 2nd ed. London: Nicholas Brealey Publishing.Brunning, H., 2007. Six domains of executive coaching. In: H. Brunning, ed. *Executive coaching: Systems psychodynamic approach*. London: Karnac Books, pp.131–151.

Buckingham, D., 2008. *Introducing identity*. London: Open University Press.

Cascio, J., 2020. *Facing the age of chaos*. Open the Future, [blog] 18 April. Available at: https://www.openthefuture.com/2020/04/facing_the_age_of_chaos.html [Accessed 5 May 2025].

Cilliers, F. and Koortzen, P., 2005. Working with conflict in teams – the CIBART model. *HR Future*, October, pp.51–52.

Corbett, D. 2007. *Portfolio Life: The new path to work, purpose, and passion after 50*. San Francisco: John Wiley and Sons.

Czander, W., 1993. *The psychodynamics of work and organisations: Theory and application*. New York: The Guilford Press.

Daminger, A. 2019. 'The cognitive dimension of household labor', American Sociological Review, 84(4), pp. 609–633. doi: 10.1177/0003122419859007.

Daringer, A. 2024. A Cognitive Labor of Love. Retrieved from: https://behavioralscientist.org/a-cognitive-labor-of-love/#:~:text=Women%20do%20more%20cognitive%20labor,important%20decisions%20for%20the%20household

Diamond, M., 2013. Psychodynamic approach. In: J. Passmore and D. Peterson, eds. *The Wiley-Blackwell handbook of the psychology of coaching and mentoring*. San Francisco, CA: John Wiley and Sons, pp.365–384.

Diamond, M.A. and Allcorn, S., 2009. *Private selves in public organisations*. New York: Palgrave Macmillan.

Ebrahim, R. 2023. *South Africa's Landmark Ruling on Parental Leave Equality*. Retrieved from: https://legalese.co.za/south-africas-landmark-ruling-on-parental-leave-equality/#:~:text=The%20court%20declared%20that%20all,four%20months%20of%20parental%20leave

Fearon, J., 1999. What is identity as we now use the word? [online] Stanford University. Available at: https://web.stanford.edu/~jfearon/papers/iden1v2.pdf [Accessed 25 Apr. 2025].

Fox Eades, J., 2011. Childhood transitions and celebrating strengths. In: S. Palmer and S. Panchal, eds. *Developmental coaching: Life transitions and generational perspectives*. Hove: Routledge, pp.31–50.

Goldin, N.M., 2017. *Systems psychodynamic coaching for leaders in career transition*. Doctoral thesis. University of South Africa.

Gratton, L. and Scott, A., 2017. *The 100-Year Life*. London: Bloomsbury.

Halliday, D.L., 2012. *Managing the gap – the psychology of personal transition*. Doctoral thesis. Boston University School of Education.

Halpert, J.A. & Burg, I.J. 1997. 'Mixed messages: Co-worker responses to the pregnant employee', Journal of Business and Psychology, 12(2), pp. 241–253. doi: 10.1007/BF02294878.

Hoyle, L. and Pooley, J., 2004. Working below the surface: The emotional life of contemporary organizations. In: C. Huffington, D. Armstrong, W. Halton, L. Hoyle and J. Pooley, eds. *Working below the surface*. London: Karnac Books, pp.171–190.

Huffington, C., James, K. and Armstrong, D., 2004. What is the emotional cost of distributed leadership? In: C. Huffington, D. Armstrong, W. Halton, L. Hoyle and J. Pooley, eds. *Working below the surface: The emotional life of contemporary organizations*. London: Karnac Books, pp.67–82.

Kilburg, R., 2004. When shadows fall: Using psychodynamic approaches in executive coaching. *Consulting Psychology Journal: Practice and Research*, 564, pp.246–268.

Kimpotgieter.com, n.d. *Retirement life planning*. [online] Available at: https://kimpotgieter.com/retirement-life-planning/ [Accessed 25 Apr. 2025].

Makola, S. 2018. *Exploring first-time mothers' perceptions of their pregnancy, maternity leave and post-partum return to work in Gauteng, South Africa*. Retrieved from: https://www.academia.edu/95619652/Exploring_first_time_mothers_perceptions_of_their_pregnancy_maternity_leave_and_post_partum_return_to_work_in_Gauteng_South_Africa

Martincekova, L. and Skrobakova, Z., 2019. Transition from work to retirement: Theoretical models and factors of adaptation. *Journal of Adult Development*, [details needed].

McAlpin, K. and Wilkinson, D., n.d. *Coaching through transition*. [online] Performance Coaching International. Available at: https://www.performancecoachinginternational.com/coaching-through-transition/ [Accessed 25 Apr. 2025].

Millward, L.J. 2006. The Transition to Motherhood in an Organizational Context: An interpretative phenomenological analysis. *Journal of Occupational and Organizational Psychology*, 793:315 – 333

Nicholson, K.C. and Torrisi, J., 2006. Performance anxiety. *Theme Magazine*, Issue 7. Available at: http://www.thememagazine.com/stories/performance-anxiety [Accessed 25 Apr. 2025].

Parkes, M., 1971. Psycho-social transitions: A field for study. *Social Science and Medicine*, 52, pp.101–115.

Pooley, J., 2004. Layers of meaning: A coaching journey. In: C. Huffington, D. Armstrong, W. Halton, L. Hoyle and J. Pooley, eds. *Working below the surface: The emotional life of contemporary organizations*. London: Karnac Books, p.176.

Potgieter, K. and Willcox, G., 2015. *Retiremeant: Get more meaning from your money*. Cape Town: Metz Press.

Purvis, J. 1991. 'Gender and education: The social construction of gendered subjectivities', British Journal of Sociology of Education, 12(3), pp. 301–311. doi: 10.1080/0142569910120304.

Rousseau, D.M. (1995) Psychological contracts in organizations: Understanding written and unwritten agreements. Thousand Oaks, CA: Sage Publications.Sandberg, S. 2013. *Lean In: Work, and the Will to Lead*. New York: Alfred A. Knopf.

Savickas, M.L., 2007. Occupational choice. In: H. Gunz and M. Peiperl, eds. *Handbook of career studies*. Thousand Oaks, CA: Sage Publications, pp.79–97.

Scheepers, C., 2012. *Coaching leaders: The 7 'P' tools to propel change*. Randburg: Knowres Publishing.

Sievers, B., ed., 2009. *Psychoanalytic studies of organizations*. London: Karnac Books.

Stapley, L.F. (2006) Individuals, groups, and organisations beneath the surface: An introduction. London: Karnac Books.

Terblanche, N.H.D., Albertyn, R.M. and Van Coller-Peter, S., 2017. Designing a coaching intervention to support leaders promoted into senior positions. *South African Journal of Human Resource Management*, 150, pp.1–10.

U.S. Army War College. 1987. VUCA: Volatility, Uncertainty, Complexity and Ambiguity. Carlisle, PA: U.S. Army War College.

Ulrich, D., 2000. Coaching CEO transitions. In: M. Goldsmith, L. Lyons and A. Freas, eds. *Coaching for leadership: How the world's greatest coaches help leaders learn*. San Francisco, CA: Jossey-Bass/Pfeiffer, pp.189–198.

Volkan, V.D. and Zintl, E., 1993. *Life after loss: The lessons of grief*. New York: Charles Scribner's Sons.

Chapter 7 References

Almeida, M.-L. & Frumar, C. 2023. *Help your employees cope with stress*. [online] Gallup. Available at: https://www.gallup.com/workplace/509726/help-employees-cope-stress.aspx [Accessed 29 Apr. 2025].

Bryant, A. & Kazan, A.L. 2012. *Self-leadership: How to become a more successful, efficient, and effective leader from the inside out*. New York: McGraw-Hill Education.

Cavanagh, M.J. & Spence, G.B. 2013. Mindfulness in coaching: Philosophy, psychology or just a helpful skill. In: J. Passmore, D.B. Peterson & T. Freire, eds. *The Wiley-Blackwell handbook of the psychology of coaching and mentoring*. Chichester: Wiley-Blackwell, pp.112–134.

Chamine, S. 2012. *Positive Intelligence: Why Only 20% of Teams and Individuals Achieve Their True Potential and How You Can Achieve Yours*. New York: Greenleaf Book Group.

González-García, M., de Diego, A., & González López, J. 2018. Mindfulness and Coaching: Promoting the Development of Presence and Full Awareness. *MLS Psychology Research*, 1(1), 79–94.

Gu, X. et al. 2022. The effects of loving-kindness and compassion meditation on life satisfaction: A systematic review and meta-analysis. *Applied Psychology: Health and Well-Being*, 14(3), pp.1081–1101. doi:10.1111/aphw.12367.

Huppert, F.A. 2009. Psychological well-being: Evidence regarding its causes and consequences. *Applied Psychology: Health and Well-Being*, 1(2), pp.137–164.

Jha, A.P. 2021. *Peak Mind: Find Your Focus, Own Your Attention, Invest 12 Minutes a Day*. New York: Harper Wave.

Juliano Jr, D. 2024. *The role of mindfulness in leadership coaching*. Doctoral dissertation. Walden University.

Kabat-Zinn, J. 2013. *Full catastrophe living: Using the wisdom of your body and mind to face stress, pain, and illness*. New York: Bantam Books.

Killingsworth, M.A. & Gilbert, D.T. 2010. A wandering mind is an unhappy mind. *Science*, 330(6006), p.932. doi:10.1126/science.1192439.

Manga, E., 2019. *Breathe: Strategising energy in the age of burnout*. Johannesburg: Jacana Media.

Manz, C.C. 1986. Self-leadership: Toward an expanded theory of self-influence processes in organizations. *Academy of Management Review*, 11(3), pp.585–600.

Ryan, R.M. & Deci, E.L. 2017. *Self-determination theory: Basic psychological needs in motivation, development, and wellness*. New York: Guilford Publications.

Seppala, E.M. et al. 2014. Loving-kindness meditation: A tool to improve healthcare provider compassion, resilience, and patient care. *Journal of Compassionate Health Care*, 1(5). doi:10.1186/s40639-014-0005-9.

Shapiro, S.L. et al. 2006. Mechanisms of mindfulness. *Journal of Clinical Psychology*, 62(3), pp.373–386. doi:10.1002/jclp.20237.

Virgili, M. 2013. Mindfulness-based coaching: Conceptualisation, supporting evidence and emerging applications. *International Coaching Psychology Review*, 8(2), pp.40–57.

Willcox, G. 1982. The Feeling Wheel: A tool for expanding awareness of emotions and increasing spontaneity and intimacy. *Transactional Analysis Journal*, 12(4), pp.274–276. doi:10.1177/036215378201200411.

Chapter 8 References

Bachkirova, T. 2024. *Why coaching needs real intelligence, not artificial intelligence. Philosophy of Coaching: An International Journal*, 9(2), pp.6–15.

Boyatzis, R.E., Smith, M.L., Van Oosten, E. and Woolford, L. (2013) 'Developing resonant leaders through emotional intelligence, vision and coaching', *Organizational Dynamics, 42(1), pp. 17–24. doi:* 10.1016/j.orgdyn.2012.12.003.

Diller, S., Stenzel, L.-C., and Passmore, J. 2024. 'The coach bots are coming: Exploring global coaches' attitudes and responses to the threat of AI coaching', Human Resource Development International, 27(4), pp. 597–621. doi: 10.1080/13678868.2024.2375934.

Holm, J.R., Lorenz, E., Lundvall, B.Å., & Valeyre, A. 2022. 'The impact of artificial intelligence on skills at work in Denmark', AI & Society, 37(1), pp. 1–17. doi: 10.1007/s00146-021-01222-4.

Isaacson, S. 2021. *How to thrive as a coach in a digital world*. Maidenhead: McGraw Hill–Open University Press.

Isaacson, S., Kong, S., Leech, D. & Tee, D. 2024. *Unlocking Potential: AI Coaching in the NHS.*

Kline, N., 2009. *More time to think: The power of independent thinking*. London: Fisher King Publishing.

Larson, G. (n.d.) *Oh, crap! Was that TODAY?* [Cartoon]. Available at: https://za.pinterest.com/pin/funny-gifts--416864509233101388/ [Accessed 29 Apr. 2025].

Leonard, D. (2008) 'The impact of coaching on leadership development: A study of coaching effectiveness in a healthcare organization', Journal of Leadership Studies, 2(2), pp. 17–27. doi: 10.1002/jls.20060.

Mai, V., Neef, C., and Richert, A. (2022) '"Clicking vs. Writing" – The impact of a chatbot's interaction method on the working alliance in AI-based coaching', Coaching | Theorie & Praxis, 8(1), pp. 15–31. doi: 10.1365/s40896-021-00063-3.Emerald+2

Passmore, J. and Tee, D. (2023) 'Can chatbots like GPT-4 replace human coaches: Issues and dilemmas for the coaching profession, coaching clients and for organisations', The Coaching Psychologist, 19(1), pp. 47–54. doi: 10.53841/bpstcp.2023.19.1.47.

Terblanche, N., Haan, E. and Nilsson, V., 2022a. *Coaching at scale: Investigating the efficacy of artificial intelligence coaching. International Journal of Evidence Based Coaching and Mentoring*, 20, pp.20–36.

Chapter 9 References

Aephoria Group, *Home*. Available at: https://www.aephoriagroup.com/ (Accessed: 29 April 2025).

Chestnut Paes Enneagram Academy, *Enneagram Learning*. Available at: https://www.Enneagramlearning.com/ (Accessed: 29 April 2025).

Chestnut, B. 2013. *The Complete Enneagram: 27 Paths to Greater Self-Knowledge*. Berkeley, CA: She Writes Press.

Chestnut, B. and Paes, U. (n.d.) *Enneagram 2.0 Podcast*. Available at: https://podcasts.apple.com/us/podcast/Enneagram-2-0-with-beatrice-chestnut-and-uranio-paes/id1499745500 (Accessed: 29 April 2025).

Cron, I.M. (n.d.) *Typology Podcast*. Available at: https://www.typologypodcast.com/ (Accessed: 29 April 2025).

Cron, I.M. and Stabile, S. 2016. *The Road Back to You: An Enneagram Journey to Self-Discovery*. Downers Grove, IL: InterVarsity Press.

Daniels, D. and Price, V. 2009. *The Essential Enneagram: A Comprehensive Guide to Self-Understanding, Personal Development, and the Nine Personality Types*. New York: HarperOne.

Integrative 9, *iEQ9 Enneagram Assessments*. Available at: https://www.integrative9.com/ (Accessed: 29 April 2025).

International Enneagram Association (IEA), *Credentialled Professionals, Membership, Ethics and Guidelines*. Available at: https://www.internationalEnneagram.org/ (Accessed: 29 April 2025).

Lapid-Bogda, G. (n.d.) *The Enneagram at Work. Big Self School Podcast*. Available at: https://www.bigselfschool.com/podcast/the-Enneagram-finds-you-with-ginger-lapid-bogda (Accessed: 29 April 2025).

Lapid-Bogda, G. n.d. *What Type of Leader Are You? Using the Enneagram System to Identify and Grow Your Leadership Strengths and Achieve Maximum Success*. [Place of publication not identified]: [Publisher not identified].

Lapid-Bogda, G., *The Enneagram in Business*. Available at: https://www.gingerlapidbogda.com/ (Accessed: 29 April 2025).

Riso, D.R. and Hudson, R. 1999. *The Wisdom of the Enneagram: The Complete Guide to Psychological and Spiritual Growth for the Nine Personality Types*. New York: Bantam Books.

The Enneagram Institute, *Home*. Available at: https://www.Enneagraminstitute.com/ (Accessed: 29 April 2025).

The Narrative Enneagram, *Home*. Available at: https://www.narrativeEnneagram.org/ (Accessed: 29 April 2025).

Chapter 10 References

Arakawa, R. and Yakura, H. (2024) *Coaching Copilot: blended form of an LLM-powered chatbot and a human coach to effectively support self-reflection for leadership growth.* Available at: https://arxiv.org/abs/2405.15250 (Accessed: 29 April 2025).

Bandura, A., 1977. *Social learning theory.* Englewood Cliffs, NJ: Prentice-Hall.

Brown, B., 2010. The power of vulnerability. TEDxHouston, [video] June. Available at: https://www.ted.com/talks/brene_brown_the_power_of_vulnerability [Accessed 5 May 2025].

Covey, S.R. 1989. *The 7 Habits of Highly Effective People.* New York: Free Press.

Covey, S.R. 1989. *The 7 habits of highly effective people: powerful lessons in personal change.* New York: Free Press.

Forbes Coaches Council. 2023. *Pros and cons of coaching with AI, Forbes.* Available at: https://www.forbes.com/councils/forbescoachescouncil/2023/05/04/pros-and-cons-of-coaching-with-ai/ (Accessed: 29 April 2025).

Ibarra, H. n.d. Quoted in: *Technology is breaking down barriers in coaching, making it possible to scale personalized development across entire organizations and societies.* London Business School.

Institute of Coaching. n.d. *Unlocking potential: how artificial intelligence can help in executive coaching.* Available at: https://instituteofcoaching.org/blogs/unlocking-potential-how-artificial-intelligence-can-help-executive-coaching (Accessed: 29 April 2025).

International Coaching Federation. n.d. *Technology & AI in coaching.* Available at: https://coachingfederation.org/research/coalition-technology-in-coaching (Accessed: 29 April 2025).

Skinner, B.F., 1953. *Science and human behavior_Edi.* New York: Macmillan.

Thaler, R.H. and Sunstein, C.R. 2008. *Nudge: Improving decisions about health, wealth, and happiness.* New Haven: Yale University Press.

ENDNOTES

1   Whitmore, 2009.
2   Côté & Gilbert, 2009.
3   Rogers, 1951.
4   Whitmore, 1992.
5   ICF, 2023.
6   Kahn, 2014.
7   Clutterbuck, 2010.
8   Clutterbuck, 2010
9   Kline, 1999.
10   Kline, 2025.
11   Kline, 2019.
12   Kubler-Ross, 1969.
13   Harris, as cited in Eves, 1988.
14   Sinek, 2021.
15   Gallup, 2020
16   McKinsey, 2020
17   Bain, HBR 2014
18   Novotney, 2019.
19   Ames & Kammrath, 2004.
20   Clear, 2018.
21   Gallup, 2022.
22   McKinsey, 2022.
23   Gallup, 2022
24   Pedriquez, 2025.
25   Edmondson, 2018.
26   Browne, 2025.
27   Rath & Conchie, *"Strengths Based Leadership" pg 251 -254 by Tom Rath and Barry Conchie
28   Aristotle, 2009.
29   Bar-On, 1985.
30   World Economic Forum, 2023.
31   Halliday, 2012.
32   Bridges, 2003, p. 3.
33   Terblanche, Albertyn and van Coller-Peter, 2017.
34   Biggs, 2003, p.373.
35   Goldin, 2017.
36   Parkes, 1971.
37   Bridges, 2003.
38   Ulrich, 2000, p. 189.
39   Cilliers & Koortzen, 2005, p. 52.
40   Scheepers, 2012.
41   Pooley, 2004, p.176.
42   Sievers, 2009, p. 2.
43   Diamond, 2009.
44   Czander, 1993.
45   Nicholson and Torrisi, 2006.
46   Amado & Elsner, 2007.
47   Amado and Elsner, 2007, p. 170.
48   Elsner, 2007.
49   Amado and Elsner, 2007.
50   Czander, 1993.
51   Sievers, 2009.
52   Armstrong, 2005.
53   Amado & Elsner, 2007.
54   Stapley, 2006.
55   Fox Eades, 2011, p. 34
56   Diamond, 2013, p. 370.
57   Volkan & Zintl, 1993, p. 13.
58   Volkan and Zintl , 1993.
59   Pooley, 2004.
60   Brunning, 2007, p. 143.
61   Kilburg, 2004.
62   Huffington et al., 2004.
63   Diamond & Allcorn, 2009.
64   Huffington, James & Armstrong, 2004.
65   Pooley, 2004.
66   Pooley, 2004.
67   McAlpin & Wilkinson, n.d.
68   U.S. Army War College, 1987.
69   Cascio, 2020.
70   Millward, 2006.
71   Bridges, 2003.
72   Sandberg, 2013.
73   Bridges, 2003.
74   Halpert & Burg, 1997.
75   Daminger, 2019.
76   Ebrahim, 2023.
77   Rousseau, 1995.
78   Makola, 2018.
79   Daminger, 2024.
80   Bridges, 1980.
81   Gratton & Scott, 2017.
82   Corbett, 2007.
83   Potgieter & Willcox, 2015.
84   Potgieter & Wilcox, 2015.
85   Huppert, 2009.

86 Gallup, 2024.
87 Manga, 2019
88 Kabat-Zinn, 2013.
89 Shapiro, 2006.
90 Virgii, 2013.
91 González-García, de Diego & González López, 2018.
92 Ryan & Deci, 2017.
93 Manz, 1986.
94 Bryant and , 2012.
95 Shapiro, 2006.
96 Killingsworth, 2010,
97 Wilcox, 1982.
98 Juliano, 2024.
99 Juliano, 2024.
100 Cavanagh, 2013.
101 Juliano, 2024.
102 Juliano, 2024.
103 Gu X, 2022.
104 Seppala, 2014.
105 Gonzalez, 2018.
106 Jha, 2021.
107 Chamine, 2012.
108 Isaacson, 2021.
109 Kline, 2009.
110 Terblanche et al, 2022.
111 Isaacson et al, 2024.
112 Larson, n.d.
113 Bachkirova, 2024.
114 Diller, Stenzel, & Passmore, 2024.
115 Mai, Neef & Richert, 2022.
116 Passmore & Tee, 2023.
117 Terblanche et al., 2022a.
118 Terblanche et al., 2024.
119 Holm, Lorenz, Lundvall & Valeyre, 2022.
120 Diller et al., 2024.
121 Passmore & Tee, 2023.
122 Terblanche et al., 2022.
123 Terblanche et al., 2022a.
124 Boyatzis et al., 2013.
125 Leonard, 2008.
126 Covey, 1989.
127 Brown, 2010.
128 Thaler & Sunstein, 2008.
129 Skinner, 1953.
130 Bandura, 1977.

INDEX

www.ingramcontent.com/pod-product-compliance
Lightning Source LLC
Chambersburg PA
CBHW080529220326
41599CB00032B/6256